GOODYEAR

McLAREN FORMULA 1

CAR BY CAR

John Gabrial collection

Quarto.com

First Published in 2024 by Motorbooks, an imprint of The Quarto Group,
100 Cummings Center, Suite 265-D, Beverly, MA 01915, USA.
T (978) 282-9590 F (978) 283-2742

Motorbooks titles are also available at discount for retail, wholesale, promotional, and bulk purchase. For details, contact the Special Sales Manager by email at specialsales@quarto.com or by mail at The Quarto Group, Attn: Special Sales Manager, 100 Cummings Center, Suite 265-D, Beverly, MA 01915, USA.

29 28 27 26 25 3 4 5

ISBN: 978-0-7603-8512-8

Digital edition published in 2024
eISBN: 978-0-7603-8513-5

Library of Congress Control Number: 2024931471

Design: Cindy Samargia Laun
Cover Image: James Mann
Back Jacket Image: Motorsport Images
Back Jacket Flap Images, from top to bottom: Andrew Ferraro, Motorsport Images

Printed in China

Dedication

Dedicated to the memory of Jasmine Codling, 2006–2023.

Acknowledgments

Thanks to Zack Miller and Brooke Pelletier at Motorbooks for their eternal patience. Likewise my equally long-suffering wife, Julie. Thanks also to Kevin Wood, guardian of the LAT Images archive and the Jim Clark mug. Special thanks to Neil Oatley for running an experienced eye over the facts.

EVERY RACE CAR SINCE 1966

McLAREN FORMULA 1

CAR BY CAR

STUART CODLING

Foreword by Mika Häkkinen

Contents

FOREWORD by Mika Häkkinen

McLaren is the team with whom I won 20 Grands Prix and two world championships, so it has notably played a big part in my life. When Ron Dennis invited me to join McLaren as a test driver in 1993, I knew McLaren had the ability to create championship-winning cars. I also benefited from good advice: My friend and manager Keke Rosberg, Finland's first F1 champion, had raced for McLaren. He was confident it was the right home for me. James Hunt had also mentored me when I was a junior driver. He is famous for his brilliant world championship win driving for McLaren in 1976. I liked James a lot, and his best advice was to be sure to enjoy myself!

Over my nine years at McLaren, I was teamed with Michael Andretti, Ayrton Senna, Martin Brundle, Nigel Mansell, Mark Blundell, and lastly David Coulthard. All were talented, but Ayrton is particularly remembered for his time at McLaren, winning 35 grands prix and three world championship titles. My six-year partnership with David remains the longest driver pairing in McLaren's history. Together we won the Constructors' Championship in 1998.

I drove McLarens powered by Ford, Lamborghini, and Peugeot engines, but it was with Mercedes-Benz that we achieved our greatest success. Having scored my first race win in 1997, I was able to win consecutive drivers' titles in 1998 and 1999. Under the leadership of Zak Brown, McLaren remains highly competitive today, and I have really enjoyed watching the success achieved by Lando Norris and Oscar Piastri.

I am delighted to have been invited to write this foreword for Stuart Codling's *McLaren Formula 1 Car by Car*, and I hope you enjoy reading about the incredible machines which have made McLaren such a formidable part of the Formula 1 story.

Monaco, December 2023

Mercedes-Benz
Mobil 1
BOSS
HUGO BOSS
West

INTRODUCTION

John Gabrial Collection

Stocky of build and walking with a slight limp—the result of a childhood illness that left him hospitalized for nearly three years—Bruce Leslie McLaren cut a slightly unusual figure in the increasingly glamorous world of motor racing in the late 1950s and early 1960s. But this New Zealand native would become the youngest Grand Prix winner of all time in 1959—a record that stood until 2003—and found an organization that remains one of the most successful in Formula 1 history.

His secret, apart from the ability to drive a car quickly, was a contagious enthusiasm. The challenges he faced as a youngster led to his later capacity to excel. Not being allowed to walk unaccompanied until the age of 12, missing out on the ball sports he'd loved before the onset of Perthes' disease, and having to be taught by a tutor instead of attending school with his classmates—all instilled in him a determination to succeed.

"If Bruce arrived at the workshop one morning and said, 'Okay guys, today we're going to walk across the Sahara desert,'' recalled Howden Ganley, employee number three of Bruce McLaren Motor Racing Ltd., in a talk at the Monaco GP in 2015, "there'd have been no complaints in response, just, 'Right, Bruce, when do we start?'"

McLaren was born on August 30, 1937. His father, Leslie, ran a service station and had a passion for motor racing. With this background it was virtually inevitable that Bruce would develop similar passions as well as a sound knowledge of mechanical engineering. He passed his driving test at the age of 15 and attempted his first competitive outings at the wheel of a second-hand Austin Ulster he'd spent two years restoring himself.

McLaren continued to race while studying engineering at Auckland University. There he struck up a correspondence with Jack Brabham, the Australian dirt-track racer who was then making a name for himself on the European racing scene. Brabham introduced McLaren to the Cooper Car Company's racing organization after the young driver won the New Zealand International Grand Prix Association's "Driver to Europe" scholarship.

Soon after, Bruce McLaren booked passage from New Zealand to Europe in March 1958, aged 21. Sharing a rented room in a pub with his friend and sometime mechanic Colin Beanland, Bruce made himself useful at Cooper, building up chassis and helping designer Owen Maddock at the drawing board.

Later that year the German Grand Prix organizers bolstered their grid by admitting Formula 2 cars. Bruce secured a reserve entry in an F2 Cooper. He qualified 15th, was fifth into the first corner, and took the checkered flag fifth, the first F2 driver across the line.

As his reputation grew, so did his doubts that Cooper had what it took to be a winning constructor in the long term. The company had pioneered the mid-engined configuration that gave better primary handling balance, but in other ways it was run like a stubbornly parochial small business by Charles and John Cooper.

There was a certain resistance to change at Cooper, an attitude that a winning car needed no development. In the drawing office Bruce witnessed arguments about

Bruce McLaren (left) with John Cooper.

In 1960 McLaren was one of just six drivers to finish the Belgian Grand Prix, during which two other competitors were killed.

McLaren (26) leads John Surtees out of the Station Hairpin at Monaco in 1961.

development between the mechanically gifted Brabham and Maddock. The Australian engineer Ron Tauranac was writing to Brabham with new ideas, and this tacit assistance—plus Brabham's sheer force of will—led to the successful "low-line" Cooper T53. The process convinced Brabham that it was time to carefully decouple himself from Cooper and set up a business of his own in partnership with Tauranac.

By 1963 Bruce was ready to follow the same route. He was a well-known Grand Prix driver and had recently gotten married, but he was still sharing a one-room apartment with a friend in southwest London. He needed a break.

Cooper's F1 fortunes were in decline as others outpaced them with innovation, and it was at this point McLaren took the initiative and broke free. His company, Bruce McLaren Motor Racing Ltd., was incorporated later in 1963. Ostensibly set up to contest the Tasman series in the Southern Hemisphere that winter, McLaren had his eyes on bigger goals over the horizon.

McLaren's business partner was American lawyer Edward "Teddy" Mayer, a member of the "RevEm" Formula Junior team with his brother Timmy and Peter Revson, heir to the Revlon cosmetics empire. Though devastated by Timmy's fatal accident at the Longford Tasman round in February 1964, Teddy found purpose in helping Bruce manage the company's dealmaking.

Other close friends became McLaren's first employees: Bruce's mechanic Wally Wilmott; Mayer's mechanic Tyler Alexander; and aspiring racer Ganley, initially hired as a gofer. Working in a dirt-floored workshop in the corner of an earthmoving equipment warehouse, Bruce designed the space frame for the first in-house McLaren, the M1 sports car. The initial design's outline was literally marked in the dirt.

As he worked toward a Formula 1 entry, Bruce recognized that he needed more design support. This came in the form of Robin Herd, a double-first physics and engineering graduate of Oxford University who had worked on the Concorde supersonic aircraft project. Herd shared Bruce's compulsion to try out unusual solutions in the name of continuous improvement, as their first F1 car would prove.

"No matter how well a car handles, it is never perfect," wrote McLaren in his book *From The Cockpit*, "bearing in mind that the following year's models will be even faster. So it is best to try changes, then set out to test their worth. . . ."

6

CHAPTER 1

1960s

Inspired by his friend and mentor, Bruce McLaren took on the role of constructor and team owner in much the same way as Brabham had. He took small steps, reducing his ties with Cooper while quietly amassing the resources to go into business for himself—and to compete in F1 under his own name.

The nascent McLaren marque benefited from the noisy grudge match evolving between Ford and Ferrari at Le Mans. Bruce's work on Ford's GT program, including the troubled J-car iteration of the GT40, gave him an inside view into aerodynamic matters that complemented his innate engineering ability. And it brought a lucrative tire-development contract with Firestone.

While Brabham's company focused on building single-seaters, McLaren branched out profitably into "big-banger" sports prototypes. Successful factory campaigns in the Can-Am series yielded direct revenues in prize money, along with an income stream from Elva Cars, which built Can-Am designs for McLaren under license.

His Formula 1 project got off to a stuttering start, though, and Bruce McLaren Racing Cars Ltd. remained a hand-to-mouth business. "We would always sell works cars we had no further use for," Teddy Mayer recalled in an interview with racing historian Doug Nye. "It was team policy: if it was standing still and not earning its keep, sell it."

←
Bruce McLaren's young team quickly acquired a reputation for engineering excellence.

CASTROL
DAILY
14

M2B

Just before Christmas in 1965, Bruce McLaren invited members of the specialist press to attend an informal gathering at his company's new premises in David Road, Colnbrook, UK. Based under Heathrow's flightpath, the walls regularly shook with the sound of passing aircraft, but it had a solid concrete floor and was more spacious than the Belvedere Works. In this otherwise unremarkable industrial estate, Bruce was about to reveal Grand Prix racing's worst-kept secret.

Sitting on axle stands in one corner of the workshop was a tubular space frame single-seater chassis, ready to accept suspension geometry based on the M1 sports prototype. This was the M3 customer club-racing car, based on McLaren's evocation of the concept. His colleagues affectionately dubbed it the "whoosh-bonk." McLaren explained, "You can take the suspension off the sports car—whoosh—knock up a chassis and—bonk—there's the car."

Of greater interest to the members of the press was the other, more complete car available for inspection: the M2B, in which McLaren intended to contest the 1966 Formula 1 World Championship. Bruce had been testing the prototype M2A in what was meant to be secret since its completion in September. The pretense was that, since he was still competing for Cooper in F1, he and his team had built the car solely for the purpose of testing tires for Firestone. With its intriguing technical details in place—albeit shorn of a rear wing that had been tested at Zandvoort—the finished race car was ready to be seen properly.

Like the M2A prototype, the M2B was based on a monocoque chassis design in which the D-shaped side-members were made not from sheet metal but from Mallite, a composite material used in aircraft cabins. Sheets of 26-gauge aluminum were bonded to ⅛-inch (3.2-millimeter) end-grain balsa wood to form a sandwich that offered greater torsional stiffness than plain aluminum sheeting. Manufacturer William Mallinson & Sons delivered a special batch of this material with variable-thickness skin, enabling it to be carefully rolled into D-shaped side pontoons and then bonded and riveted to fabricated steel bulkheads. The pontoons were sealed internally to enable them to store fuel.

M2B SPECIFICATIONS

Engine	Ford 2,995cc 90-degree V-8 Serenissima 2,996cc 90-degree V-8	**Suspension**	Lower wishbones with upper rocker arms and inboard coil springs, telescopic dampers (front), upper radius rods and outboard coil springs, telescopic dampers
Power	300bhp @ 9,600 rpm / 260bhp @ 9,500 rpm	**Brakes**	Discs f/r
Gearbox	Four/five-speed manual	**Tires**	Firestone
Chassis	Mallite sheet and steel panel monocoque	**Weight**	535 kilograms (1,179 pounds)

←
Despite being blessed by a priest before leaving the factory, the Serenissima V-8 was underpowered and unreliable. Still, it powered the M2B to McLaren's first world championship points in the 1966 British Grand Prix.

2

Elsewhere convention reigned, with lower wishbones in the front suspension with upper rocker arms actuating inboard coil springs and dampers and rear suspension via lower wishbones, outboard coil-over dampers and twin radius rods.

McLaren's biggest challenge was an engine supply: F1 had become a 3.0-liter formula and everyone was scrambling for a suitable powerplant. Bruce and Teddy Mayer used their US connections to sound out Ford, but no financial support was forthcoming. McLaren bought five of Ford's 4.2-liter Indy V-8s, which new recruit Gary Knutson converted with the assistance of Traco Engineering. Ultimately, despite the evaluation of several bore-stroke permutations, this engine never delivered the anticipated power.

As a result, Bruce had to pass up the annual winter trip Down Under to the lucrative Tasman series, testing the M2B in California alongside Ford's Le Mans car instead. Plans for a two-car F1 entry had to be shelved, since only one engine was ready for the Monaco season opener, where the Ford's weight and shallow rev range told the tale: Bruce qualified 10th. To compound this low-key F1 debut, an oil union worked loose in the race and Bruce parked the M2B rather than blow its engine.

For the Belgian Grand Prix, McLaren adapted the M2B to accommodate a sports car–derived engine from Count Volpi's fledgling Serenissima company, but the Italian V-8 spun a bearing in practice so Bruce had to quit the event. The only McLaren on track for the race was an M3, driven by 1961 champion Phil Hill and carrying cameras for John Frankenheimer's movie, *Grand Prix*.

It was a slim return for McLaren's new company: just two points finishes all year, one with the rebuilt Serenissima at Brands Hatch and another with the revised Ford at Watkins Glen. This meager showing led Bruce and Robin Herd to conclude they needed another crack at F1 with a new package.

←
The M2B's best championship finish was fifth place at Watkins Glen with a revised version of the Ford engine.

↓
While the M2B's Indy-derived V-8 made an almighty noise, it was too heavy and didn't respond to the adjustments that were intended to widen the power band.

←
Engine supply issues meant Bruce McLaren was a solo entry for his new team's maiden Grand Prix appearance at Monaco in 1966.

16

M4B

The engine-supply quandary continued to dominate McLaren's Formula 1 agenda into 1967. While Ford *had* been convinced to bankroll an F1 engine—Walter Hayes, head of the Blue Oval's British arm, had persuaded the board to underwrite a V-8 designed and built by Cosworth—this would be exclusive to Lotus for the year. The Indy Ford and Serenissima V-8s were a bust, despite the charming quirk of the latter manufacturer in summoning a priest to bless the engines as they were loaded onto the McLaren van. Bruce himself had his eye on BRM's forthcoming V-12, but this project was running late.

As a stopgap, he ran the so-called M4B, an M4A Formula 2 chassis modified at the rear to mate to a 2.1-liter BRM V-8, ballasted up to the F1 weight limit and fitted with larger fuel tanks on either side of the cockpit. In contrast to the M2B, the M4A and M4B were utterly conventional aluminum "bathtub" monocoques with outboard suspension and fiberglass body panels. Herd had learned from the team's first F1 car to rein in the innovation.

"On our initial [F1] design we erred," he remembered, "and tended toward technical ingenuity and bullshit rather than race-winning engineering."

McLaren contested just two championship races in the sole M4B, running as high as third place in Monaco as the car's nimbleness ameliorated the smaller engine's lack of grunt. Despite a long pit stop to replace a flat battery, McLaren finished fourth, although Lorenzo Bandini's fatal accident meant no one was in a celebratory mood at the outcome of this race.

For the following round, at Zandvoort, the nature of the circuit did not flatter the M4B, and Bruce qualified just 14th. On pole position and 3.1 seconds faster around the 2.6-mile circuit was Graham Hill in the new Lotus 49, powered by the Ford-Cosworth V-8. As Hill's teammate Jim Clark surged through the field to take the lead and win, McLaren crashed on the fourth lap.

He decided against taking the M4B to Spa and accepted an offer to race one of Dan Gurney's Eagle T1Gs for three further rounds before the BRM V-12 was ready. The repaired M4B was used for tire testing but was destroyed after it caught fire at Goodwood.

←
The M4B required additional fuel tank space on either side of the cockpit to last the distance of a Grand Prix.

M4B SPECIFICATIONS

Engine	BRM 2,070cc 90-degree V-8	**Suspension**	Lower wishbones with top links and radius arms, coil springs, and telescopic dampers
Power	280bhp @ 10,500 rpm	**Brakes**	Discs f/r
Gearbox	Five-speed manual	**Tires**	Goodyear
Chassis	Aluminum monocoque	**Weight**	500 kilograms (1,102 pounds)

GOODYEAR

M5A

While McLaren completed the monocoque chassis of their 1967 Formula 1 challenger in February, it was not destined to see action until August in the Canadian Grand Prix at Mosport, east of Toronto. By then the BRM P101 V-12 engine was finally ready, while the works team persisted with the ungainly H16 (of which Jackie Stewart was fond of saying "carried more petrol, water, and oil than the Queen Mary").

While the M5A shared a few similarities with the M4B, it presented greater packaging challenges since the V-12 was longer and thirstier than the 2.1-liter V-8. A rounder monocoque profile provided more space for rubber-bag fuel tanks in the pontoons on either side of the driver, but these had to be augmented with additional fuel capacity in the chassis members, which cradled the engine, plus auxiliary tanks above and below the driver's legs.

Unlike Ford-Cosworth's DFV, the P101's block wasn't engineered to act as a structural element of the car. This meant it required bulkheads at each end as well as bracing members on each side. It arrived late, leaving time for just one brief shakedown at Goodwood before being freighted across the Atlantic. The engine proved longer than expected since various ancillaries had been placed at the end of the block. McLaren decided to remove the alternator, figuring there would be little drain on the battery because the fuel pump was mechanically driven.

This decision proved costly at Mosport, as Bruce had to chase down the leaders after an early spin in wet conditions. The battery lost charge earlier than expected—possibly as a result of its location under the oil catch tank, exposed to heat—and the engine started misfiring. He finished seventh, four laps down, after a stop for a new battery, but the car's performance could have offered so much more.

←
For the M5A's final Grand Prix under McLaren ownership, it was repainted papaya orange. The soon-to-become-iconic color was first used on the company's Can-Am cars.

M5A SPECIFICATIONS

Engine	BRM 2,998cc 90-degree V-12	**Suspension**	Lower wishbones with top links and radius arms, coil springs, and telescopic dampers
Power	370bhp @ 9,750 rpm	**Brakes**	Discs f/r
Gearbox	Five-speed manual	**Tires**	Goodyear
Chassis	Aluminum monocoque	**Weight**	535 kilograms (1,179 pounds)

↓
The late arrival of BRM's V-12 entailed a number of compromises when the M5A made its first appearance at Mosport in Canada.

↓
When Ferrari could field only one car for the Italian Grand Prix, the officials withdrew their demand that McLaren paint the M5A green.

Come the Italian Grand Prix weekend, the M5A's red paintwork created a scandal at scrutineering. While the era of cars racing in national colors rather than in liveries dictated by sponsors was shortly to be ushered into the pages of history, at Monza in 1967 McLaren's color scheme led to something close to an international incident, with red being reserved for Italian entries. At the end of practice the officials backed down, reversing their decree that the car should be resprayed green: the fact that only one Ferrari had been entered for the race was something of an embarrassment, one now compounded by its showing as only the fourth fastest. Bruce had qualified on the front row.

A broken cylinder liner eliminated Bruce after forty-six of the sixty-eight laps. At Watkins Glen he qualified ninth after differential trouble in practice, then spun and dislodged a coolant hose in the race. In Mexico City, 7,200 feet (2,195 meters) above sea level, the BRM struggled to run cleanly in the thinner air and appeared to be using more oil than expected. Bruce halted after forty-five laps when the pressure gauge hit zero; when the car was recovered, there was plenty of oil left in the tank.

It was an intriguing mystery, but Bruce and his colleagues didn't have the time or energy to solve it, given their dovetailing campaign in the Can-Am series. As he watched his Can-Am teammate Denny Hulme finish third for Brabham in Mexico and win the world championship, Bruce was visualizing a 1968 F1 campaign with two cars, both powered by the Ford-Cosworth DFV rather than the vexatious BRM V-12.

McLaren's successful Can-Am car, the M6A, was the first to wear what would become the team's signature color: bright papaya orange, chosen because Teddy Mayer believed it would make the car 'ping' even on a monochrome TV. Resprayed in this hue the sole M5A would make one further appearance for McLaren before being sold to Swiss privateer Joakim Bonnier—who later hung the car on the wall of his home as a decoration.

→
After Joakim Bonnier finished racing the M5A, he had it mounted on the wall of his Swiss home.

Gulf

M7A/B/C/D

Already a dominant force in Can-Am by 1968, McLaren came of age in Formula 1 that year with Robin Herd's final design for the team. Herd had laid down the monocoque before he left while Bruce himself took responsibility for the suspension geometry, work on which was completed by Gordon Coppuck.

Having drawn an enclosed monocoque for the M5A, Herd reverted to the open-top bathtub style, which had a nonstructural fiberglass panel covering the driver's legs and extending on either side of the cockpit. Three fabricated-steel bulkheads formed the heart of the structure, each acting as suspension mounting points as well as anchoring the aluminum and magnesium sheet skins, which were bonded as well as riveted. There was no need for a subframe to carry the engine and transmission because Bruce had negotiated a supply of Ford's Cosworth-built DFV V-8s, which had been designed to act as stressed elements of the chassis.

While posterity enshrines this landmark engine as a positive and democratizing influence that lowered barriers to entry and broadened the field, at the time many observers lamented the homogeneity it brought. What is undeniable is that having one engine in the majority of cars made aerodynamics and quality of engineering a differentiating factor.

One quirk of championship scheduling in the 1960s was the presence of the South African Grand Prix, usually held in late December as a season finale or early January as the opener, enabling teams to integrate this Southern Hemisphere race logistically with the Tasman series held in Australia and New Zealand. Pressed for time as team owner, lead driver, and now chief engineer, Bruce skipped the Kyalami race while Hulme took the repainted M5A to fifth place. By early spring the M7As were ready and Bruce and Denny each won non-championship races in the UK against respectable fields.

←
High-mounted rear wings were already being challenged by officials when McLaren arrived at the 1969 Monaco Grand Prix weekend with the M7C sporting a second aerofoil at the front. A ban on these devices followed and it ran in this configuration only on the Thursday of the race weekend.

M7A/M7B/M7C/M7D SPECIFICATIONS

Engine	Ford 2,993cc 90-degree V-8	**Suspension**	Lateral links and radius arms (f), lateral top links and reversed lower wishbones (r), coil springs and telescopic dampers
Power	410bhp @ 9,000 rpm	**Brakes**	Discs f/r
Gearbox	Five-speed manual	**Tires**	Goodyear
Chassis	Aluminum monocoque	**Weight**	520 kilograms (1,146 pounds)

McLaren retains an M7C in "high-wing" spec as a static exhibit (though the "guillotine" was unpainted in period).
James Mann

A single M7A chassis—thought to be #3, Bruce's Belgian Grand Prix winner—was converted to run integral side-mounted fuel tanks. It was designated M7B thereafter. When this new car proved unsuccessful, it was sold to the Colin Crabbe Antique Automobiles team and raced by Vic Elford.

Bruce believed the M7A could handle better if its fuel load were more widely distributed, as in his company's Can-Am cars. When the world championship resumed at Jarama in early May, Bruce's M7A featured outboard pannier-style fuel tanks like those of the 1954 Lancia D50. Hulme came in second while Bruce stopped to preserve his engine when it lost oil pressure.

Monaco was less auspicious. Bruce was eliminated in a crash on the opening lap, while Hulme came last of the runners in a race blighted by understeer and a late pit stop. Neither McLaren driver was satisfied with the poise of the M7As through practice, but the Belgian Grand Prix produced a remarkable result all the same. From fifth and sixth on the grid, Hulme led until a half

Fittingly, it was Bruce McLaren who recorded his marque's first world championship win, at Spa-Francorchamps in 1968. It was to be his final Grand Prix victory.

shaft failed and McLaren raced into second place, which became the lead when Jackie Stewart made a late stop for fuel. Unaware of this, Bruce was puzzled at the sight of his crew jumping for joy as he became only the second driver to win a Grand Prix in a car bearing their own name.

Improved tires did much to solve the M7A's stability issues and, after wrapping up the Can-Am championship, the team undertook further development work, including the evaluation of the high-mounted wings that were becoming *de rigueur*. Hulme won in Italy and Canada, claiming third in the championship.

For 1969 Bruce directed the team to construct a revised chassis with low and wide pannier tanks mounted integrally within a wraparound monocoque design, designated the M7B. When this proved unsatisfactory, he sold it to a privateer and raced a new chassis, designated M7C although it was based more closely on the wider wraparound monocoque of Coppuck's M10A Formula 5000 design.

A ban on high wings from Monaco onward, followed by mixed messages from the governing body over permissible alternatives, caused disruption in 1969—as did a diversion into the cul-de-sac that was the four-wheel drive. Goodyear's new generation of G18 and G20 tires arrived late in the season and made for a considerable improvement, enabling Hulme to win the last race of the year.

The M7 concept would race on into 1970, both in private hands and in the form of a third works-entered car, designated M7D, paid for by Alfa Romeo's competitions department and powered by a sports car–derived V-8.

Gulf
Gulf

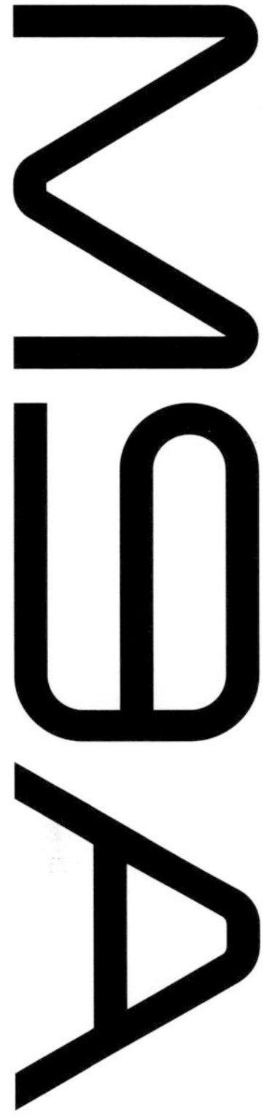

In the late 1960s, four-wheel drive was thought to be fundamental to Formula 1's future—to the extent that contemporary reporters began to airily dismiss the 2WD cars as "obsolete." History now records it as one of many dead ends.

While it might seem obvious to modern readers that adding weight and complexity to a racing car in pursuit of tenuous performance gains is foolish, at the time there were clear and pressing reasons to pursue four-wheel drive. Chief among these was the fact that engine performance was rapidly outstripping tire development. Splitting torque delivery across the axles seemed a clear win in terms of improving traction out of corners as well as from a standing start.

Robin Herd had left McLaren to join Cosworth's 4WD project, and Lotus and Matra also had 4WD cars in the works. McLaren felt compelled to follow this trend despite the failures of previous projects by Ferguson and BRM.

The M9A was a fresh monocoque by new chief designer Jo Marquart, with the Cosworth V-8 still acting as a stressed member but reversed so the power takeoff was behind the driver, whose seat was located further forward than usual to accommodate the transmission. This meant the pedals were ahead of the front axle line, requiring the driver to squeeze their legs under one of the half shafts driving the front wheels. The gearbox was a McLaren design using a small quantity of Hewland internals, and the center-mounted differential was similarly a McLaren development of Ferguson's 4WD transmission. Broadening the monocoque to accommodate the propeller shafts passing along the left side gave the M9A a distinctively stubby appearance.

Bruce wasn't keen after testing it, likening the "very disconcerting" experience to "trying to write your signature with someone constantly jogging your elbow." It raced just once, in Derek Bell's hands at the British Grand Prix at Silverstone, where it retired after a rear suspension carrier broke. After a few more tests the M9A was shelved and focus returned to M7 development; among the key issues was that the ideal torque split for peak traction made the M9A's steering too heavy.

↗
Plumbing for the M9A's front-mounted radiator had to take a rather complex path around the front suspension and driveshafts.

←
Four-wheel drive was briefly seen as the future of Formula 1, but McLaren's M9A driven by Derek Bell would see action in just one Grand Prix.

M9A SPECIFICATIONS

Engine	Ford 2,993cc 90-degree V-8	**Suspension**	Double wishbones (f), lateral bottom links and upper wishbones (r), inboard coil springs and telescopic dampers
Power	410bhp @ 9,000 rpm	**Brakes**	Discs f/r
Gearbox	Five-speed manual	**Tires**	Goodyear
Chassis	Aluminum monocoque	**Weight**	570 kilograms (1,257 pounds)

Marlboro
Marlboro
James Hunt
Marlboro
TEXACO
Marlboro
CHAMPION
11
FORD

1970s

CHAPTER 2

At the foot of the South Downs, a chalk escarpment running nearly 70 miles from Winchester to Eastbourne, lies the former RAF Westhampnett, a grass airfield from where World War II fighter ace Douglas Bader flew his final mission. After the war, motor racing enthusiasts (including the landowner, the Duke of Richmond and Gordon) pressed its perimeter roads into service as a racetrack. Though racing there ended in 1966, Goodwood remained a popular testing venue.

Tuesday, June 2, 1970, was a day like any other. Shortly after noon, Bruce McLaren was test-driving the new M8D Can-Am car when the rear bodywork became unclipped as he accelerated out of Lavant Corner, spinning him at high speed into a concrete wall. He was killed instantly.

The news reached Teddy Mayer by phone. In a daze he called together the small group of multiskilled engineers, fabricators, and mechanics who were friends as well as employees. A lesser organization would have been felled by the loss of the individual whose energies had created and sustained it, but Bruce's spirit outlived him. Instead, the day after McLaren's death, his team were drawn inexorably back to the factory. They picked up their tools and carried on preparing for their next race, a Can-Am event in Canada.

"We all owe it to Bruce to race," Mayer told them. "So we might as well get to it."

Over five decades have elapsed since these events, but the team bearing Bruce's name is still animated by this hunger to compete.

←
The remarkable M23 claimed two world titles.

M14A/D

Racing in America had shored up the team's finances and informed a number of business decisions. A key one was the partnership with Goodyear, made with the understanding that McLaren would target the Indy 500 as well as racing in Can-Am. Hence Gordon Coppuck focused on the M15 Indy car design over the winter of 1969; at the same time, Jo Marquart produced an evolution of the M7C concept for F1, aiming to improve both handling and aerodynamics while tidying the structure.

Adopting double wishbones for the front suspension gave more steering lock and enabled the deletion of an intermediate chassis bulkhead that had been required to provide an anchoring point for the previous configuration of lateral links. This in turn freed up space to extend the fuel cells in each side pontoon and thereby narrow the chassis slightly without reducing overall capacity.

While the Cosworth V-8 engine acted as a structural member of the chassis and required no subframes, it was partially enclosed by bodywork to smooth the airflow and act as a mounting point for the rear spoiler. Reducing unsprung weight was another priority, achieved by adopting a new upright design on the front suspension and shifting the rear brake discs inboard. After a dalliance with 13-inch (33-centimeter) front wheels at the beginning of the season, the team adopted 15-inch (38-centimeter) rims all round; the drivers felt these gave better handling and braking characteristics at the expense of a little additional weight.

The 1970 Grand Prix season turned out to be competitively peculiar, as well as ultimately tragic. The innovative, wedge-shaped Lotus 72 would prove to be a game-changer, though not in its original form with feel-sapping rising-rate suspension. A schism with Matra meant the 1969 championship-winning team, Tyrrell, fielded a customer March chassis. In turn, Matra, having gone their own way, suffered from reliability problems and barely figured in competition. Ferrari took time curing teething troubles with their new 312B. And Brabham's first monocoque chassis was fast but not always reliable.

Against this background McLaren might have prospered with a strong development of the previous year's car, but it was not to be. Hulme was second to Brabham in the South African season opener, but Bruce McLaren's engine failed. In Spain Hulme was second on the grid but dropped out early on while Bruce recovered from a suboptimal 10th-place grid spot to finish second, albeit

M14A/M14D SPECIFICATIONS

Engine	Ford 2,993cc 90-degree V-8	**Suspension**	Double wishbones (f), lateral top links and reversed lower wishbones (r), coil springs and telescopic dampers
Power	430bhp @ 9,000 rpm	**Brakes**	Discs f/r
Gearbox	Five-speed manual	**Tires**	Goodyear
Chassis	Aluminum monocoque	**Weight**	536 kilograms (1,182 pounds)

←
Peter Gethin was a front-runner in Formula 5000 but was unable to replicate this form in F1.

a lap down, to Jackie Stewart's March. Both races had been marked by severe attrition. In Monaco Denny qualified third but made a poor start, recovering to fourth at the checkered flag, by which time Bruce had long since parked his M14A with a suspension breakage.

The Tuesday after Monaco, Hulme was severely injured during practice at Indianapolis: his M15 caught fire at speed and the methanol fuel's characteristic of burning with an invisible flame meant help arrived late. His hands were so badly burned there was a fear that some of his fingers might be amputated. Three days after the Indy 500, where Peter Gethin and Carl Williams acted as stand-in drivers, Bruce was killed testing the new M8D Can-Am car at Goodwood.

Stunned by these developments, Bruce's friends and colleagues coped the only way they knew how—by carrying on. Adapting one M14A to accommodate Dan Gurney as a stand-in provided focus, as did building an M14D to suit Andrea de Adamich and his Alfa Romeo arrangement. When Gethin crashed the second M14A chassis at Zandvoort and bent the tub, it was rebuilt with thicker-gauge aluminum.

A sponsorship clash meant Gurney stood down in favor of Gethin after three rounds, while Hulme made a stoic return to the cockpit at the French Grand Prix, new skin still lifting and blistering beneath his gloves. There would be no F1 wins that season, but not for want of pure grit.

↖
Chassis M14A-3 was modified for testing with new front suspension geometry in period and the current owner races it in this form. *James Mann*

←
Peter Gethin (*right*) ready for action in his M14A at Zandvoort in 1970, while Andrea de Adamich (*left*) was destined to miss out on qualifying in his new M14D, denied by 0.01 seconds by George Eaton in a BRM (*top*).

→
Goodyear had introduced an almost treadless tire at the 1971 season opener, but Firestone hit back with a full "slick" in Spain a month later.

GOODYEAR
10

GOODYEAR
McLAREN CARS
26
26

M19A/C

The loss of Bruce McLaren not only ripped the heart out of his team, it also robbed them of a skilled driver and engineer. Events in 1971 would serve up continuous reminders of what they had lost.

To make up for some of the design shortfall and enable Coppuck to focus on the wedge-shaped M16 Indy car, Teddy Mayer hired ex-Brabham designer Ralph Bellamy to assist Marquart in creating the M19A F1 chassis. Early in the car's development this role would be reversed, for Marquart was in the process of setting up his own company—Huron Auto Racing Developments—in partnership Canadian sometime Formula Libre racer Jack Smith and British salesman Roy Ireland.

→
While Lotus relocated its coolers amidships for better balance, McLaren persisted with front-mounted radiators until rolling out the M23.

←
The M19A's rising-rate suspension geometry gave many theoretical advantages, but it proved frustratingly unresponsive to setup changes. In Holland in 1971, Denny Hulme could do no better than 12th.

The M19A was a full 5 inches (13 centimeters) longer in the wheelbase than its predecessor, with the aim of accommodating more of the fuel load behind the driver, a concept that also informed the gently swelling monocoque profile around the cockpit. The combination of this and a long, protuberant nose led to the press dubbing it "the Alligator." For impact protection the outer monocoque surfaces were formed in 16-gauge aluminum alloy.

As the Ford-Cosworth engine was rapidly becoming a common denominator across the grid, tires, suspension geometry and aerodynamics became avenues through which teams sought to gain a competitive advantage. Bellamy specified the M19A with inboard coil-over dampers front and rear, actuated by a combination of pushrods and rocker arms to give rising-rate characteristics. The aim here was to give a soft initial response, theoretically boosting grip and traction, but stiffening as the deflection increased.

Lotus had experimented with rising-rate suspension on their innovative and championship-winning 72 car the previous year but removed it mid-season when the drivers complained that it sapped them of critical feel. McLaren and their drivers also struggled to find a setup sweet spot, particularly as the tire development war between Goodyear and Firestone intensified. At the opening round in South Africa, Goodyear introduced a

M19A/M19C SPECIFICATIONS

Engine	Ford 2,993cc 90-degree V-8	**Suspension**	Double wishbones (f), lateral top links and reversed lower wishbones (r), inboard coil springs, and telescopic dampers
Power	430bhp @ 9,000 rpm	**Brakes**	Discs f/r
Gearbox	Five-speed manual	**Tires**	Goodyear
Chassis	Aluminum monocoque	**Weight**	565 kilograms (1,246 pounds)

↑
The lightened M19C enabled Denny Hulme to claim a run of podiums in 1972 and enshrine McLaren as "best of the rest" behind Lotus and Tyrrell. Peter Revson, shown here in Italy, also claimed three podiums with it.

→
Mark Donohue, who finished third on his Grand Prix debut at Mosport, in his Penske-entered M19A in 1971. Donohue had an instinctive grasp of engineering and was instrumental in developing the car.

virtually treadless tire offering a larger contact patch, only to be trumped by Firestone bringing a completely slick tire to the second round in Spain just over a month later.

McLaren also missed Bruce's assured touch as a development driver. Dan Gurney had stepped in for a handful of races following Bruce's death in 1970, but his personal sponsorship from Castrol made it untenable for him to remain with Gulf-backed McLaren. Peter Gethin, twice a British Formula 5000 champion in a McLaren M10A and M10B, lacked experience at this level and started the season in an M14A until a second M19A chassis was ready. On track he was generally shown the way by Denny Hulme and he moved to BRM late in the season, where he ameliorated his otherwise indifferent year by winning an eight-car lunge for the tape in the Italian Grand Prix.

Hulme gave the team cause for optimism by leading the almost intolerably hot opening round at Kyalami until lap seventy-six of the seventy-nine, when a bolt dropped out of his rear suspension. But this would be the M19A's most competitive showing in an otherwise disappointing year. During the handful of non-championship events between the first two rounds, Hulme finished third on aggregate in the one-off Questor Grand Prix in California, the M19A's highest placing until Mark Donohue claimed a podium in his Penske-run car in the Canadian Grand Prix.

Donohue's input helped McLaren address some of the car's issues, such as the rising-rate setup, which was dropped in favor of a conventional arrangement at the rear for 1972. This, combined with reprofiled wings and a better understanding of the new Goodyear slicks' characteristics, brought a performance uplift as Hulme and new teammate Peter Revson, in M19As bedecked in the colors of new title sponsor Yardley Cosmetics, claimed a win and two other podiums. A lightened variant, designated the M19C (there was no B) netted ten podiums before being retired early in 1973.

PENSKE
K.F. WHITE
McLAREN
GOODYEAR
10
SUNOCO

TEXACO
TEXACO
5

M23

Following Ralph Bellamy's departure for Brabham, Coppuck assumed control of McLaren's F1 development. A new car would be required as soon as possible: the M19 was at best sporadically competitive and, more critically, rules mandating deformable structures around the fuel tanks were due to come into force during the Spanish Grand Prix weekend at the end of April 1973.

Coppuck's M23, based on his experience creating the 1972 Indianapolis 500–winning M16, would prove so competitive and responsive to development that it would claim two world championships and remain a pillar of McLaren's works F1 program until 1977. Adopting the fashionable wedge profile and relocating the radiators from the nose to just ahead of the rear wheels would prove transformative, as would a chassis notably stiffer than its predecessor. At the front, Coppuck specified a mildly redesigned version of the late-model M19's rising-rate front suspension, retaining an aerodynamically optimal setup: lower wishbones, with the springs and dampers and sophisticated rocker links and pullrods mounted inside the nose cavity and actuated by upper rocker arms. The rear suspension, a conventional setup of upper radius rods and reversed lower wishbones, offered a small degree of rising rate via nonlinear coil springs.

Radiators mounted on the car's "hips" enabled a lower frontal area as part of the overall wedge shape, saved weight—no need for all those pipes ducting coolant from rear to front and back again—and shifted mass advantageously to within the wheelbase. The squared-off ducts acted as the first line of defense in side impacts to comply with the new regulations and were integral to the car's structure; at the border between these and the main "tub" the aluminum panels were double skinned and the void filled with impact-absorbent foam.

The first M23 chassis was completed in late February and, after a day testing at Goodwood, Denny Hulme pronounced it ready to race in the forthcoming South African Grand Prix, round two of the season. Peter Revson and young hotshot Jody Scheckter both drove M19s. Hulme qualified on pole and led the opening laps until picking up a puncture from debris, and his charge back toward the points was stymied by a second pit stop when he mistakenly believed his front left tire was deflating. Scheckter entertained his local crowd by leading briefly before being passed by Jackie Stewart.

M23 SPECIFICATIONS

Engine	Ford 2,993cc 90-degree V-8	**Suspension**	Double wishbones (f), lateral top links and reversed lower wishbones (r), inboard coil springs and telescopic dampers; rocker arms and adjustable anti-roll bar (f) from 1975
Power	440–465bhp @ 9,000 rpm	**Brakes**	Discs f/r
Gearbox	Five-speed manual (six-speed from 1976)	**Tires**	Goodyear
Chassis	Aluminum monocoque	**Weight**	575 kilograms (1,268 pounds)

←
Emerson Fittipaldi developed the M23 to suit his style in 1974 and claimed McLaren's first drivers' and constructors' championships.

↑
McLaren's Gordon Coppuck had been reluctant to follow Lotus's lead in building a wedge-shaped F1 car, believing such profiles were only a benefit on oval circuits. By 1973 the whole grid was going that way.

↑
It took time to shape the M23 into a winner. Here, in Spain in 1973, Peter Revson qualified fifth and finished fourth—but a lap down on the podium finishers.

It would be midseason before the M23 properly delivered on its early promise: Hulme claimed a dramatic victory in Sweden, hustling back into contention after sticking throttle slides threatened to derail his race early on. Home hero Ronnie Peterson was on course to win for Lotus until his left rear tire began to deflate, allowing Hulme to pass him on the penultimate lap. Revson took the M23's second win after an attritional race at Silverstone in which Scheckter, back in the occasional third McLaren, bolstered his reputation as a troublemaker by causing an accident at the end of the first lap; this eliminated nine cars, three of which belonged to John Surtees. Scheckter had to be hurriedly smuggled out of the circuit incognito by team manager Phil Kerr to avoid an encounter with the incandescent 1964 world champion.

The M23's third and final win of the season came in contentious circumstances as the safety car was deployed for the first time in the Canadian Grand Prix following an on-track accident. The pace vehicle was driven by local car dealer Egbert "Eppie" Wietzes, a race winner in US Formula A in a McLaren M18; he came immediately after drying conditions had prompted a flurry of pit stops for slick tires. In this era of manual lap charts, confusion reigned over who was actually in the lead, and Wietzes inadvertently picked up the wrong car to head the field. After hours of postrace wrangling, Revson was enshrined as victor to the detriment of Howden Ganley. A former McLaren mechanic—employee number three—Ganley had driven an Iso-Marlboro and believed that he was the winner.

Over the winter McLaren recruited 1972 champion Emerson Fittipaldi to replace Revson, who had fallen out of favor with Teddy Mayer. Fittipaldi gained sponsorship from Texaco and Marlboro, which necessitated some maneuvering to accommodate Yardley. This was achieved by Kerr running a third M23 with Yardley branding as a satellite entry with multiple motorcycle champion Mike Hailwood driving.

Fittipaldi threw himself into the testing process energetically while Hulme took the opportunity to go on holiday. It was a decision the 1967 champion would come to regret as Fittipaldi found improvements that better suited his own particular driving style. Wider track (by 2 inches [5 cm]) combined with a longer wheelbase (via a spacer on the gearbox bell housing) to improve weight distribution and stability.

In 1974 Tyrrell was less of a factor: Jackie Stewart had retired, and Lotus was tied up in knots with the 76, a flawed successor to the 72. The resurgent Ferrari proved to be McLaren's biggest opposition, although Scheckter won two Grands Prix for Tyrrell and Peterson three for Lotus (having reverted to the 72). Though Niki Lauda was ostensibly Ferrari's team leader, a number of retirements meant it was teammate Clay Regazzoni who went to the championship finale level on points with Fittipaldi. They started ninth and eighth at Watkins Glen but Regazzoni got the better start and moved ahead—and then, as befitted his reputation as a driver whose etiquette was more appropriate for the wrestling ring, he swerved to defend his position as Fittipaldi looked to go past at Turn 2. Emerson slithered through regardless, with two wheels on the grass. An eventual fourth place was enough to claim the drivers' title, and confirm McLaren's first constructors' championship, as Regazzoni dropped back with handling problems. Hulme's final Grand Prix ended with a blown engine.

Jochen Mass became Fittipaldi's full-time teammate in 1975 and the M23 underwent aerodynamic revisions along with a new rocker arm front suspension setup. Lauda and Ferrari remained tantalizingly out of reach, though, and by midseason those closest to Emerson spoke of him contemplating retirement. No one expected what actually happened: having finished second in 1975, he announced he would be leaving McLaren to join his brother Wilson's new Copersucar team, delivering the news to Mayer from a pay phone in the Zurich airport.

Fittipaldi's departure coincided with James Hunt suddenly becoming available when his Hesketh team ran out of money. What panned out in 1976 was a season like no other, later dramatized (with some artistic license) in the Hollywood movie *Rush*. Battles raged on and off the track as Hunt was disqualified from two victories (one reinstated after protest) and Lauda missed several rounds after suffering horrific burns in a crash at the Nürburgring. Hunt was three points behind going into the final round at Fuji Speedway in Japan, where the weather was so foul Lauda elected to park his Ferrari on the second lap, deeming the conditions too dangerous. The track began to dry out, but the final laps were no less dramatic. Hunt was one of several drivers forced to pit with tire problems, and he had to fight his way to the third place—which earned him the championship.

Though the replacement M26 had been on the drawing board since 1975, the M23 saw service into 1977 when the new car proved surprisingly truculent.

←
After Fittipaldi quit by pay phone, McLaren recruited James Hunt at the last minute for 1976. With similar abruptness, a ban on high-mounted airboxes came into force during the Spanish Grand Prix weekend.

↑
Fittipaldi won two grand prix in 1975 in M23-9, later raced by James Hunt and Jochen Mass in 1976 and 1977. Its current owner, US entrepreneur and collector Greg Galdi, also races it in historic events. *James Mann*

↑
Talent-spotted by James Hunt in Formula Atlantic, Gilles Villeneuve got his F1 break in a McLaren in the 1977 British Grand Prix.

John Gabrial Collection

Marlboro
TEXACO
Marlboro
GOOD YEAR
GOOD YEAR
7
7
Marlboro

M26

Arriving at a follow-up to the successful M23 was always going to be a challenge, and the M26, whose engineering philosophy relied on flawed theoretical aerodynamic principles, is rightly considered one of McLaren's lesser models even though it won three Grands Prix. The design began to take shape in 1975 but was set aside as attention focused on developing the M23 as well as the M16E and M28 Indy cars.

McLaren brought the first M26 chassis to the Österreichring for the 1976 Austrian Grand Prix but, after fuel pickup problems during practice, Hunt reverted to his regular M23. Teammate Jochen Mass gave the M26 its race debut in the Dutch Grand Prix at Zandvoort. It was not an auspicious first outing: untameable understeer contributed to a crash in practice and, from 15th on the grid, Mass struggled to a lapped ninth place. The M26 wasn't seen again in public until the third round of the 1977 season, in South Africa, where a sudden tire deflation (caused by a front brake component failure) during practice pitched Hunt into a high-speed impact with a barrier, severely damaging the car. The fact that the team constructed two new M23 chassis for the factory racing effort in 1977 (plus another for privateer Brett Lunger) was indicative of the state of affairs.

While the M26 was very much a sequel to the M23, sharing the same suspension configuration as the 1976-spec M23s, its aerodynamic concept was more extreme both above and below the surface. The cockpit structure was aggressively narrow and minimalist, the sidepods minimal and containing only the oil coolers (initially) while the radiators sat ahead of the rear wheels. Underneath, Coppuck had pursued an idea first evaluated on the M23: plastic "spoiler" strips to deflect airflow from under the car.

Coppuck's belief—which he subsequently recognized to be incorrect—was that the underfloor would produce negative pressure, sucking the car toward the ground and boosting grip, if air could be channeled around the car rather than under it. In fact, as Lotus would demonstrate with their 78 model introduced in 1977, the key to generating negative pressure was to accelerate the flow under the car.

←
As part of ongoing attempts to solve the M26's issues, McLaren relocated the radiator to the sidepods and the oil cooler to the nose when the car was reintroduced in mid-1977.

M26 SPECIFICATIONS

Engine	Ford 2,993cc 90-degree V-8	**Suspension**	Rocker arms and lower wishbones (f), lateral top links and reversed lower wishbones (r), inboard coil springs and telescopic dampers
Power	465bhp @ 9,000 rpm	**Brakes**	Discs f/r
Gearbox	Six-speed manual	**Tires**	Goodyear
Chassis	Aluminum monocoque with Nomex honeycomb	**Weight**	589 kilograms (1,299 pounds)

McLaren built a new M26 chassis for Hunt to use in the Spanish Grand Prix, round five, but he found its handling unpredictable and qualified no higher than ninth. In the race itself, high engine temperatures contributed to his misery and, though attrition helped him rise to third place, a misfire halted him before the checkered flag. The defending champion was by now a distant fifth in the title race.

Hunt and Mass reverted to M23s for Monaco before McLaren wheeled out an improved M26 for Hunt in Belgium, with reshaped sidepods (now accommodating the radiators) and the oil cooler relocated to the nose, where it was fed by a squared-off aperture. Over subsequent races the team experimented with the location of the underfloor strips and even cut a duct to channel air out through the cockpit.

This coincided with an upswing in form: Hunt won from pole position at Silverstone and registered two more victories late in the season. At Fuji Speedway Hunt quietly infuriated officials by skipping the podium ceremony to hurry off to his plane. Had he known this would be his final Grand Prix victory and the last for McLaren until 1981, he might have savored the moment.

McLaren allowed themselves to be fooled by the M26's apparent improvement, missing the opportunity to copy the Lotus ground-effect aerodynamic concept as they approached 1978. When they did take up the design, testing an M26E with Lotus-style sidepod enclosures at Brands Hatch, it was ineffectual. Having finished third in the constructors' championship in 1977, McLaren slumped to eighth, registering one podium finish as Lotus dominated. Frustrated, Hunt was beginning to make mistakes and was let go at the end of the season.

←
McLaren unveiled the M26 (*left of picture, alongside the M23*) in July 1976, but it would not race in earnest until the following season.

↑
Persistent cooling problems in testing delayed the planned introduction of the M26 in 1976. Jochen Mass raced it at Zandvoort but labored to a lapped ninth place.

↑
McLaren's attempt to convert the M26 into a ground-effect car was disastrous. The so-called M26E appeared just once, at Brands Hatch in 1978.

Marlboro
Marlboro
castrol
8
GOODYEAR
GOODYEAR

M28/B/C

The "missing" M27 demonstrates the extent to which the team had lost their way in the late 1970s. During this period rivals pushed ahead with innovations that McLaren failed either to understand promptly or copy effectively.

During the winter of 1977–1978, James Hunt and new teammate Patrick Tambay briefly tested what Hunt described as an M26.5, essentially an M26 with different (and ugly) rear bodywork that continued the effort to divert air away from the underfloor and expedite its passage between the rear wheels and the gearbox area. The ideas that would have formed the M27 were ultimately shelved, as Gordon Coppuck began to pursue concepts similar to what Lotus was attempting.

That McLaren still hadn't quite grasped the fundamentals of ground effect was demonstrated by the appearance of the short-lived M26E at the British Grand Prix that summer: for all its boxy sidepods, à la the Lotus 79, these features were empty. The Lotus sidepods employed venturi to accelerate the airflow and were sealed by skirting between the bottom of the bodywork and the track surface, preventing air from being drawn in from the side and dissipating the suction effect.

The M28, McLaren's first ground-effect car, therefore missed the boat by at least a season. Tambay tested the first chassis at Silverstone nine days after the final round of 1978. Both driver and team needed good news. Just over a year earlier, having signed for McLaren, Tambay had a meeting with Enzo Ferrari during which Enzo told him, "You've made a terrible mistake." Events on track had borne that out. More recently the brilliantly talented Ronnie Peterson had died following a first-lap crash at Monza, just days after signing a deal with McLaren to replace Hunt for the 1979 season.

Further winter testing at the Circuit Paul Ricard in the south of France, then in Brazil and Argentina ahead of the season opener in the Autódromo Oscar Gálvez in Buenos Aires, suggested that the M28 could be competitive. New recruit John Watson was quick in testing, but problems soon manifested: chief among these was a lack of structural integrity.

←
By the time they reached Monaco in 1979, McLaren had a C-spec M28 ready for John Watson. The track exposed this cumbersome car's weaknesses and Patrick Tambay, shown here, failed to qualify his M28B.

M28/M28B/M28C SPECIFICATIONS

Engine	Ford 2,993cc 90-degree V-8	**Suspension**	Rocker arms and lower wishbones with inboard coil springs and telescopic dampers
Power	470bhp @ 9,000 rpm	**Brakes**	Discs f/r
Gearbox	Six-speed manual	**Tires**	Goodyear
Chassis	Aluminum monocoque with Nomex honeycomb	**Weight**	625 kilograms (1,378 pounds)

Coppuck had doubled down on ground effect, creating a very large car with a 113-inch (287-centimeter) wheelbase and large sidepods fixed to an ultranarrow monocoque, the aim being to maximize the area under the car that could generate negative pressure. But with size came weight and, in an effort to mitigate this, Coppuck had made extensive use of chemical bonding rather than rivets to join the Nomex honeycomb monocoque panels to the cast magnesium elements within the structure. These bonds were failing and the team was slow to realize the main cause was the monocoque's lack of rigidity.

The bonds were strengthened for the opening round in Argentina, where Watson finished third from sixth on the grid. This would remain the car's best championship result, for at Interlagos it demonstrated the flaws that eventually defined it: draggy and slow on the straights, stymied by its weight under acceleration and braking. Through testing and the first round, the performance of Goodyear's latest tires had flattered the car, but now its weaknesses were exposed. Watson salvaged eighth, while Tambay crashed in practice and raced the spare car, an M26.

Despite sidepod revisions, the M28s continued to be abject at Kyalami and Long Beach. For round four, at Jarama in Spain, McLaren introduced a B-spec, which was 5 inches (12.7 centimeters) shorter and featured new front suspension geometry, a narrower track front and rear, and relocated rear springs and dampers. Watson was two-and-a-half seconds off pole position. By Monaco the C-spec was ready, distinguished by a longer and narrower nose section with the suspension pickups, springs and dampers mounted further inboard, and another new sidepod design; Watson managed fourth (out of six finishers) from 14th on the grid while Tambay failed to qualify his M28B.

By this point McLaren had already decided to cease development of a car Watson described as "a disaster" and Teddy Mayer called "ghastly." Tambay give it a final outing at the British GP while Watson introduced the new M29.

←
John Watson finished third from sixth on the grid in the 1979 season opener in Argentina. The M28 would never better this result in a Grand Prix.

↑
The B-spec M28 introduced in Spain featured relocated rear springs and dampers, mounted as far inboard as possible.

→
For the US Grand Prix West at Long Beach, McLaren secured additional sponsorship from Löwenbräu beer.

Marlboro
Marlboro
Marlboro
Marlboro
Marlboro
Castrol

M29B/C/F

Just two and a half months elapsed between Teddy Mayer giving the order to abandon M28 development and the new M29 making its Grand Prix debut at Silverstone, round nine of 15 in the 1979 season. During the opening races, McLaren had taken stock of the competitive picture in Grand Prix racing: the previously dominant Lotus 79 and its short-lived replacement, the 80, were now being roundly beaten by Ligier's JS11 and the Williams FW07. Ferrari's new 312T4 was a regular winner in the hands of Jody Scheckter and Gilles Villeneuve. Lotus, like McLaren with the M28, had prioritized peak downforce through ground effect and was suffering because the cars were structurally weak and unreliable. The teams setting the pace all used ground effect to some extent but hadn't compromised strength and efficiency in order to obtain it.

Certain engineering features of the M28 had made it difficult and expensive to modify: it had three fuel tanks, two of which were in the sidepods. The Nomex honeycomb monocoque elements and bonding system also militated against rapid change, so for the M29 Gordon Coppuck moved the driver forward in a chassis that made greater use of conventional aluminum sheeting and consolidated the fuel capacity into a single reservoir within it. The suspension was largely carried over from the M28 since this wasn't believed to be the issue.

Unfortunately, as with the M28, the new car's most convincing performance was its first one. Watson gave the first M29 chassis its race debut in the British Grand Prix at Silverstone, where it lapped almost two seconds faster than the M28's previous best. Patrick Tambay managed to qualify his M28C 18th and was classified seventh, two laps down after running out of fuel, while Watson had a dramatic race from seventh on the grid, dropping back after a poor start and battling to fourth despite an unplanned pit stop. But he was still a lap down on Clay Regazzoni's race-winning Williams, and Regga's teammate Alan Jones had been on pole by a 0.6-second margin, leading imperiously until water pump failure ruled him out.

M29/M29B/M29C/M29F SPECIFICATIONS

Engine	Ford 2,993cc 90-degree V-8	**Suspension**	Rocker arms and lower wishbones with inboard coil springs and telescopic dampers
Power	470bhp @ 10,500 rpm	**Brakes**	Discs f/r
Gearbox	Six-speed manual	**Tires**	Goodyear
Chassis	Aluminum monocoque	**Weight**	587 kilograms (1,294 pounds)

←
For 1980 Gordon Coppuck revised the venturi within the sidepods for the B-spec M29, but poor performance dictated a C-spec.

↑
Developed in a little over two months and carrying over the suspension (but little else) from the M28, the M29 was introduced at the 1979 British Grand Prix.

Successive rounds demonstrated that the M29 was no race winner, as Watson and an increasingly disenchanted Tambay generally qualified outside the top ten and were contenders for only minor placings. New suspension geometry for the Italian Grand Prix failed to yield improvement, so after the end of the season Coppuck made further revisions to the rear end, moving the brakes to an outboard location, and with revised venturi within the sidepods.

This B-spec showed greatly improved pace during a test at Paul Ricard where, among other drivers being evaluated as potential teammates for Watson in 1980, French and European Formula 3 champion Alain Prost was eager to make his mark. Feeling he was being invited to a shootout for the seat, Tambay quit. Marlboro had already offered Prost a drive in the spare McLaren at the season finale, but he turned it down, fearing he would not be able to show his talent effectively in a new car on an unfamiliar circuit. Within a handful of laps at Ricard, Mayer was scrambling to get Prost's signature on a contract.

McLaren's title sponsor intervened again during the course of a troubled 1980 campaign. In Argentina Prost finished sixth in the first round, but he described the M29B experience as "like driving on ice." A C-spec with revised weight distribution, achieved by lengthening the gearbox bell housing and angling the front wishbones rearward, was introduced at Long Beach, and low-drag bodywork evaluated at Brands Hatch—but both Prost and Marlboro were growing impatient for change. Coppuck's M30, introduced for Prost at Zandvoort, failed to persuade the Frenchman to stay on for 1981.

Modified to comply with new rules banning sideskirts, the M29 would live on in F-spec into 1981, but only as a placeholder for an entirely new car executed by a new design and management team.

↓
Patrick Tambay contested six Grands Prix in an M29 and retired from all but one.

↑
The M29 soldiered on until the early races of 1981 in a much-modified F-spec.

Marlboro
8

CHAPTER 3

1980s

In September 1980 McLaren was reborn. A team that had once been a benchmark for innovative thinking, backed up by engineering of peerless quality, had been running on the increasingly vaporous remnants of past glories since 1977. Title sponsor Marlboro, its patience spent, engineered a shotgun marriage between Teddy Mayer's Bruce McLaren Motor Racing Ltd. and Project 4. The latter was the ambitious Formula 2 organization run by Ron Dennis, who had entered motor racing aged eighteen as a mechanic for Cooper.

Along with John Barnard, Tyler Alexander, and Project 4 backer Creighton Brown, Dennis and Mayer became directors of the new McLaren International company. Dennis and Mayer didn't savor the arrangement, the former having coveted a Marlboro-backed Formula 1 entry in his own right while the latter resented interference in the business he had set up with Bruce McLaren.

Politically F1 existed in a febrile state at the turn of the decade as rancor grew between motor racing's governing body and the Formula One Constructors' Association (FOCA), a body founded by Brabham owner Bernie Ecclestone and March cofounder Max Mosley. In mobilizing (and, in effect, unionizing) the majority of the teams to squeeze better deals from race promoters and expand F1's reach on television, Ecclestone and Mosley made enemies within the blazer-wearing coterie of national racing clubs. Friction between the governing body and entrants would rumble on for decades.

Dennis set about rebuilding McLaren in his own image: punctilious, professional, and forward looking. He moved the company out of Colnbrook as rapidly as possible and, by the end of 1982, Mayer had given up in the battle of wills and accepted Dennis's offer to buy out his shares.

But for all that this connection with the company's history had been severed, McLaren would once again build a reputation as high-tech pioneers.

←
The car that became the MP4/1 had been taking shape at Project 4 before the merger with McLaren. Its composite construction would revolutionize F1.

McLaren
GOODYEAR
itg
Prost
8
Castrol
bmcgroup
SmartRoom
Masters

M30

Designed in a hurry and rushed into service at the Dutch Grand Prix of 1980, the M30 was as much a political gesture as a racing car. Gordon Coppuck's former assistant John Barnard had blossomed while working in the US, creating—among other class-defining designs—the Chaparral 2K ground-effect Indy car. Upon returning to the UK in 1979, he had linked up with Ron Dennis, boss of the Marlboro-backed Project 4 Formula 2 team, with the intention of entering F1 with an all-carbon-fiber car. Marlboro was interested in the concept, but not in financing two F1 teams; noting McLaren's poor recent form, they suggested a merger.

This was an arrangement that Dennis and Mayer disliked. Who would be in charge? Additionally Barnard had no intention of answering to Coppuck as he worked on his new vision.

Nevertheless Marlboro began to put pressure on McLaren through 1980 as the M29 proved stubbornly resistant to development, even when Robin Herd was brought in as a freelance consultant to suggest aerodynamic changes. Alain Prost, the recently signed new star, also burned with ambition to get in a better car. In the hope of retaining Prost and keeping Marlboro from forcing the merger through, Mayer greenlit the design of a new car with two key benchmarks: greater stiffness than the M29 and more aerodynamic efficiency. Shorter and wider than the M29, the sole M30 was handed to Prost to race at Zandvoort.

If the point of the M30 was to prove McLaren had no need for outside help, it failed: John Watson outqualified Prost by half a second in an M29 while the new car was plagued with oversteer. Watson held onto a comfortable seventh until his engine failed, while Prost picked up a point in sixth place.

This was the only point the M30 would score. Within weeks Marlboro pushed through the merger and Coppuck was dismissed. The resurgent Watson continued to get the better of Prost in qualifying thanks to a number of setup changes Barnard suggested for the M29, such as raising its ride height. The M30 proved less responsive to Barnard's input despite a new floor. Suspension failure after an early collision gave Prost a scare in Canada, followed by a huge accident during practice for the season finale at Watkins Glen, again thought to be the result of a breakage. Nothing could now persuade him to remain at McLaren.

The damaged M30 was later sold and rebuilt around a spare tub, enjoying a competitive second life in UK Formula Libre events in the hands of Irishman Alo Lawler.

←
The sole M30 chassis built (pictured here in Singapore in 2014) was uncompetitive in period. It was sold into private hands and raced by subsequent owners in Formula Libre and historic events with some success.

M30 SPECIFICATIONS

Engine	Ford 2,993cc 90-degree V-8	**Suspension**	Rocker arms and lower wishbones with inboard coil springs and telescopic dampers
Power	485bhp @ 10,750 rpm	**Brakes**	Discs f/r
Gearbox	Six-speed manual	**Tires**	Goodyear
Chassis	Aluminum monocoque	**Weight**	600 kilograms (1,323 pounds)

7
Marlboro
SAIMA
Marlboro
MICHELIN

MP4/1B/C/D/E

With the MP4/1—initially known just as MP4—McLaren dragged Formula 1 not entirely willingly into the space age. Carbon fiber, an advanced composite material blending great strength with light weight, became the de facto construction method of F1 cars in the coming years, but only after the MP4/1 destroyed many preconceptions. Chief among these was the fear that the car would explode in a shower of dust in the event of an impact.

Though the MP4/1 was seen as a signal of intent by McLaren's new regime after the merger, the concept predated it. Having demonstrated his understanding of ground effect with the Chaparral 2K IndyCar, John Barnard returned to the UK in 1979 with the intention of building the ultimate ground effect F1 car. Key to this was a tub no wider at the bottom than the Cosworth V-8, maximizing room for underwings. Form, structure, and material choice therefore followed function as Barnard explored carbon fiber in preference to aluminum, which was insufficiently strong, and steel, which was too heavy.

This wonder material was not without its challenges. Carbon fiber requires a complex process to achieve tensile strength: first woven into sheets, it is then cut into shape, layered, and glued together and baked under pressure to avoid air pockets forming between the layers. Barnard recognized the mistake that other designers made in using carbon fiber in F1—they thought of it as a direct replacement for sheet steel or aluminum—and saw that the complete monocoque had to be molded as a unit. To do this he would need to learn how many layers to specify and in what alignment—then he'd have to find someone prepared to build it.

He was rejected when he approached British Aerospace, which rebuffed him for what were considered unreasonable production terms, but this led to a useful contact with composites expert Arthur Webb. McLaren eventually succeeded in having the monocoques molded by Hercules in the US. Together with Webb, Hercules' Steve Nichols, and Alan Jenkins—a refugee from the moribund Rebaque team—Barnard arrived at a design where unidirectional carbon fiber layers sandwiched an aluminum honeycomb, enabling the team to incorporate the engine mountings and suspension pickups into the structure.

MP4/1, MP4/1B, MP4/1C, MP4/1D, MP4/1E SPECIFICATIONS

Engine	Ford 2,993cc 90-degree V-8; TAG 1,496cc 80-degree turbocharged V-6	**Suspension**	Upper rocker arms and lower wishbones with inboard coil springs and telescopic dampers (f), double wishbones with inboard coil springs and telescopic dampers (r)
Power	485bhp @ 10,750 rpm / 800bhp @ 11,000 rpm	**Brakes**	Discs f/r
Gearbox	Six-speed manual	**Tires**	Michelin
Chassis	Carbon fiber and aluminum honeycomb monocoque	**Weight**	585 kilograms (1,290 pounds)

←
Last-minute rule changes ahead of the 1983 season required the MP4/1 to undergo surgery to become a flat-bottom car. The regulations also disrupted development of the MP4/2.

↑
By the end of the 1981 season the MP4/1 had dispelled doubts about the performance benefits and safety of carbon-fiber construction. A rather disappointing showing here at the Las Vegas finale, where John Watson and Andrea de Cesaris finished seventh and 12th, showed there was room for improvement.

→
McLaren evaluated a number of different front-wing configurations through 1981 in an attempt to reduce the severity of aerodynamic "porpoising."

Though unsure whether Project 4 had the budget to spend a year developing the car before entering it in F1 for 1981, Barnard was persuaded by Dennis—on the promise that his salary would be paid even if money to build the car didn't materialize. Despite Dennis's energetic attempts to wrangle potential sponsors, finances were running out in mid-1980 when the first tub was nearing completion. The merger with McLaren saved the carbon-car program, but now the pressure was really on: Dennis had promised Marlboro a win in its first season. The sponsor's significance is such that some debate still remains as to whether MP4 stands for McLaren Project 4 or Marlboro Project 4.

Barnard now had more engineering resources at his disposal, but also more battles ahead as he sought to impose his vision of how business should be transacted. For years McLaren's mechanics and engineers, skilled fabricators all, had improvised when making parts, with the result that no two cars were exactly alike. Under Barnard, though, the company held to a policy that everything was to be made exactly according to the drawings signed off by the design office. The inevitable clashes between the old guard and the newcomer led to Tyler Alexander nicknaming the occasionally combustible Barnard the "Prince of Darkness."

While the first chassis was completed in time for John Watson to drive at Long Beach, problems with the exhausts splitting and burning the bodywork meant it did not see action until round three in Argentina. At least initially it seemed the new car was not as transformative as promised. Teething issues pegged it back, as did the team's switch to Michelin tires, which had been designed for the turbo-powered Renaults and Ferraris. The lighter McLaren, powered by a less ferocious engine, struggled to warm up the rear tires sufficiently. There were also problems with "porpoising," a phenomenon where the underbody aerodynamics would enter a cycle of losing and regaining downforce, causing the car to bounce. Racing's governing body had tried to legislate ground effect out of the picture by banning the sliding sideskirts that sealed the underfloor, but teams had responded with fixed skirts that required ultrastiff spring settings and exacerbated the bouncing.

↑
Niki Lauda made a million-dollar return to the F1 cockpit in 1982, driving the aerodynamically redeveloped MP4/1B. He claimed his first win here in Long Beach after race leader Andrea de Cesaris missed a gearshift while shaking his fist at a recalcitrant backmarker.

As McLaren began to work out these issues, results improved—at least for Watson, who scored a memorable win at the British Grand Prix. While Marlboro was appeased, Dennis and Barnard were under no illusions: Watson had driven brilliantly, yes, but he had been assisted by the failure of turbo-powered cars. There was also the problem of his teammate, Andrea de Cesaris, the son of a European Marlboro distributor. De Cesaris came as part of the sponsorship package and was occasionally quick, but always erratic and prone to crashing. Because of this, he was a liability to the team, and Dennis was relieved when no less a talent than double world champion Niki Lauda approached McLaren with a view to making an F1 comeback.

Lauda was initially unsure if he could master the new generation of cars, but he needed the money for his struggling airline business and he drove a hard bargain. Accordingly he became F1's first million-dollar driver. His new teammate's salary bruised Watson's ego, and it didn't help matters when he emerged, albeit unhurt, from a serious accident at Monza in 1981. At least this mishap served to prove the carbon car's safety credentials.

Advancements in design the following year continued to improve performance. New inwardly angled sideskirts, applied in tandem with extended sideskirts and underbody, defined the MP4/1B of 1982, but it was becoming increasingly clear a turbo engine would be required. During the season, matters came to a head between

Barnard and Mayer, resulting in Mayer and Alexander negotiating their exit from the organization. One of the issues related to the choice of turbo engine (see the next chapter), but there would be further political turbulence through 1983 as Lauda began to grow impatient for the turbo's introduction.

New rules mandating a flat underfloor meant a redeveloped aero package for the 1983 MP4/1C, with swept-in bodywork at the rear and carbon brake discs, but the cars were regularly outclassed by turbo entries. In summer Lauda went straight to Marlboro Europe boss Aleardo Buzzi with a blunt assessment that they would likely fail to qualify unless the new TAG Porsche was shoehorned into the MP4/1. Barnard was furious—the engine had been developed in parallel for the forthcoming MP4/2 and optimized for it—but Marlboro threatened to cut funding if McLaren did not comply.

The original MP4/1 prototype was pressed into service as a test hack with 1982 bodywork, christened the MP4/1D, and the "definitive" MP4/1E in 1983-legal trim was ready for Lauda in the Dutch GP. The hurriedly completed model recorded only one race finish, but it at least enabled Barnard to improve the brake disc design for 1984.

↙
In October 1983, British Formula 3 champion Ayrton Senna tested a McLaren alongside his F3 rival Martin Brundle and rising star Stefan Bellof. Ron Dennis would later say, "He came across as arrogant . . . he was clearly impressive, no question, but he was still young."

↓
Designer John Barnard was furious when Niki Lauda went to the Marlboro bosses to demand the early introduction of the TAG-Porsche turbo engine in 1983. But shoehorning it into the MP4/1 served a useful purpose: the V-6's greater power exposed shortcomings in McLaren's new carbon brakes.

Marlboro

MP4/2

Early in the operation of the MP4/1, it became apparent that McLaren needed a turbocharged engine. Introduced by Renault in 1977, in a car derided as "the yellow teapot," forced induction had gone from laughingstock to must-have in the space of four seasons. For various reasons, though, John Barnard disliked the options on the table: Renault's V-6 was insufficiently tidy, with its ancillaries sitting around it, while the BMW straight four was based on a stock block and needed a subframe. Teddy Mayer's insistence on the Renault crowned a number of disagreements over engineering matters and led to Barnard issuing an ultimatum: either Mayer had to go or he would leave the company.

Barnard's ideal engine would be tailor-made to fit the next-generation car taking shape in his head, and Porsche were happy to act as consultant and manufacturer—but they weren't willing to pay for development. This suited McLaren, enabling the team to own the engine—provided that money could be found. A solution came in the form of a new partnership: there was enough in McLaren's coffers to fund the initial design phase, with the rest coming when Ron Dennis charmed Mansour Ojjeh's Techniques D'Avant Garde (TAG) company away from Williams.

Based on the fundamentals of the MP4/1, the MP4/2 was conceived as the ultimate ground-effect car, facilitated by the narrowness of the 80-degree V-6 and its carefully packaged ancillaries (Barnard absolutely would not compromise on the "envelope," leading to some friction with Porsche). This changed during the engine's development, when the governing body eliminated ground effect by mandating flat floors for 1983.

Previous McLarens had been shaped chiefly by heuristics and practical experimentation, with little time or money available for wind tunnel research. Under the new regime

←
Earning second place to teammate Alain Prost in the 1984 season finale at Estoril was enough for Niki Lauda to clinch his final drivers' title by half a point. A year later, Prost's greater pace would grind Lauda down to the extent that he announced his retirement.

MP4/2 SPECIFICATIONS

Engine	TAG 1,496cc 80-degree turbocharged V-6	**Suspension**	Double wishbones with pushrod-actuated inboard coil springs and telescopic dampers (rear upper rocker arms, 1984)
Power	800bhp @ 11,000 rpm	**Brakes**	Carbon discs f/r
Gearbox	Five-speed manual, six-speed manual (MP4/2C)	**Tires**	Michelin (1984), Goodyear
Chassis	Carbon fiber and aluminum honeycomb monocoque	**Weight**	540 kilograms (1,191 pounds)

Barnard was able to validate his designs' aero surfaces scientifically, using the National Physical Laboratory's rolling-road wind tunnel in the affluent London suburb of Teddington. The initial MP4/2 concept featured massive underwings within the sidepods—Barnard would recall "the numbers we were getting in the wind tunnel were phenomenal"—but the abrupt move to flat-bottomed chassis in 1983, midway through the car's development cycle, forced a change of direction.

The MP4/2 was finally ready in time for its scheduled debut in the 1984 season. Its shape would incorporate concepts found to have worked in the hurried conversion of the MP4/1 to flat-bottom spec, particularly the so-called "Coke-bottle" waist of the bodywork behind the sidepods. A hybrid of ideas put forward by Barnard and Alan Jenkins, this look became a standard feature of F1 cars for decades to come. But to maximize the sweep, Barnard relocated the twin KKK turbochargers further forward and at a sharper angle, which compromised power a little. He also added new housings to allow for higher boost pressures, a feature that was retained from the Monaco Grand Prix onward. Barnard's obsessive attention to detail drove another midseason change: mirrored turbochargers that turned in opposite directions from each other, giving a small but significant improvement in stability when the driver came off the throttle. They also meant the exhaust layouts could be symmetrical.

Accommodating a more powerful engine required the MP4/2 to have more robust running gear and higher cooling capacity than its predecessor, as well as stronger brakes. Running the engine in the MP4/1E at the end of 1983 had taken the car's recently added carbon brake discs beyond their capacity. In solving this problem, Barnard arrived at a new means of integrating the carbon and aluminum components of the suspension and braking system in a way that allowed for the different expansion characteristics of these materials when subjected to extreme heat. The MP4/2 would also be the first F1 car to feature carbon discs with drilled cooling vents.

A new and highly sophisticated engine-management system by Bosch featured sequential fuel injection. Offering greater tuneability for different operating conditions as well as better fuel efficiency, the system—like any pioneering technology—was troublesome at first. McLaren considered themselves lucky that the majority of such problems occurred during practice.

Alain Prost returned in place of John Watson for 1984 and won seven races to Lauda's five—but Lauda claimed more minor placings over the season and took the title by half a point. While the records convey a tale of McLaren domination, there were many close calls, including reliability issues with the chassis—particularly nuts in the brake disc bells working loose—and with the engine. And the MP4/2 wasn't always the fastest car, especially in qualifying, where it sat on pole just three times. The 3.2 bar boost level was conservative compared with rivals, but it could be sustained over a full race distance while several rivals ran out of fuel.

For 1985 Barnard looked to optimize the car while responding to regulatory changes that outlawed side extensions to the rear wings. As well as new bodywork elements on the B-spec MP4/2, there were new uprights and hubs and, at the rear, pushrod actuation for the springs and dampers rather than a rocker arm. A new gearbox replaced the one that was struggling to cope with the TTE PO1 V-6's output. Michelin's withdrawal at the end of 1984 also enforced a move to Goodyear tires.

Lauda had the principal share of mechanical and electrical failures during the season and announced his retirement at the Austrian Grand Prix, leaving Ferrari's Michele Alboreto as the chief rival to Prost for the drivers' title. Five wins and a measured end to the season got Prost over the line as Alboreto's campaign fizzled out with five consecutive breakdowns.

The tub design was largely carried over for the 1986 MP4/2C, but with the driver leaning back further, a change enabled by the Fédération Internationale de l'Automobile (FIA), which mandated a smaller, 195-liter (52-gallon) fuel tank. The turbochargers were relocated again with the aim of achieving more inlet flow and higher power.

The year proved challenging for several reasons. Still heavily in debt and insecure about how to follow his "perfect" F1 car, Barnard had sold his shares in the company at the end of 1984 and become a contract employee. This would change the dynamic between him and Dennis in unforeseen ways: arguments of ever greater magnitude ensued over technical policy and money and, throughout 1986, Barnard negotiated a new job at Ferrari.

New driver Keke Rosberg struggled with the MP4/2C's understeer balance and Barnard refused to accommodate his setup requirements until the Monaco Grand Prix. Prost achieved four more wins against the headwind of Williams-Honda's technical superiority: the Honda was now as frugal as the TTE PO1 engine, as well as more powerful. A surprise to all, Prost scored a victory and the world championship in the final round as Williams was beset by tire failures.

↑
In launch spec the MP4/2 featured lateral extensions to the rear wing, exploiting loopholes in the regulations to improve cornering performance and traction—a key limiting factor run the turbo era. *James Mann*

→
Alain Prost forged a strong relationship with race engineer Alan Jenkins (*center*) and would later recruit him as technical director of his eponymous F1 team. Chief mechanic Dave Ryan (*right*) worked for McLaren for over thirty years in various roles.

←
Initially conceived as the ultimate ground-effect car, the MP4/2 proved competitive even though underbody aerodynamics were legislated out of existence before its debut.

Marlboro
Johansson
BOSS
MEN'S FASHION
Marlboro
Marlboro

MP4/3

The first post-Barnard McLaren was completed under the supervision of Steve Nichols. There had been little that was blatantly wrong with the existing MP4/2C, however, so the MP4/3 was more of an evolution than a step change. The suspension geometry was carried over, but the monocoque design was new with a view to making the car's aerodynamic profile sleeker. Wind tunnel research suggested that side-ducted radiators would offer the same cooling characteristics within a slightly lower sidepod profile. Another reason for redesigning the tub was to optimize it for the 195-liter (52-gallon) fuel tank introduced in 1986.

Throughout the 1987 season, the MP4/3 was troubled by inconsistent handling and an even greater predilection for understeer than its predecessor. The TAG turbo V-6 was also beginning to run out of development road. Honda's equivalent produced more power, especially in qualifying where drivers had the facility to turn the boost up considerably. Fuel efficiency had always been the TAG's forte, but bumping up the compression ratio to augment this had diminished its smoothness and reliability. New rules mandated that turbo engines have pop-off valves, limiting boost to 4.0 bar, but the TAG rarely went this high. In fact, when the valves opened they confused the engine-management system's induction sensors.

While Prost won the first round of the season, in Brazil, he earned it through guile, making fewer pit stops than Nelson Piquet's faster Williams. The following rounds were more indicative of how the season would pan out: a snapped alternator belt eliminated Prost early on while he was challenging Nigel Mansell for the race lead. New teammate Stefan Johansson seemed set for second place when part of his front wing broke off.

Prost notched up just two more wins during the season and remained only a fringe candidate for the championship, even though Piquet was hiding the effects of a concussion sustained during the San Marino weekend. Johansson endured even more bad luck on the reliability front and was stymied by two cracked ribs after hitting a deer during practice for the Austrian Grand Prix.

Having recruited former Williams engineer Neil Oatley to work with Prost through 1987, Ron Dennis expanded his team once more by poaching technical director Gordon Murray from Brabham and signing Ayrton Senna to drive alongside Prost in 1988—with Honda engines replacing the TAGs.

←
John Barnard's departure meant the depleted engineering team had to settle for evolution in 1987, tweaking elements of the existing design (such as reworking the sidepods for a lower profile) to create the MP4/3.

MP4/3 SPECIFICATIONS

Engine	TAG 1,496cc 80-degree turbocharged V-6	**Suspension**	Double wishbones with pushrod-actuated inboard coil springs and telescopic dampers
Power	800bhp @ 11,000 rpm	**Brakes**	Carbon discs f/r
Gearbox	Six-speed manual	**Tires**	Goodyear
Chassis	Carbon fiber and aluminum honeycomb monocoque	**Weight**	540 kilograms (1,191 pounds)

Marlboro
POWERED by
HONDA
Marlboro
Shell
TAG HEUER
Marlboro
HONDA
12
Shell
Shell
GOODYEAR

MP4/4

The ever-changing nature of the competition in Formula 1, and the growth and evolution of its calendar, make it difficult to define any single car as the greatest or most successful ever. Yet few would argue that the McLaren MP4/4's was a contender for that title. Fifteen wins out of sixteen races contested, including a streak of eleven consecutive victories—a benchmark only recently equaled—make it at least the defining car of the turbo era.

The MP4/4 project was ambitious: Dennis had bravely signed off on it knowing full well that F1's rules were about to undergo a major change, rendering the car a one-off. For 1988 motor racing's governing body sought to undermine the superiority of turbo cars by reducing fuel tank size yet again, by 45 liters (12 gallons), to 150 (40 gallons) and cutting maximum boost from 4.0 bar to 2.5 bar. Turbos would be banned altogether in the following year. In the interim the naturally aspirated cars would get yet another performance break in the form of being able to run 40 kilograms (88 pounds) lighter. In an age in which many competitors stretched the life of a car over two seasons or more, these were powerful reasons not to build a new turbo chassis.

F1's rule makers hadn't reckoned on McLaren and Honda's resolve. The team had already been running an MP4/3-based test car with a Honda engine; the engineering compromises this involved, along with the car's inherent handling issues, fed into Dennis's decision to greenlight the MP4/4. A single new component made it all possible, unlocking a host of possibilities: a carbon clutch with a 5.5-inch (14-centimeter) plate, 1.75 inches (4.45 centimeters) smaller in diameter than their rivals. It had already been proven by new McLaren recruit Ayrton Senna in a Lotus during the 1987 racing season. Honda agreed to develop an all-new engine with a lower crankshaft to exploit the smaller clutch. The logical choice was to design a new car to maximize all other opportunities to lower the center of gravity.

McLaren had fewer than six months to create the MP4/4. New technical director Gordon Murray had persuaded Dennis that building the chassis in-house would deliver quality benefits that justified the expense of acquiring specialized equipment such as autoclaves.

←
McLaren won fifteen of the sixteen Grands Prix in 1988, but here, in Monza, came the outlier result: Alain Prost had a misfire that ultimately caused his engine to fail, but not before he had turned the mixture up, forced the pace, and tried to lure teammate Ayrton Senna into chasing him. In the closing laps, Senna had to lean his mixture off and carry high corner speeds to eke out his diminished fuel load. Hurrying a pass on backmarker Jean-Louis Schlesser, he was tipped into a spin when the inexperienced Schlesser botched his attempt to get out of the way.

MP4/4 SPECIFICATIONS

Engine	Honda 1,494cc 80-degree turbocharged V-6	**Suspension**	Double wishbones with pullrod-actuated inboard coil springs and telescopic dampers (f), rocker arm-actuated inboard coil springs and telescopic dampers (r)
Power	680bhp @ 12,500 rpm	**Brakes**	Carbon discs f/r
Gearbox	Six-speed manual	**Tires**	Goodyear
Chassis	Carbon fiber and aluminum honeycomb monocoque	**Weight**	540 kilograms (1,191 pounds)

↑
Every aspect of the MP4/4 was designed to achieve a low-slung aerodynamic profile, including the engine's crankshaft height and the step-up gearbox. *James Mann*

↑
During qualifying at Monaco in 1988, Ayrton Senna lapped so quickly he had a transcendent experience in the cockpit: he was so far ahead in the race that his engineers instructed him to slow down, at which point he lost concentration and crashed.

A separate design team led by Neil Oatley (doing double duty as Alain Prost's race engineer) started work on the 1989 car outline for a larger, naturally aspirated engine, while Steve Nichols led work on the MP4/4.

Nichols departed from the Barnard monocoque concept, specifying a straight-sided tub rather than one tapering toward its base: the flat-bottom regulations had long since rendered the taper irrelevant. Periscope induction scoops on the outer bodywork replaced the flat inlets used previously. A completely new dry-sump gearbox design by David North and Pete Weismann used a three-shaft step-up arrangement to exploit the low crankshaft height while maintaining a relatively flat driveshaft angle (any steeper and the joints would be more likely to break under duress).

Positioning the driver at a laid-back angle delivered center-of-gravity benefits and worked in combination with lower, slimmer sidepods to deliver cleaner airflow to the rear wing, reducing drag. Recently an ugly disagreement has developed between Murray and the rest of the McLaren design team over authorship of the MP4/4, and this is one of the disputed areas: Murray says the concept was drawn from the audacious but flawed low-line BT55 he created for Brabham, while Nichols and his colleagues (including aerodynamicist Bob Bell) say they were focusing on center of gravity and clean airflow anyway and, in any case, the BT55 was a lemon they did not wish to imitate.

↖ Senna chats with the architects of the MP4/4's success. *Left to right*: Gordon Murray, Steve Nichols, and Osamu Goto.

← Alain Prost led from the start of the 1988 Japanese Grand Prix after teammate Senna stalled on the grid. Having bump-started his car using the track's downward slope, Senna charged back to win the race and the drivers' championship.

Motor racing can be dangerous even when the cars aren't moving. Here Ayrton Senna risks receiving chemical burns if his mechanic spills that fuel.

To counter the rule makers' intentions, Honda worked closely with Shell on a bespoke fuel formulation laden with exotic hydrocarbons, to the extent that it had to be preheated before the car was filled up. The new blend helped mitigate any power losses caused by lower boost pressures while also being highly resistant to preignition during the compression phase.

The MP4/3 mule car was so underwhelming in a public preseason test in Rio that Honda began to agitate for the MP4/4's arrival. The car was ready just in time for the first race of the season on April 3, 1988, achieving just one shakedown test at Imola a week and a half before. There Prost immediately went two seconds a lap quicker than the mule car.

McLaren's mechanics had to pull all-nighters during the Rio race weekend to get the cars ready, not clocking out until 5:30 a.m. on the Sunday of the Grand Prix. Senna qualified on pole but was then disqualified from the race after his gear linkage broke on the formation lap and he started from the pits in the spare car. No matter: Prost led from start to finish, learning to live with his dislike of the laid-back driving position.

It was at round two in San Marino where the true dominance of the MP4/4 was revealed as the McLarens qualified 1–2, with Senna on pole 3.3 seconds faster than third-place Nelson Piquet's Lotus. While Piquet had the same engine and a new car, Lotus hadn't invested in a new gearbox and had to mount their powertrain tilted upward at the rear to avoid a steep driveshaft angle. Their much-vaunted active suspension system didn't add enough performance to mitigate this inherent compromise.

Having won at Imola, Senna secured another pole at Monaco, 1.4 seconds quicker than Prost, with a lap where he said later he entered a separate plane of consciousness. In the race he was nearly a minute ahead of Prost when the pit wall told him to slow down—at which point he lost concentration and crashed.

Senna had come to McLaren with a mission to test himself against Prost, whom he saw as the best in the business. Theirs was a rivalry for the ages, but the 1988 season unfolded in relative harmony for them as Senna emerged a clear victor in the world championship. And it would likely have ended in sixteen straight victories for McLaren had Senna not tangled with a backmarker while leading the Italian Grand Prix at Monza. The MP4/4 maintained its superiority throughout the year, thanks in part to a series of engine upgrades. (McLaren funded a Japanese Formula 3000 campaign for test driver Emanuele Pirro, so he was always available for private runs at Honda's home circuit, Suzuka.) Still Monza remains the one that got away.

Marlboro
Berger
BOSS
Marlboro
POWERED by
HONDA
Marlboro
COURTAULDS
Shell
Shell
BOSS
HONDA
GOODYEAR

MP4/5B

McLaren entered Formula 1's new naturally aspirated era immaculately prepared, having spent the latter half of 1988 testing Honda's new 72-degree, 3.5-liter (.92-gallon) RA109E V-10 extensively in a mule car based on the MP4/4. The experience of this running persuaded Osamu Goto and his design team to specify a chain-driven camshaft in place of the initial belt-drive arrangement for reliability reasons—although this had implications for the unit's weight.

Mass and its distribution proved one of the MP4/5's ongoing issues as Gordon Murray and designer Neil Oatley tried to shave weight off the car strategically so as not to upset the handling. From the first tests, Prost and Senna both voiced complaints about the car's balance, even though it was competitively quick.

While sharing some design themes with the MP4/4, the MP4/5 had to accommodate a larger fuel tank as well as a longer engine, which entailed a slight increase in the wheelbase to 114 inches (290 centimeters). Different cooling architecture dictated redesigned sidepods that no longer needed to accommodate engine air intakes, since this function had been consolidated into a single scoop above the driver's head.

McLaren continued to attack the weight and handling issues into the 1989 season, introducing Pete Weismann's new transverse gearbox at the British Grand Prix. But the team's biggest challenge wasn't car performance, as Senna racked up pole positions and both he and Prost claimed wins and podium finishes—it was the relationship between the two drivers. No longer entirely cordial, it descended into full-blown rancor after round two in San Marino, where Prost claimed Senna had reneged on a prerace agreement not to attack each other in the opening corners. From this point on, both drivers conducted themselves in the manner of sulking children, communicating with each other only via intermediaries, and each nursing unfounded suspicions that the team favored the other man.

This foolishness built to a peak—though not for the last time—in the decisive Japanese Grand Prix, the penultimate round of the season, when they collided at the Suzuka Circuit's chicane having left their competitors in their wake. Senna was able to get going again, pitted

MP4/5, MP4/5B SPECIFICATIONS

Engine	Honda 3,493cc 72-degree V-10	**Suspension**	Double wishbones with pullrod-actuated inboard coil springs and telescopic dampers (f), pushrod-actuated inboard coil springs and telescopic dampers (r)
Power	680–710bhp @ 13,500 rpm	**Brakes**	Carbon discs f/r
Gearbox	Six-speed manual	**Tires**	Goodyear
Chassis	Carbon fiber and aluminum honeycomb monocoque	**Weight**	500 kilograms (1,102 pounds)

←
A slimmer aerodynamic profile kept the MP4/5B competitive into 1990. By the Mexican Grand Prix, McLaren boss Ron Dennis, flanked by drivers Ayrton Senna and Gerhard Berger, celebrated Honda's fiftieth Grand Prix win.

↑
Honda and McLaren had been testing the new naturally aspirated V-10 since the summer of 1988 in an MP4/4-based mule car. McLaren even funded a season in Japanese Formula 3000 for Emanuele Pirro (pictured here at Circuit de Jerez in December 1988), so he was always available for testing at Suzuka.

for a new nose cone and charged back into the lead, only to be disqualified for receiving a push start. This handed Prost the championship. Senna's vociferous complaints that the French-run governing body was favoring the French driver earned him and McLaren a $100,000 fine each and a threat of exclusion from the 1990 season.

Prost's departure to Ferrari, replaced by Gerhard Berger, brought the promise of better relations on track—once the fines had been paid and relations with the FIA and Jean-Marie Balestre, its autocratic president, had been smoothed over. The MP4/5 was revised into a B-spec for the 1990 season, featuring a larger fuel tank to mitigate the revised V-10's increase in power and redesigned aerodynamics with a greater focus on efficiency. Ferrari's performance through 1989 had been clouded by unreliability—their V-12's vibrations tended to dislodge the alternator belt, causing

↓
The transition to a larger, naturally aspirated V-10 for the MP4/5 gave McLaren several challenges to solve in terms of packaging and weight distribution.

↓
"If you no longer go for a gap," Ayrton Senna said, "you are no longer a racing driver." Here at Suzuka in 1990 he arguably pushed that maxim too far, taking himself and bitter rival Alain Prost out of the race at the first corner.

electrical shutdowns—and McLaren realized it was no longer possible to boost cornering performance with huge wings while Honda's power offset the drag. Smaller front and rear wings, slimmer sidepods, and a turbulence-reducing cockpit shroud distinguished the MP4/5B, along with a much larger underfloor diffuser between the rear wheels.

Two further engine steps arrived midseason, in Germany and Belgium, as McLaren and Honda juggled in-season development with the design of a new V-12–powered car for 1991. Prost, in the revamped and now more reliable Ferrari, took the championship down to the wire, and Japan was once again the scene of a controversial incident between him and Senna. In a moment of madness, the Brazilian ace took his rival out at the first corner while they were flat out in fifth gear. Miraculously neither driver was injured and the world title fell, controversially, to Senna.

GOODYEAR
Marlboro
1
Marlboro
Shell
27
Shell

CHAPTER 4

From chumps to multiple champs: having begun the 1980s as a team out of time, struggling to adapt to Formula 1's evolution, McLaren closed the decade as a virtually unbeatable fighting force who defined the state of the art. Remaining in that position, though, would be a challenge, as the team encountered headwinds both technical and political.

As rivals such as Ferrari and Williams pioneered semiautomatic gearboxes and led the way in sophisticated performance-assistance technologies such as traction control, anti-lock braking, and active suspension, McLaren's apparent reliance on sheer Honda horsepower carried a hint of complacency. The failure to secure a competitive power supply immediately after Honda's withdrawal led to wasted years and a schism with iconic title sponsor Marlboro. The arrival of Mercedes, new sponsorship, and the design genius of Adrian Newey set in motion a revival on track, but Formula 1 remained a game in which the rules were constantly changing.

The chief architect of this flux was Max Mosley—now the FIA president but working, as ever (if not now explicitly), with his old business partner Bernie Ecclestone. For all the fears about safety and spectacle, F1's audience was robust and growing. When the Concorde Agreement, F1's commercial settlement, came up for renewal in 1996, its timing—just as Ecclestone transferred the British TV rights to a different broadcaster for many times the previous rate—led many teams to realize just how much money Ecclestone was now making while their own share of the commercial revenues had stagnated. McLaren boss Ron Dennis was one of the holdouts, a position that would bring him into a conflict with Mosley whose final chapter ended painfully, years later.

←
World champion Alain Prost's defection to Ferrari for 1990 added a thrilling new dimension to his battle with nemesis Ayrton Senna (left).

1
McLaren
POWERED by
HONDA
Shell
GOODYEAR

MP4/6

Ex-McLaren technical director John Barnard might have departed Ferrari at the end of 1989, but the Scuderia's competitive resurgence continued through 1990 as Alain Prost was joined by his former McLaren engineer, Steve Nichols. Honda was in the process of launching the NSX sportscar, which they had benchmarked against Ferrari's equivalent road car—and to that end insisted on developing a V-12 F1 engine to emphasize their Ferrari-beating credentials on track. Many within McLaren were skeptical, but Honda would not be denied.

Although it would have virtually the same displacement as the V-10, a V-12 would inevitably be longer, especially when Honda opted for an oversquare design with the aim of chasing a higher rev ceiling. As well as the packaging implications, more cylinders meant greater weight and more reciprocating elements to manage, along with the potential for greater thirst and frictional losses. Ayrton Senna and Gerhard Berger, along with test drivers Emanuele Pirro and Allan McNish, were unimpressed when they evaluated the first iteration of the new engine in the MP4/5C mule car in late summer 1990. But only Senna had the status to tell Osamu Goto and his engineers what he thought.

Since Gordon Murray was increasingly occupied with his pet project, the McLaren F1 road car, Neil Oatley took a greater executive role in the design of the MP4/6, assisted by new head of aerodynamics Henri Durand, a recent recruit from Ferrari. Atop the priorities list was limiting the potential downsides of the new engine, which would require a slight increase in wheelbase to 117 inches (297 centimeters), and a larger fuel cell, as well as different cooling architecture within the sidepods—which were necessarily taller than before.

To offset the higher drag induced by the sidepods and wider engine, McLaren made one key departure from the MP4/5's mechanical concept. Shifting to pushrod actuation for the front springs and dampers and mounting them in line with the nose cone rather than vertically enabled a slightly narrower nose cone. Higher-modulus carbon fiber in the structure along with detailed weight-saving work throughout the car largely offset the engine's weight, though that would still have an effect on the car's balance.

MP4/6 SPECIFICATIONS

Engine	Honda 3,493cc 60-degree V-12	**Suspension**	Double wishbones with pushrod-actuated inboard longitudinal coil springs and telescopic dampers
Power	720–780bhp @ 13,500–14,800 rpm	**Brakes**	Carbon discs f/r
Gearbox	Six-speed manual	**Tires**	Goodyear
Chassis	Carbon fiber and aluminum honeycomb monocoque	**Weight**	505 kilograms (1,113 pounds)

←
Ayrton Senna's MP4/6 spits flames at Hockenheim in 1991. Metering issues with Shell's new fuel blend proved costly midseason.

Senna led the 1991 Brazilian Grand Prix from the start and then drove one of the finest races of his life, bringing his MP4/6 home in first place when it became stuck in sixth gear.

McLaren was developing a semiautomatic gearbox, as pioneered by Ferrari in 1989, but felt it wasn't ready for competition. The prudence of this decision soon became evident as Senna won four consecutive races at the start of the season: while Ferrari's new 642 proved disappointing, the Renault V-10–powered Williams FW14 had McLaren-beating pace but was let down by its fragile semiautomatic transmission.

Senna's key rival through 1991 would not, therefore, be Prost—who was fired by Ferrari before the season's end after voicing criticism of his equipment— but Williams' Nigel Mansell. The double world champion might not have had the best car-engine package at his disposal, but he was at the peak of his driving powers. In the Brazilian Grand Prix, Senna was leading, delighting his home crowd, when his gearshift first became recalcitrant and then failed to engage altogether. Rain in the final laps added to the challenge as Senna brought his MP4/6 home in sixth gear and had to be lifted, physically spent, from the cockpit and helped to the top step of the podium.

Senna's winning streak gave him a points advantage, and his defense of it was boosted by further developments from Honda and Shell, although the new fuel blend caused metering issues that forced Senna to soft-pedal unnecessarily in France and then run out of fuel before the flag in Britain and Germany. Honda delivered new engine specs in Monaco, Britain, and Hungary that cut overall mass and reciprocating weight and furnished an even higher rev ceiling. Allied to further weight-saving measures on the car, this enabled Senna to mount a successful rearguard action against the Williams challenge, securing his third world title by leading a McLaren 1–2 in the penultimate round—appropriately enough, at Suzuka.

↗
Honda insisted on developing a V-12 to emphasize their Ferrari-beating credentials, but weight, thirst, and frictional losses offset any power advantage.

→
A 1–2 finish for McLaren at Suzuka after Nigel Mansell (*at rear*) spun out with braking issues sealed the championship win for Ayrton Senna.

Marlboro
Marlboro
HONDA
Shell
CAMEL
RENAULT
elf
5
Canon
Labatt's
Bull

Ayrton Senna's third and final world championship was costly. McLaren would not begin to appreciate exactly how costly until the early phases of what would be, by this team's standards, a catastrophic 1992 campaign. First, Honda's development push on the initially disappointing RA121E V-12 through 1991 had sapped resources from the 1992 engine project, a V-12 with very different architecture, including a wider 75-degree vee angle. Dyno testing didn't begin until December 1991, forcing McLaren to delay their new car project. Once ready the new engine delivered little performance uplift despite its new pneumatic valve actuation; a mandatory shift to regular unleaded pump fuel had reduced outputs across the board.

The new plan was to introduce the MP4/7 at the beginning of the European season—round four, in Spain—and use the MP4/6 until then on the grounds that it had been competitive enough to win both world championships in 1991. But McLaren hadn't reckoned on developments at Williams. They also planned to delay introduction of their new FW15 while proving out a new active suspension system in a B-spec of the already rapid FW14. Both teams would be forced to change course: the FW14B proved so dominant that the FW15's debut was pushed back to 1993, while Ron Dennis was so aghast at the FW14B's pace in preseason testing that he directed his engineers to fast-track the MP4/7's completion.

Aerodynamically the MP4/7 retained the general sidepod envelope of the MP4/6, but with smaller and more optimized radiator venting. The multielement rear wing was restructured so that the lower beam element was mounted to the gearbox by two short fixings rather than a tall central pillar. Perhaps most noticeably, the entire nose cone was much slimmer, though McLaren continued to eschew the high-nose concept first used by March and Tyrrell.

While the outer surfaces of the new car followed a familiar theme, the chassis required a total rethink. Ever since John Barnard's pioneering MP4/1, McLaren had used a conventional male-mold methodology in which the carbon fiber sheets are cut and layered onto the

←
Fans and marshals celebrate a thrilling end to the 1992 Monaco GP. Although a new floor had ameliorated the MP4/7's chassis flex, it was still nowhere near as quick as Nigel Mansell's active-suspension Williams FW14B. A suspected puncture forced Mansell to make an extra stop and Senna fended him off in the closing laps.

MP4/7 SPECIFICATIONS

Engine	Honda 3,493cc 75-degree V-12	**Suspension**	Double wishbones with pushrod-actuated inboard longitudinal coil springs and telescopic dampers
Power	790bhp @ 14,800 rpm	**Brakes**	Carbon discs f/r
Gearbox	Six-speed semiautomatic	**Tires**	Goodyear
Chassis	Carbon fiber and aluminum honeycomb monocoque	**Weight**	506 kilograms (1,116 pounds)

outside of a preshaped "buck." Wider industry practice (and Barnard himself, most recently at Benetton F1) had been following the female-mold technique, where the material is layered inside the mold, reducing the possibility of weak points at corners and giving a smoother finish to the outer surface of the finished item. Adopting this different methodology for the MP4/7 would require McLaren's engineers to relearn design and manufacturing techniques. The first chassis they produced were prone to flexing, causing inconsistent handling.

Another new element of the MP4/7 was the gearbox, a new six-speed, semiautomatic unit with electro-hydraulic actuation. A McLaren Electronic Systems fly-by-wire control unit governed both this and the throttle.

Preseason testing can conceal many sins. It was common at the time for some teams to run their cars artificially light, either to attract potential sponsors or, in the case of Ferrari, to avoid the critical eye of senior management and the ferocious Italian press. But the first Grand Prix of 1992 showed that the

←
Although Senna won again in Hungary, Mansell had built such a lead in points that second place was enough to claim the drivers' title with five rounds remaining.

↖
Adopting a different chassis molding technique meant a difficult start for the MP4/7 and a huge effort to get the car ready for Brazil, Ayrton Senna's home race. McLaren also had three MP4/6s as spares.

Williams FW14B's prodigious pace had been anything but artificial: Nigel Mansell qualified 0.74 second quicker than Senna and romped away in the race, finishing over half a minute ahead.

The pattern continued even after McLaren had moved mountains to get the MP4/7 ready for round three in Brazil, a month earlier than originally planned. At his home race Senna qualified 2.19 seconds off Mansell and retired with engine trouble as both Williams cars finished a lap ahead of everyone else.

A new floor fitted at the Monaco Grand Prix cured the chassis flex, and Senna won when longtime leader Mansell had to make an extra pit stop. Two further wins, also opportunistic poaching jobs, brought Senna to fourth in the championship behind the Williams drivers and Michael Schumacher, the only other winner of a Grand Prix that year. Honda announced their withdrawal from F1, leaving McLaren without an engine partner. Furious, Senna tried to find a way into Williams—only to find Prost had negotiated a seat for 1993.

➔
In his final race for McLaren, Gerhard Berger ended the team's first era with Honda on a high note with victory on the Adelaide Street Circuit.

MP4/8

Over the winter as 1992 gave way to 1993, Dennis fought to stave off one of the gravest perils to his team since Marlboro had threatened to terminate their contract over the delayed introduction of the TAG turbo engines a decade earlier. He had known in advance of Honda's decision to quit F1 before the announcement in September 1992, but he still harbored hopes of running the same engines, rebadged as TAG or even Mugen (Honda's performance subsidiary), under the supervision of engine guru Osamu Goto. While Goto *did* join McLaren, albeit with a vague remit that was never properly disclosed, Honda elected not to sell their intellectual property.

As an alternative, Dennis and Mansour Ojjeh made a $20-million offer to buy the struggling French Ligier team, which ran Renault engines. The engine supplier vetoed this move, being unwilling to countenance McLaren's longstanding relationship with Shell. Elf, the nationalized oil company, was Renault's fuel-and-lubes partner both in F1 and as the official factory fill for the company's global road car range.

While juggling all this, Dennis also had to wrangle his star driver, for Ayrton Senna was burning with rage after a troubled 1992 campaign and was not looking forward to another year of being trounced by Williams—especially with his old foe Alain Prost now in the best car. Senna questioned whether he should participate at all, having heard the news that McLaren's only remaining engine option was a customer supply of Ford's V-8—below the Blue Oval's works team Benetton in the food chain and well short of the Renault V-10 on power. He had played hardball with Dennis before, famously settling an impasse over his salary in his 1988–1990 contract by flipping a coin—and now he simply refused to drive except on a race-by-race basis.

What convinced him to persist was the remarkable MP4/8. Despite carrying significant design compromise owing to uncertainty over the engine supplier, this technological tour de force enabled Senna to pull off

←
Customer Ford engines meant a step down in power, but McLaren's 1993 car was nimble and loaded with advanced electronics. This enabled Ayrton Senna to challenge the faster Williams cars when track conditions were suboptimal—such as here, on Senna's home ground in Brazil.

MP4/8 SPECIFICATIONS

Engine	Ford 3,494cc 75-degree V-8	**Suspension**	Double wishbones with pushrod-actuated inboard longitudinal computer-controlled coil springs and telescopic dampers
Power	730bhp @ 13,200 rpm	**Brakes**	Carbon discs f/r
Gearbox	Six-speed semiautomatic	**Tires**	Goodyear
Chassis	Carbon fiber and aluminum honeycomb monocoque	**Weight**	505 kilograms (1,113 pounds)

↑↑
In changeable but mostly dreadful weather conditions at Donington Park, Senna—still operating on a race-by-race deal with McLaren—excelled to win by a minute and a half.

↑
Senna was impressed enough by the Lamborghini V-12's potential in the MP4/8B mule car that he telephoned Ron Dennis straight after the test session at Estoril to enthuse about it—but McLaren ultimately opted to go with Peugeot.

five Grand Prix wins. A refined and lightened McLaren Electronic Systems control unit now provided traction control and active management of ride height as well as fly-by-wire throttle and gearbox actuation. While the MP4/8 was less aerodynamically sophisticated than the Williams FW15 (which began the year in C-spec after being held over from the previous season), it was downsized to take advantage of the Ford engine's compact dimensions.

The key advantage generated by active suspension was that it enabled a car to maintain a consistent ride height. Aerodynamicists could now be more aggressive and add elements that might previously have been too sensitive to small changes in ride height as the car accelerated, braked, and rode bumps.

New teammate Michael Andretti, a star of IndyCar racing, never really adapted to F1 and was replaced by test driver Mika Häkkinen midseason. Senna reveled in the MP4/8's nimbleness and even began to enjoy himself, especially in the European Grand Prix at Donington. In that race's changeable but largely miserable conditions, he overtook four cars on the opening lap and won by a minute and a half, humiliating Prost in the process.

In the search for a better engine, McLaren got as far as building an MP4/8B test car to evaluate Lamborghini's V-12. The Italian marque had been under Chrysler ownership since 1987 and was keen to make an impact in F1. Senna made positive noises about the V-12's power but asked if it could be tweaked for more midrange. Ultimately the alliance did not come about; the engine was already over four seasons old and the test units supplied to McLaren were not new but drawn from a pool allocated to another team. One blew up comprehensively at Silverstone with Häkkinen at the wheel.

Senna announced his departure for Williams in 1994 and Prost, having sewn up his fourth world title, quickly signaled his own impending retirement. As a parting gift, Senna took McLaren past Ferrari as F1's most successful constructor by winning the final round of the season.

↑
Many senior figures within McLaren rate the MP4/8 as one of the company's best cars. The design team rose to the challenge of having to use an engine producing up to 90bhp less than the best in the field. *James Mann*

Marlboro
BRAKES ON
PEUGEOT
Shell
GOODYEAR
EAGLE

MP4/9

It seemed like a good idea at the time. In weighing up the options on the table—a V-12 by Lamborghini, whose parent company's interest was wavering or a brand-new Peugeot V-10 with a cash subsidy from the ambitious manufacturer—Ron Dennis viewed the latter as the most prudent choice. And circumstances seemed to be proving him correct as the 1994 F1 season approached and word came that Chrysler was offloading Lamborghini to an Indonesian consortium. Would the money necessary to bring the aging design up to scratch have been forthcoming, given these developments? Surely not.

Peugeot's migration to F1 was among the desired outcomes of F1 promoter Bernie Ecclestone and FIA President Max Mosley; both had overseen the demise of the World Sportscar Championship (WSC). Having won the WSC as well as the 24 Hours of Le Mans, Peugeot Sport flirted with the idea of a works F1 program with a car designed by former Williams and Ferrari engineer Enrique Scalabroni. The board, though, was reluctant to sign off on the expense and competitions manager Jean Todt left to run Ferrari's F1 team instead. But the 3.5-liter (212-cubic-inch) V-10 engine from the now-defunct sports car program seemed ripe for porting over to F1.

The reality of the A4 engine's performance was gruesome, and it became only marginally less so once the A6 V-10 became available. Just as vexing were the politics: Peugeot wanted a French driver on the squad, but Alain Prost, having tested the MP4/9, decided no amount of money could persuade him to come out of retirement to race it. Philippe Alliot was Peugeot's next choice, a driver Dennis did not consider to be top-drawer material. As a compromise, Alliot was enshrined as chief test driver and Senna's old Formula 3 rival Martin Brundle employed on a race-by-race basis.

McLaren's engineers faced many challenges on top of adapting to an engine originally designed for a different type of racing. For the 1994 season Mosley and Ecclestone, spooked by the Williams team's dominance and the influence of technology on ever more rapid lap times, had pushed through a set of technical changes in the hopes of improving the show. Electronic driver aids such as active suspension and traction control were banned, and in-race refueling was permitted to add some

MP4/9 SPECIFICATIONS

Engine	Peugeot 3,498cc 75-degree V-10	**Suspension**	Double wishbones with pushrod-actuated inboard longitudinal coil springs and telescopic dampers
Power	760bhp @ 14,500 rpm	**Brakes**	Carbon discs f/r
Gearbox	Six-speed semiautomatic	**Tires**	Goodyear
Chassis	Carbon fiber and aluminum honeycomb monocoque	**Weight**	515 kilograms (1,135 pounds)

←
Refueling was reintroduced to Formula 1 in 1994, using technology derived from midair aviation rigs.

strategic variation. An unexpected consequence of the ban on assistance technologies was that cars whose aerodynamics were optimized around active suspension became edgy and difficult to drive.

The MP4/9 represented a step change in aerodynamic philosophy as McLaren adopted the high-nose concept in which the whole frontal section of the car was raised with the aim of increasing the volume of air flowing underneath. A splitter below the curved underside of the cockpit section then directed some of the flow around the side into the radiators while sending a portion of it under the car toward the diffuser, which accelerated the flow as it exited under the rear wing, providing downforce. Vertical bargeboards mounted away from the cockpit sides, already evaluated on the MP4/8, augmented this effect while managing the turbulent wake of the front wheels. Drivers likened the cockpit arrangement to sitting in a bathtub with their feet at the level of the taps.

Following a number of dangerous incidents, and the tragic deaths of Senna and Roland Ratzenberger during the San Marino Grand Prix weekend, the FIA rushed through a package of changes to restrict car performance. Several circuits were retrofitted with temporary chicanes, while all cars had to be adapted with smaller front wings with raised endplates, smaller diffusers, reinforced suspension, and better lateral impact protection around the cockpit. In later races slots had to be cut in the rear of the airbox and a wooden plank mounted on the floor to enforce a higher ride height.

This year marked McLaren's first winless season since 1980, as Brundle and Mika Häkkinen suffered a number of retirements between recording just eight podium finishes. Despite three major performance upgrades, the Peugeot engine continued to be unreliable and the atmosphere was not helped by the company's tendency to blame the drivers or the team. It was with a measure of relief that Ron Dennis concluded a deal with Mercedes for 1995 and Brundle ended the benighted season with a podium finish in Australia, albeit helped by a collision that eliminated title protagonists Damon Hill and Michael Schumacher.

← Bargeboards became an aerodynamic feature as McLaren adopted the raised-nose design philosophy.

↙ Martin Brundle scored McLaren's best finish of the year with second place in Monaco, but Mika Häkkinen was later upgraded from third place on the road here at Spa-Francorchamps when Michael Schumacher was disqualified for a technical infringement.

→ Martin Brundle's MP4/9 belches smoke on the grid at Silverstone after shooting flames out the back. Tiresome politics ensued as Peugeot issued a press release blaming Brundle for retiring the car; the pyrotechnics were caused by "piston-ring flutter" temporarily pressurizing the crankcase, forcing oil through various seals.

Marlboro
Mercedes-Benz
Marlboro
TENCEL
Mobil 1
BOSS
Marlboro
Mobil 1
8
GOODYEAR
GOODYEAR
LOCTITE
ABAC

MP4/10B/C

A new engine package was just one of many adaptations McLaren had to face in 1995, for title sponsor Marlboro now wanted an established star driver—ideally a world champion—after the disappointing 1994 season. On top of this the FIA had brought in a new set of technical regulations that rendered existing F1 cars obsolete.

Owing to the heated nature of the discussion between the various stakeholders, the new rules weren't published until September 1994, three months *after* leading teams would customarily begin work on cars for the new season. The headline changes were a reduction in engine power achieved by cutting displacement to three liters; better safety through mandatory impact-absorbing structures within the chassis and more stringent crash testing; and reduced cornering speeds via further aerodynamic changes. Removing the minimum fuel tank size of 200 liters (53 gallons) enabled designers to accommodate some of the new impact structures and move the cockpit area further back. But the aero changes, including a 50-millimeter (2-inch) step under the chassis and an exclusion zone around the front wheels for bodywork with aerodynamic influence, was reckoned to cut downforce by up to 40 percent.

Another seemingly insignificant but important change governed how the minimum weight was calculated. This figure was raised to 595 kilograms (1,311 pounds), ostensibly to allow leeway for the new crash structures, but it now also included the weight of the driver.

The MP4/10 had a higher, narrower nose than its predecessors, coming to a sharp point at the tip. The height of the nose followed broader design trends across the grid, supporting teams' desire to maximize airflow under the car to extract more performance from the smaller diffuser. Indeed the entire chassis was built to be as narrow as possible at floor level to exploit the step. Likewise the new engine, underwritten by Mercedes-Benz but built at Ilmor in Brixworth, Northamptonshire, was designed with a relatively wide 75-degree vee angle so that ancillaries such as the water and oil pumps could be packaged within the vee rather than alongside the block.

Other measures to claw back lost downforce included a more elaborate rear wing and a subsidiary wing mounted behind the airbox. Chief aerodynamicist Henri Durand would later admit his team erred in prioritizing downforce over efficiency, resulting in higher drag than anticipated as well as an aero balance that was biased to the rear.

MP4/10, MP4/10B, MP4/10C SPECIFICATIONS

Engine	Mercedes 2,997cc 75-degree V-10	**Suspension**	Double wishbones with pushrod-actuated inboard longitudinal coil springs and telescopic dampers
Power	690bhp @ 15,600 rpm	**Brakes**	Carbon discs f/r
Gearbox	Six-speed semiautomatic	**Tires**	Goodyear
Chassis	Carbon fiber and aluminum honeycomb monocoque	**Weight**	595 kilograms (1,311 pounds)

←
McLaren introduced a C-spec MP4/10 in Portugal with a lower center of gravity, but neither McLaren cracked the top ten in qualifying.

Rear wing extensions and an airbox-mounted winglet were among McLaren's solutions to new aerodynamic restrictions. Mark Blundell, pictured in Monaco, drove for the remainder of the season after Nigel Mansell canceled his planned comeback.

Mercedes-Benz's increasing investment in development of the Ilmor-built engine was reflected both in the badging on the V10's cam covers and its high-profile transfer to McLaren from the relatively obscure Sauber team.

Nigel Mansell, 1992 world champion, was lured back after a successful sojourn in US IndyCar racing, but his recruitment hit an immediate snag: the MP4/10's cockpit was too small for him. Even Mika Häkkinen and test driver Mark Blundell, who stood in for Mansell in the opening rounds, found it constrictive.

The MP4/10's inherent understeer balance, exacerbated by a simplistic front wing that was perhaps too literal an interpretation of the new rules, proved a limiting factor in the opening round at Interlagos, although both McLarens finished in the points. But the team's focus was necessarily on developing a B-spec car with a wider cockpit to accommodate Mansell's broader frame.

The MP4/10B was ready for round three at Imola, but it was still no match for the dominant Williams and Benetton cars, the latter having acquired the Ligier team to obtain its Renau t engine supply. Worse still, Mansell loathed the MP4/10B's handling. At round four in Spain he was struggling to keep the car on the track as Michael Schumacher's Benetton came up to lap him. Mansell drove straight to the McLaren pits, parked, and never drove the car again. Blundell took over for the remainder of the season.

Despite the introduction of a revised engine at the British Grand Prix—and a C-spec car with lower center of gravity in Portugal—McLaren's best results were a pair of second-place finishes for Häkkinen at Monza and Suzuka. And the season ended on an ominous note as Häkkinen required an emergency tracheotomy after a crash during qualifying in Adelaide.

After a run of four consecutive retirements, Mika Häkkinen finished second at Monza, benefiting from the elimination of faster cars ahead.

Marlboro
MILD SEVEN
Mobil
8
Red Bull

Marlboro
Mobil 1
Mercedes-Benz
Marlboro
Marlboro
BOSS
CAMOZZI
LOCTITE

MP4/11B

The 1996 season began much as 1995 had ended, with an Australian Grand Prix. Adelaide had been usurped by Melbourne as the venue, and the race promoter had been able to secure the prestigious season-opener slot. Elsewhere there were more changes in Formula 1, as Michael Schumacher moved to Ferrari and the FIA brought in augmented lateral impact measures for car cockpits in response to Mika Hakkinen's near-fatal crash in Adelaide.

Both McLaren and Mercedes sought to learn from the previous season's missteps. This was apparent in the almost totally revised MP4/11, which shared less than 10 percent of the componentry used in its predecessor. One of the updated features in the design was a new longitudinal gearbox. While the engine's issues had chiefly been a lack of reliability rather than power, Mercedes committed to a performance uplift as well as better durability in the third iteration of the FO 110—which also had very little carryover from the 1995 unit.

Steve Nichols had returned from Ferrari and designed a new suspension layout in which the wishbones had a solid mounting to the chassis instead of a conventional attachment via ball joints. Thanks to the increasing fidelity of finite element analysis tools in computer-aided design software, the necessary flexibility could now be engineered into the construction of the wishbones at the point where they met the chassis.

David Coulthard joined from Williams and McLaren were delighted when Häkkinen made a successful return to the cockpit in a test at Paul Ricard in February. But, given Coulthard's newness and the uncertainty over Häkkinen's fitness, the team turned to Alain Prost to shake down the MP4/11 at Estoril ahead of its launch. Both he and the race drivers reported poor handling balance and, after the first three rounds, McLaren began to develop a short-wheelbase configuration in which both axles were repositioned by 5 centimeters (1.9 inches), though this was tunable to give a more rearward weight distribution.

McLaren ran in short-wheelbase form for the first time in Monaco but, after introducing the MP4/11B at Silverstone, generally preferred to run the longer setup with more rear weight bias. There were also detail changes to shape the front suspension wishbones for aerodynamic benefit, and the front wing mounting was augmented to prevent flex.

The results were more positive in 1996: Coulthard led the San Marino Grand Prix confidently, there were fewer retirements, and McLaren claimed six podiums. But fourth in the constructors' standings wasn't enough for Marlboro, who decided to focus on Ferrari from 1997 onward.

←
The short-wheelbase MP4/11B was introduced in Monaco, where David Coulthard (wearing a helmet borrowed from Michael Schumacher when his own suffered persistent visor misting) finished second in mixed conditions.

MP4/11, MP4/11B SPECIFICATIONS

Engine	Mercedes 2,997cc 75-degree V-10	**Suspension**	Double wishbones with pushrod-actuated inboard longitudinal coil springs and telescopic dampers
Power	720bhp @ 15,700 rpm	**Brakes**	Carbon discs f/r
Gearbox	Six-speed semiautomatic	**Tires**	Goodyear
Chassis	Carbon fiber and aluminum honeycomb monocoque	**Weight**	600 kilograms (1,323 pounds)

BOSS
Mobil 1
Mercedes-Benz

MP4/12

While technical regulations remained relatively stable into 1997—the biggest requirement being a new, deformable crash structure at the rear—McLaren approached the new season with yet another largely new car design. Almost every component had been further optimized: most of the outer surfaces, except for the sidepods, bore the signs of careful revision. The latest version of Mercedes' FO 110E engine retained the 75-degree vee angle but was 0.2 inches (0.5 centimeter) lower, owing to a new intake system design; this in turn yielded center-of-gravity benefits as well as the potential for a lower engine cover.

The MP4-12 tested in an orange livery that harked back to the team's 1960s roots, before the definitive silver and black (based on new title sponsor Reemtsma's West cigarette brand) was unveiled during the official launch at London's Alexandra Palace, where popular artists of the time, including the Spice Girls and Jamiroquai, serenaded visitors. The event was a stage for McLaren to trumpet its new identity, and further developments were in the works: media groupthink had blamed the team's recent fallow period on Ron Dennis's policy of not hiring a superstar designer while relying on "groups of faceless engineers." Now Dennis had poached the acknowledged genius of the time, Adrian Newey, the principal architect of four championship-winning Williams cars.

A highly competitive and ambitious individual, Newey wanted even more say in the team's direction but was never going to get it at Williams. When they fired world champion Damon Hill in favor of Heinz-Harald Frentzen, this provided Newey his cue to leave. Litigation between the two teams meant Newey could not officially start work at McLaren until August 1997, but this didn't preclude him from sketching ideas at home.

Williams continued to have the best car—Newey's last design for them—through the 1997 season, but Frentzen and Jacques Villeneuve contrived to make heavy weather of its superiority. They were blameless, though, in their reasons for retiring from the season opener. David Coulthard won from fourth on the grid

MP4/12 SPECIFICATIONS

Engine	Mercedes 2,997cc 75/72-degree V-10	**Suspension**	Double wishbones with pushrod-actuated inboard longitudinal coil springs and telescopic dampers
Power	740bhp @ 16,000 rpm	**Brakes**	Carbon discs f/r
Gearbox	Six-speed semiautomatic	**Tires**	Goodyear
Chassis	Carbon fiber and aluminum honeycomb monocoque	**Weight**	600 kilograms (1,323 pounds)

←
A change in title sponsor after twenty-three years with Marlboro dictated a complete change in the team's visual identity.

↑
David Coulthard claimed a surprise victory from fourth on the grid in the 1997 season opener after polesitter Jacques Villeneuve made a slow getaway and collided with Johnny Herbert's fast-starting Sauber. Then the second Williams was eliminated with brake failure.

with Mika Häkkinen third, McLaren's first win since Adelaide in 1993.

Sadly it would be some time before the team hit these heights again. The new engine proved problematic, causing several retirements, and the MP4-12 was dogged by understeer. Mercedes introduced the 72-degree FO 110F engine midseason at Magny-Cours, but Häkkinen's retirement there demonstrated that the issues had not all been fixed.

After his arrival Newey contributed some ideas, including a new front wing, but a key factor in improving the MP4-12's cornering performance had been dreamed up by Steve Nichols while he sat in the bath, and implemented by R&D chief Paddy Lowe. By fitting an additional brake pedal and a secondary master cylinder, which was then plumbed into the rear brakes, McLaren made it possible for the drivers to brake just one of the rear wheels midcorner to balance out understeer. Initially it had to be set up to work on one specific side, which the team chose depending on the circuit, but a later development enabled them to direct braking effort to either side, selectable via a switch on the steering wheel. The implementation was trickier on Coulthard's car, since he used a three-pedal arrangement with a foot clutch, whereas Häkkinen used a hand clutch and braked with his left foot, but the system was reckoned to be worth up to three quarters of a second in terms of lap time.

Häkkinen and Coulthard recorded a win each and two more podiums in the latter half of the season. The "brake-steer" system generated protests from rival teams, who claimed it would cost millions for them to copy. In truth it had been derived from less than $100 in spare parts.

↑↑
McLaren's braking system caught the eye in 1997. Both cars retired here at the Nürburgring, and *F1 Racing* magazine photographer Darren Heath, tipped off by the editor via cellphone, was able to reach Häkkinen's car before it was recovered to the pits. He fired off a few shots of the mysterious extra pedal in the cockpit.

↑
Häkkinen and Coulthard finished 1–2 in the 1997 season finale when world champion–elect Jacques Villeneuve slowed in the final laps. An FIA investigation into collusion between McLaren and Williams—Häkkinen had pitted out of Villeneuve's way earlier in the race—found no evidence to press the allegation.

West
West
Schweppes
KENWOOD
Sun
BRIDGESTONE
West
8
Mobil 1
West

MP4/13

Increasing car performance, particularly in the 1997 season after Bridgestone joined the fray as a rival to Goodyear, prompted FIA President Mosley to announce another wide-ranging package of measures to contain speeds and improve safety for 1998. As usual with Mosley's impositions, these came freighted with unforeseen consequences.

Since Goodyear had signaled its withdrawal at the end of the season, McLaren swapped to Bridgestone, which would require some adaptation. Everyone in the field had to scramble for solutions as it turned out, since the new rules aimed to reduce the contact patch of the tires by the rather crude measure of mandating that they have wide grooves cut in the surface, three at the front and four at the rear. As a further measure to cut cornering speeds and (in theory) improve overtaking, the maximum track width was reduced by 12 percent, from 78.75 inches (200 centimeters) to 70.87 inches (180 centimeters). The brake apparatus also came under attack, with new restrictions on exotic materials and disc thickness.

While the safety improvements were mostly beneath the skin—the driver's survival cell had to be wider at the front, the chassis walls were reinforced, and it all had to withstand a more stringent side-impact test—one visible change was the extension of the head-protection area around the cockpit aperture. Packaging the structural reinforcement would be a key challenge given the reduction in width: F1 cars naturally had very little spare space inside to be cut. There was also a school of thought that called for cars to have shorter wheelbases by a similar proportion to the reduction in width, but Newey believed that a *longer* wheelbase would reduce loading on the outside tires.

The narrower track would also have a greater effect than anticipated on aero performance and, crucially, introduce instability. Tires not only act as an aerodynamic blockage, they produce turbulence that is difficult to simulate accurately. Moving them inboard disrupted the airflow around the sidepods and had the fundamental effect of making the cars less predictable and harder to drive, which did not improve safety.

MP4/13 SPECIFICATIONS

Engine	Mercedes 2,997cc 72-degree V-10	**Suspension**	Double wishbones with pushrod-actuated inboard torsion bars
Power	790bhp @ 17,000 rpm	**Brakes**	Carbon discs f/r
Gearbox	Six-speed semiautomatic	**Tires**	Bridgestone
Chassis	Carbon fiber and aluminum honeycomb monocoque	**Weight**	600 kilograms (1,323 pounds)

←
McLaren understood how to manage the turbulent wake of the front wheels early on in the new narrow-track era. This was one of the MP4/13's key advantages.

↓
McLaren's dominant 1–2 in the 1998 season opener magnified political pressure to ban the team's brake-steer system.

↘
Elongated sidepods, combined with curving bargeboards, encouraged turbulent air behind the front wheels to wash away from the car.

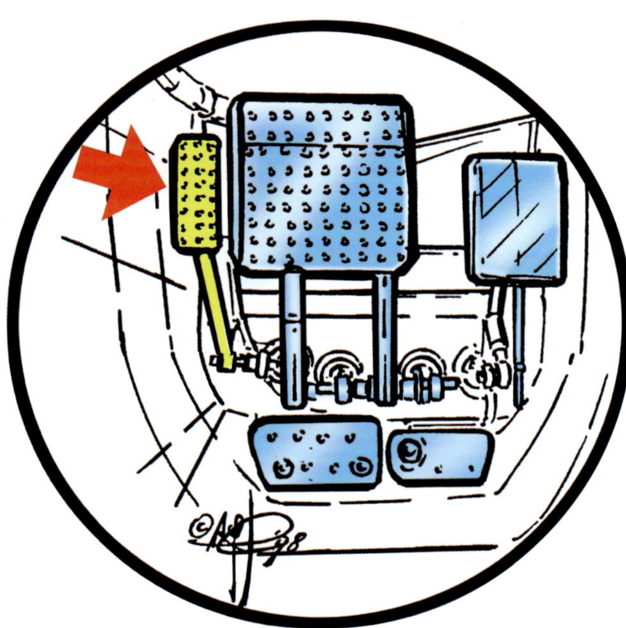

↑
An additional pedal enabled the driver to trim out understeer by applying extra braking force to one rear wheel.

Newey had found a way to circumvent the chassis height regulations by adding fins around the forward cockpit edge and head restraints. Working separately, before Newey joined McLaren in August 1997, Henri Durand's aerodynamics team had established that extending the sidepods forward helped encourage the front wheel wake to push outward rather than disrupting the car.

Despite being late to testing after a last-minute revision to the rear suspension's construction, the MP4/13 proved to be virtually unbeatable. Having recruited the 1994-1995 championship-winning Benetton technical team to join Michael Schumacher, Ferrari was close but not fast enough. And Williams, without Newey, was a spent force. Mika Häkkinen and David Coulthard qualified the MP4/13s on the front row in the Melbourne season opener and left all but Schumacher trailing in their wake. Coulthard courteously moved over to let his teammate win after Häkkinen misheard an instruction to mind his rear brake temperatures and came into the pits unnecessarily.

Newey felt the brake-steer system was making the rear brakes marginal on temperature—as borne out by Häkkinen's issues in Australia—but this was rendered academic when Ferrari's lobbying proved successful and McLaren received a directive to remove the system for round two. Nevertheless, Häkkinen won again from pole position, with Coulthard second and Schumacher third, a minute in arrears.

This pattern continued throughout the season, although Ferrari's performance improved after Bridgestone introduced a wider front tire in round three. Despite this, along with three consecutive wins during summer, Schumacher was unable to prevent Häkkinen registering McLaren's first drivers' and constructors' championships since 1991.

↑
A resurgent Ferrari, featuring Michael Schumacher, provided the greatest challenge to Mika Häkkinen's title bid.

LOCTITE
BOSS
Mobil 1
Mercedes-Benz
West
COMPUTER ASSOCIATES
1
2
Mercedes-Benz
Mobil 1
LOCTITE
West

MP4/14

McLaren's successor to the championship-winning car of 1998 had been in the wind tunnel since May of that year, so it came as little surprise that the MP4/14 closely resembled its predecessor, though with more of an Adrian Newey authorial stamp. The new nose looked broadly similar but differed in profile, with a slightly lower tip and a less pronounced downward slope underneath, while the suspension was modified to accommodate new mandatory tethers designed to prevent the wheels from detaching in an accident.

FIA President Mosley made good on his threat to restrict performance: the front tires now had four rather than three grooves, and McLaren's work on the front end of the MP4/14 aimed to bring the aerodynamic center of pressure forward to compensate for the anticipated loss of grip in that area. But in the event, Bridgestone—now the sole tire supplier to the whole grid—put so many resources into their own development of the new front tires that the rears became the chief limiting factor for performance and race strategy.

One of the issues Newey had faced with the MP4/13 was McLaren's composite expertise: the cars came in well underweight, forcing some compromises in placing ballast to optimize handling for particular circuits. Given more design time, he insisted on a far more aggressive packaging of ancillary components, requiring a new hydraulic system and a shorter gearbox.

Perhaps as a result of the edgier design, the MP4/14 proved temperamental. Mika Häkkinen and David Coulthard led the way in every prerace session during the Australian Grand Prix weekend, only for everything to go awry on race day. Häkkinen's race car never made it out of the garage and he started in the spare, fading out of the lead with throttle response problems before finally stopping. Coulthard had already been eliminated by a hydraulics system failure.

Car problems also struck Schumacher in Melbourne, so wins for Häkkinen in Brazil, Spain, and Canada, plus podiums in Monaco and France (where Schumacher won) enabled Häkkinen to build a thirty-four-point lead ahead of the midseason British Grand Prix, where Schumacher broke his leg in a crash. The championship was there for the taking.

MP4/14 SPECIFICATIONS

Engine	Mercedes 2,997cc 72-degree V-10	**Suspension**	Double wishbones with pushrod-actuated inboard torsion bars
Power	800bhp @ 17,000 rpm	**Brakes**	Carbon discs f/r
Gearbox	Six-speed semiautomatic	**Tires**	Bridgestone
Chassis	Carbon fiber and aluminum honeycomb monocoque	**Weight**	600 kilograms (1,323 pounds)

← Self-inflicted issues hampered McLaren's championship ambitions in the second half of the season. In Austria, Coulthard pushed Häkkinen into a spin on the opening lap.

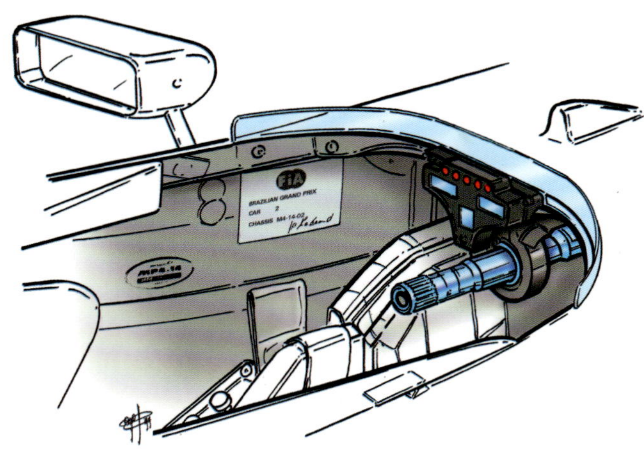

Newey has subsequently said the team "fell asleep" and "kept throwing things away." Certainly by this point much of the early season unreliability had been dialed out, at least on Häkkinen's side of the garage. Operational blunders would prove more problematic, Silverstone being a case in point: Häkkinen started on pole but exited when a wheel came off his car. Coulthard won, but Schumacher's teammate Eddie Irvine was second.

As Ferrari and substitute driver Mika Salo threw their weight behind Irvine, McLaren team errors mounted. Häkkinen qualified on pole in Austria but had to fight his way back to third after his own teammate spun him to the tail of the field on the opening lap. Coulthard then failed to prevent Irvine slipping through to win the race. Tire failure ruled Häkkinen out of the German GP, where Salo moved aside to let Irvine win and Coulthard was a lowly fifth; Häkkinen then led a McLaren 1–2 in Hungary but in Belgium he was hit again by Coulthard on the opening lap and finished second to him. In Italy Häkkinen spun off after hooking the wrong gear, then at the Nürburgring he finished fifth after the team called him in for wet-weather tires during what turned out to be a brief rain shower. The stakes rose again in the final two rounds as Ferrari recalled the now-recovered Schumacher to act (somewhat unhappily) as Irvine's wingman.

Amid a brouhaha over the legality of Ferrari's new bargeboards, Häkkinen finally sealed the drivers' title with victory at Suzuka, but Ferrari claimed the constructors' championship.

↑
A different nose profile was the biggest outward change from the previous car, but inside the MP4/14 was much more aggressively packaged.

↑
David Coulthard won the British Grand Prix, but Mika Häkkinen, who had been on pole, failed to finish when a wheel detached.

↑
After recovering from a broken leg, Michael Schumacher found himself in the unusual position of having to drive in support of teammate Eddie Irvine's title bid in the final two rounds. Here in Malaysia he did his best to block the two McLarens in the early laps.

vodafone
22
SAP
vodafone

CHAPTER 5

2000s

In 1995 McLaren had acquired a derelict mushroom farm on the outskirts of Woking with the aim of consolidating operations from various local industrial units into a new dedicated headquarters. Even on brownfield land, a construction of this scale invited considerable scrutiny and required extensive environmental mitigations. As such it wasn't until late 2001 that McLaren's aerodynamics department (now led by Peter Prodromou after Henri Durand's departure for the Prost team) was able to work in the state-of-the-art wind tunnel around which the rest of the McLaren Technology Center was taking shape.

Mercedes exercised a contractual option to acquire 40 percent of the McLaren Group, which by now included separate companies operating in the fields of electronics, marketing, and high-end catering as well as ongoing service of the F1 supercars built the previous decade. In the coming years McLaren would launch another company, bringing F1 technology to adjacent industries and rekindling an interest in road car manufacture. But the alignment with Mercedes also placed McLaren in political opposition to F1 commercial rights holder Bernie Ecclestone and FIA President Mosley, since Mercedes had formed an interest group with other manufacturers active in F1 that threatened to form a breakaway series of their own.

While Enzo Ferrari was long in his grave, the custodians of his company played the sides of this political divide against one another with a dexterity that would have made the Old Man proud. As the Ferrari team strode to successive championships in this decade, it seemed as if every decision handed down by officialdom went the way of Maranello.

"When you take on Ferrari," said McLaren Chief Operating Officer Martin Whitmarsh, "you take on City Hall as well."

←
Formula 1 reached "peak aero" in the late 2000s as the cars sprouted ever more sophisticated aerodynamic addenda.

David
Schweppes
Sun
KENWOOD
Sun
2

MP4/15

If Mika Häkkinen's title defense in 1999 had proved fraught, the events of that season would have nothing on the millennial hangover in 2000. Not that Häkkinen himself was unprepared: he arrived at the dawn of the new season looking fitter than he had in years, having spent the winter training hard. He knew he had a fight on his hands to keep Ferrari and Michael Schumacher at bay.

The atmosphere remained tired and tense within McLaren, sensations born of the growing impression that Ferrari was enjoying a favorable outcome from every technical decision presided over by the governing body. For some the removal of brake-steer after Ferrari stamped their feet still rankled. Adrian Newey was particularly frustrated by the outcome of the hearings relating to Ferrari's bargeboards, which had been introduced late in the previous season. First they were illegal, then they weren't—and in a sport where investment in innovation can be expensive, such apparent caprice was demoralizing.

While the basic aerodynamic and mechanical philosophy of the MP4/14 was carried over, Newey's engineers attempted to package the car even more aggressively while aiming to address some of the reliability problems that had stymied the 1999 title charge. Mercedes provided a new FO 100J V-10 that was 2 inches (5 centimeters) shorter than the previous spec and achieved an even higher rev ceiling. Development of this proceeded in tandem with the design of a new seven-speed gearbox to allow routing the exhaust pipes right alongside the transmission casing, exiting between the diffuser arches.

Another new idea came in the form of chimneys on each sidepod, which aimed to eject the turbulent hot air from the radiators out of the path of the rear wing. At launch McLaren management was at pains to point out that this had been checked in advance with the FIA technical delegate and declared within the rules.

The scale of the challenge facing Häkkinen's title defense became apparent when his car halted on its first test run at Jerez. The same problem—initially claimed to be hydraulic but actually caused by failed valve seals—eliminated both cars in the season opener while Häkkinen was leading Coulthard and Schumacher from pole position. Two weeks later Häkkinen retired in a cloud of smoke again while leading from pole at Interlagos, while Coulthard battled gearbox issues to finish second, only to be disqualified when postrace checks revealed his front wing endplates were

MP4/15 SPECIFICATIONS

Engine	Mercedes 2,997cc 72-degree V-10	**Suspension**	Double wishbones with pushrod-actuated inboard torsion bars
Power	815bhp @ 18,000 rpm	**Brakes**	Carbon discs f/r
Gearbox	Seven-speed semiautomatic	**Tires**	Bridgestone
Chassis	Carbon fiber and aluminum honeycomb monocoque	**Weight**	600 kilograms (1,323 pounds)

← Ferrari's competitive renaissance in 1999 pushed McLaren and Mercedes to take more design risks, with a new engine and aerodynamic philosophy.

↑
Mika Häkkinen explains driving etiquette to Michael Schumacher after the 2000 Belgian Grand Prix, where Häkkinen executed one of the most daring overtakes in F1 history after Schumacher pushed him off the track several times.

0.28 inches (0.7 centimeters) lower than permitted. McLaren protested the disqualification, saying this was a result of structural damage caused by the bumpy track surface, but their objection was given short shrift.

The Brazil race also revealed that Ferrari's car concept revolved around a small fuel tank, committing the drivers to more pit stops but potentially enabling them to achieve faster lap times between stops. This enabled Schumacher to overturn Häkkinen's lead in round three, but at least Häkkinen finished and had some points on the board.

Nevertheless Häkkinen was beginning to look like a beaten man. Three victories for Coulthard in the early half of the season enshrined him as the chief challenger to championship leader Schumacher, despite Coulthard nursing separated ribs incurred in a plane crash. In Monaco and Canada Häkkinen's qualifying form evaporated and his race performances were muted, to the point where Ron Dennis suggested he take a break.

Austria provided a turning point as Häkkinen won while Schumacher was eliminated in an opening-lap crash. "Now it starts," Mika told reporters afterward, although the drama continued after McLaren were fined and docked their constructors' points for the race when the engine's electronic control unit (ECU) was found to be missing one of its mandatory seals.

Further wins in Hungary and Belgium—where Häkkinen executed a daring overtake on Schumacher using another car's slipstream—enabled him to move into the championship lead. But another engine failure, this time at Indianapolis, proved costly. Victory at the penultimate round in Japan, with Häkkinen second, enabled Schumacher to win a first drivers' championship for Ferrari since Jody Scheckter in 1979.

↑
Häkkinen returned to form after a midseason waver, moving into the championship lead with victory in Hungary. He was boosted by the addition of new aerodynamic tweaks and an engine upgrade.

West

MP4-16

A further set of rule changes, mostly in the name of safety but one having a crucial impact on car performance, dictated an all-new design for McLaren in 2001. The chassis cross section was increased to allow for a 25-millimeter (0.9-inch) layer of padding around the driver's legs, the roll hoop had to be reinforced to meet new crush tests that were four times more forceful than before, the number of wheel tethers was doubled, and the safety cell now had to resist intrusion as well as impact. While laudable, these measures naturally brought increased weight and, in the case of the roll hoop, a higher center of gravity.

The FIA also tried to peg back car performance by mandating smaller, simpler rear wings and higher front wings. The rear wing was limited to two main planes, with the lower one restricted to a single element and mounted even lower on the car, and the upper plane restricted to three distinct elements.

While this had an effect on overall downforce levels, it was the comparatively innocuous-sounding 1.97 inches (50 millimeters) increase in the minimum front wing height that had more significant implications. The front wing in effect dictates the aerodynamic map of the car, influencing flow to everything downstream—hence the requirement for a clean-sheet design. But what the FIA did not realize at the time was that the higher wing was more prone to disruption by the turbulent wake of the car ahead, preventing cars from following each other closely around corners and militating against overtaking opportunities.

As well as winning both championships in 2000, Ferrari scored another victory in the off-season by successfully lobbying to have aluminum-beryllium banned from engines and their components. McLaren's Ilmor-built Mercedes engines had featured aluminum-beryllium pistons for at least a year. The material offered an attractive cocktail of performance virtues: it was stiffer than aluminum and offered better thermal conductivity properties, but it was rare and difficult to work with—and therefore expensive (some in the paddock referred to it as "unobtainium").

The ban forced another all-new engine design, but in-season development was stymied after Ilmor cofounder Paul Morgan died in a crash of his vintage fighter plane. His business partner, Mario Ilien, was overstretched by having to take on the commercial aspects of the company following Morgan's death, and within months Mercedes began to tighten their control over Ilmor by increasing their shareholding.

MP4-16 SPECIFICATIONS

Engine	Mercedes 2,997cc 90-degree V-10	**Suspension**	Double wishbones with pushrod-actuated inboard torsion bars
Power	830bhp @ 18,500 rpm	**Brakes**	Carbon discs f/r
Gearbox	Seven-speed semiautomatic	**Tires**	Bridgestone
Chassis	Carbon fiber and aluminum honeycomb monocoque	**Weight**	600 kilograms (1,323 pounds)

←
After podium finishes in the first two rounds, David Coulthard won in Brazil, establishing himself as McLaren's chief title contender after teammate Mika Häkkinen's difficult start.

↑
Suspension failure caused a concussion-inducing crash for Häkkinen in Australia. Two rounds later, another dangerous moment occurred when his car stalled on the grid in Brazil. These unfortunate events gave him second thoughts about continuing in F1.

↗
By the Italian Grand Prix, Ferrari's fans were celebrating the end of McLaren's dominance.

Two further developments further complicated the competitive picture in 2001: the arrival of Michelin as a rival to Bridgestone—which sparked a development war—and the return of traction control from round five onward. The relaxation of the ban on traction control was in effect a capitulation on the FIA's part. It had been impossible to police, and suspicion was rife that at least one major team had been using a device that momentarily cut the ignition when it detected wheelspin or used sophisticated mapping to mimic that effect.

Defending champion Michael Schumacher won the season opener in Australia from pole position for Ferrari, with David Coulthard in second place. Mika Häkkinen suffered a mild concussion in a heavy accident after his front suspension broke. The McLaren teammates were then third and sixth when Ferrari called changing conditions better in Malaysia. In Brazil Häkkinen had another hair-raising moment when his car stalled at the start; he was lucky not to be hit from behind.

In the races that followed, it became increasingly obvious Häkkinen's mojo had left him. He won at Silverstone and Indianapolis, but by the time the F1 circus reached the US, he had announced he would be taking a sabbatical in 2002. He never raced in F1 again and, years later, admitted the events of Australia and Brazil in 2001 informed his decision to step away.

Coulthard won two races but had problems with the new traction control system on the starting line in Spain and Monaco, finishing a distant second to Schumacher in the championship.

↑
Victory in the British Grand Prix came too late to rescue Häkkinen's title ambitions.

FOSTER'S
West
SIEMENS

MP4-17

The turbulence of the 2001 season was reflected in the development of the car for 2002. Challenges arose for the MP4-17 despite being the first McLaren to benefit from time in the team's new wind tunnel. Relations were cooling between Newey and Dennis, with Newey claiming that he'd been offered a new contract that essentially included a pay cut. McLaren's star technical director went as far as signing a contract to join his old friend Bobby Rahal at Jaguar Racing before Newey got cold feet. While he was probably wise to stay where he was, as Rahal soon joined the swelling ranks of former Jaguar bosses, Newey's relationship with Dennis suffered from the affair.

Dennis was determined to keep Newey in the fold—and to keep him from going elsewhere to design cars—but he moved to reduce Newey's authority, instituting a matrix management system with multiple layers for reporting and a design committee of performance creators. This system begat what Newey would describe as "a bit of a clumsy design, certainly not one of my best."

Although evolutionary in many respects, the MP4-17 bore key differences from previous McLarens at both ends. At the front it embraced the twin keel concept pioneered by the Sauber team the previous year, with a sharply undercut nose section. On each side of this, short vertical extensions provided a mounting point for the angled lower wishbones. While this theoretically delivered an aerodynamic advantage by creating a larger area under the nose, it compromised suspension rigidity, which is why some teams, notably Ferrari, did not adopt the philosophy until much later.

At the rear a completely reprofiled engine cover and lowline deck concealed another all-new V-10. As was becoming fashionable at the time, Mercedes had opened the vee out to 90 degrees in the pursuit of aerodynamic advantages and a lower center of gravity. Others went further—Renault to 100 degrees—but Mercedes felt this was the ideal compromise.

←
Revised into D-spec, the MP4-17 proved to be an unlikely challenger in 2003 when the troublesome MP4-18 had to be delayed, then shelved.

MP4-17 SPECIFICATIONS

Engine	Mercedes 2,997cc 90-degree V-10	**Suspension**	Double wishbones with pushrod-actuated inboard torsion bars
Power	850bhp @ 18,500 rpm	**Brakes**	Carbon discs f/r
Gearbox	Seven-speed semiautomatic	**Tires**	Michelin
Chassis	Carbon fiber and aluminum honeycomb monocoque	**Weight**	600 kilograms (1,323 pounds)

While Mercedes did not suffer quite the same performance and reliability issues as Renault, the FO 110M engine was one of the key weak spots of the McLaren package throughout 2002 and often had to be run below peak revs to avoid blowups. The BMW P82 V-10 motivating Williams was believed to be the most powerful in the field, but the best all-round car was the Ferrari F2002, which was introduced in round three and flew to fourteen victories.

Having swapped to Michelin tires, McLaren suffered as a result of not being able to test the new rubber until January. Although the suspension was designed with adjustability in mind, this brought inherent compromise.

New recruit Kimi Räikkonen finished third in the opening round but registered just three more podiums among a host of failures to finish, mostly related to reliability. Coulthard's victory in Monaco was the high point of the season. A potential win for Räikkonen in France fell off the table when marshals failed to signal the presence of oil on the track and he spun out of the lead.

Revised into D-spec over the winter and carrying the new FO 110P engine, the MP4-17 was destined for retirement after the first three rounds of 2003—only to see out the end of the season when the new MP4-18 proved problematic. While the MP4-17D was unexpectedly competitive, enabling Räikkonen to win in Malaysia and notch up sufficient podiums to run Schumacher close for the championship, the ongoing MP4-18 project sapped resources and focus.

Team management would concede that the distraction cost McLaren a shot at the title, but there was another reason: Michelin's front tires had been cleverly designed so that their contact patches expanded once the car was running. After a Ferrari protest—naturally—the FIA brought in new postrace measurements at Monza, forcing Michelin to rush new tires through design and production in a matter of weeks.

→
Charlie Whiting, the FIA's race director and technical delegate (jobs fulfilled by at least three people in the modern era) examines the MP4-17's front suspension on the grid in Austria. The complicated lower-wishbone arrangement offered aerodynamic benefits but compromised rigidity and suspension geometry.

←

A wider engine vee facilitated a lower rear deck but called for rerouting the exhausts from the top rather than behind the gearbox, as on the MP4-16.

↑

Although Kimi Räikkönen (carrying race number 4) suffered the majority of the technical issues in 2002, McLaren still finished third overall. *James Mann*

Sun
Sun
6
SAP
Mobil
1
SIEMENS
mobile

MP4-18

When the initial races of 2002 and the arrival of Ferrari's dominant new car package suggested that the MP4-17 would fall well short of being a championship contender, McLaren opted to take a completely new design direction for 2003. The MP4-18 would be much more tightly packaged, lower and lighter all round, with a much narrower nose cone and a lighter gearbox with a carbon fiber casing.

Initial testing revealed a number of fundamental problems that McLaren struggled to grasp and failed to address promptly, thanks in part to the design-by-committee matrix management system. The drivers complained of frightening instability, the new nose was difficult to engineer to crash-resistance standards, and the tight packaging made it difficult and time consuming for mechanics to work on. Testing was also disrupted by a number of small fires caused by the proximity of the exhaust pipes to the floor: McLaren was trying to use hot air to blow the diffuser, unaware that this would require specialized engine mapping to exploit fully.

In Newey's autobiography, the technical director states his belief that the aerodynamic instability was caused by vortices generated by beam wings in front of the sidepods bursting, an issue that could only be properly fixed by redesigning the chassis itself. His solution was voted down by his fellow "performance creators," however, who thought design resource would be better used on developing the MP4-17. Others party to the car say its problems were more deep seated, many related to radically lightweight materials proving insufficiently robust. The suspension was particularly fragile, and breakages caused several crashes in testing—which management blamed on driver error.

The MP4-18's race debut was repeatedly moved back from the planned San Marino Grand Prix; from May onward, when it began testing in public, the problems were obvious. Test driver Alexander Wurz appeared to be shouldering the majority of the work, and speculation was rife that Kimi Räikkonen had refused to drive it again after being blamed for a breakage-induced shunt.

After summer, McLaren ceased to put a date on the MP4-18's introduction, and indeed it would never race—at least, not under that name.

←
With its narrow nose, wavy front wing profile, and aggressively low center of gravity, the MP4-18 represented a completely new direction for McLaren. But test driver Alex Wurz lapped faster than the MP4-17D in it only once.

MP4-18 SPECIFICATIONS

Engine	Mercedes 2,997cc 90-degree V-10	**Suspension**	Double wishbones with pushrod-actuated inboard torsion bars
Power	850bhp @ 18,500 rpm	**Brakes**	Carbon discs f/r
Gearbox	Seven-speed semiautomatic	**Tires**	Michelin
Chassis	Carbon fiber and aluminum honeycomb monocoque	**Weight**	600 kilograms (1,323 pounds)

West
West
14
MICHELIN
DU PONT
MICHELIN
BECKS
HSBC
HSBC
SIEMENS
SAP
Mobil 1
Sun
BOSS
6

MP4-19B

Even before the MP4-19's launch, insiders were whispering to compliant journalists that it was in effect the MP4-18, though rebadged to spare further embarrassment after that car failed to enter a race. Using the same monocoque but with a raft of redevelopments, the MP4-19 was the embodiment of McLaren's matrix management system fulfilling its purpose of giving a formal voice to a broader group of creatives: Adrian Newey had wanted to design a new tub to improve the aerodynamics, but the committee believed it possible to solve the car's problems without going that far.

Thus the MP4-19 bore a close resemblance in its layout to the final spec of the MP4-18 tested late in 2003: new rear bodywork reflected a change in exhaust configuration from floor-level exits to Ferrari-style chimneys at the rear of the sidepods. On the MP4-19 the hoods were much taller, facilitating the exit of hot air from the radiators and the exhaust pipes projected further. While the nose was narrower and the front wing more curvaceous, the bargeboards and sidepod leading edges remained broadly similar to the abortive 2003 car.

Mercedes' new FO 110Q V-10 was built to comply with the latest Max Mosley cost-saving edict: engines now had to last a full race weekend or incur a ten-place grid penalty per change. Mosley had intended to introduce this in 2003, but the proposal had been met with such resistance he had delayed it and settled for imposing other changes. These included a new two-part qualifying system and new parc fermé rules in which cars were impounded between qualifying and the race itself. This had been unpopular enough: Williams and McLaren threatened to take the FIA to arbitration and Ron Dennis had complained the governing body was "trying to 'dumb down' Formula 1."

Dissatisfaction with the FIA's supervision of sporting matters was just one thread in the tapestry of rancor between the road car manufacturers and their aligned teams on one side and the governing body and F1 commercial chief Bernie Ecclestone on the other. Money, naturally, was the chief motivator: in 2001 Mosley had granted Ecclestone an unprecedented hundred-year lease of the commercial rights for a fire-sale price, only to have the German media company that was a

MP4-19, MP4-19B SPECIFICATIONS

Engine	Mercedes 2,997cc 90-degree V-10	**Suspension**	Double wishbones with pushrod-actuated inboard torsion bars
Power	870bhp @ 18,500 rpm	**Brakes**	Carbon discs f/r
Gearbox	Seven-speed semiautomatic	**Tires**	Michelin
Chassis	Carbon fiber and aluminum honeycomb monocoque	**Weight**	600 kilograms (1,323 pounds)

←
After a hairy first corner, Räikkönen took his first win of the season in Belgium.

FOSTER'S
West
SAP
Mobil

major shareholder go bust and leave the business in the hands of creditor banks. Mercedes and their allies wanted a bigger share of the commercial revenues and threatened to launch a championship of their own if they didn't get it.

A putative ban on traction control was also abandoned as impractical. Not that this would have had much effect on McLaren's 2004 season, since the MP4-19 proved suboptimal in many areas. In Australia Kimi Räikkonen and David Coulthard qualified a miserable 10th and 12th, and Räikkonen became the first retirement of the year when his engine dumped its coolant after nine laps. Coulthard picked up a solitary point in eighth place.

Initially the team blamed unseasonably low temperatures at the season opener for the car's handling instability, and it was clear the engine was down on power compared with Ferrari, BMW, and perhaps even the resurgent Renault. As the failures to finish mounted, engine durability again proved questionable, but the handling issue did not disappear in warmer temperatures.

Newey belatedly got his way and work began on a B-spec that was to be introduced at the French Grand Prix, round 10 of 18. By this point McLaren were a very distant fifth in the constructors' championship with just seventeen points. Ferrari's dominant F2004 car had propelled the Scuderia to 142 points.

A new monocoque and completely redesigned cooling architecture enabled Newey to reprofile the sidepods and bargeboards, resolving the aerodynamic instability. There was no catching Ferrari, but Räikkonen took pole position at Silverstone and was able to register a win in Belgium in an improved second half of the season.

↖
By round three, at the new Bahrain circuit, McLaren had dropped the multicurve front wing in favor of a simpler design.

↑
A B-spec MP4-19 introduced at the midseason French Grand Prix performed better, but by this point McLaren was fifth in the constructors' championship and over one hundred points behind the leaders.

←
Against technical director Adrian Newey's wishes, the MP4-18's tub design was retained and a slightly less extreme version of the same concept was built around it. Struggles in the season opener proved there was more work left to do.

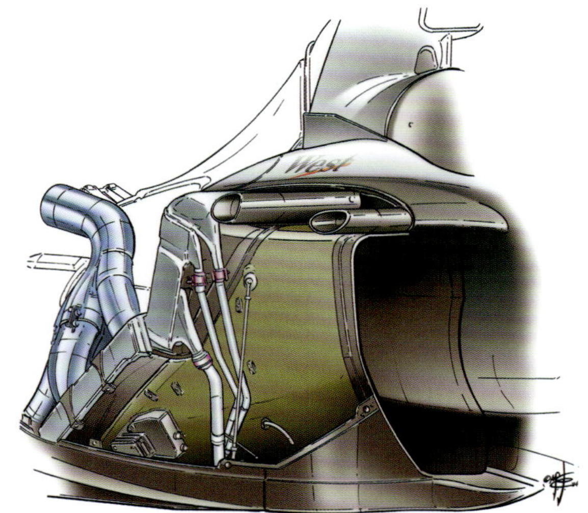

→
The MP4-19B's reshaped sidepods included sophisticated radiators with three separate elements integrating the oil-cooling function, all canted forwards at an angle to increase surface area within a given height and width.

SIEMENS
AT&T
9
SIEMENS
SAP
Mobil 1
SIEMENS

MP4-20

The sheer speed of the cars in 2004 has rarely been matched since. Michael Schumacher's 2004 lap record in Ferrari's era-defining F2004 at Shanghai International Circuit still stands as of 2023. This situation led to yet more tweaks to Formula 1's technical and sporting format with the aim of containing car performance and improving "the show." It was a tough balancing act, since the widespread perception was that the dominant team enjoyed political favor, an impression solidified ahead of the 2005 season when Ferrari split from the other manufacturers and reached a separate deal with Ecclestone to renew the Concorde Agreement, F1's commercial contract.

The qualifying format changed yet again under the redrawn sporting regulations, this time into a pointlessly abstruse system in which a driver's grid position was determined by a time aggregated from laps set in two separate sessions (one on the Saturday, the other on Sunday morning), the latter with the car carrying its race fuel load. In these sessions, as in the previous year, the drivers would go out one by one and have a single opportunity to set a time. This unwieldy aggregate format would be abandoned after five Grands Prix in 2005.

Along with the potentially dangerous diktat banning in-race tire stops, the FIA mandated that the cars' rear wings be moved forward by 5.9 inches (15 centimeters) and the front wing end sections raised by 1.97 inches (5 centimeters). Once again the intention of the aerodynamic changes was to enable cars to follow one another more closely around corners, creating overtaking opportunities, but it had the opposite effect because the higher front-wing sections were more sensitive to wake turbulence. And as McLaren discovered during computational fluid dynamics (CFD) research, vortices set up by the front-wing endplates to accelerate airflow down the car were now hitting the lower wishbones of the front suspension, damaging efficiency.

For the MP4-20, the design team solved this problem by raising the entire suspension assembly so that the

MP4-20 SPECIFICATIONS

Engine	Mercedes 2,997cc 90-degree V-10	**Suspension**	Double wishbones with pushrod-actuated inboard torsion bars
Power	920bhp @ 19,000 rpm	**Brakes**	Carbon discs f/r
Gearbox	Seven-speed semiautomatic	**Tires**	Michelin
Chassis	Carbon fiber and aluminum honeycomb monocoque	**Weight**	600 kilograms (1,323 pounds)

← Once McLaren's understanding of the new car grew, performance followed—Räikkönen claimed two consecutive wins early on, including here in Monaco.

↑
The MP4-20 was a clean-sheet design, dictated in part by new technical regulations but also as an experiment with aerodynamic innovations such as Viking horn airbox winglets.

lower wishbone connected to the wheel at the centerline rather than at the bottom of the hub. This also afforded a direct mount at the other end to the edge of the chassis, rather than a keel stub. Downstream the airflow was assisted under and around the nose by a reshaped leading edge of the chassis and an aggressively undercut sidepod leading edge.

Racing circumstances conspired to mask the MP4-20's potential in the early rounds—Kimi Räikkonen was leading in Malaysia when a rear-tire valve popped—but, as the team learned more about the car, results followed. Räikkonen won decisively in Spain and Monaco, bringing him back into contention with championship leader Fernando Alonso. Ferrari, meanwhile, was pegged back by the performance of their Bridgestone tires relative to the Michelins.

The MP4-20 featured other new technology in the form of a seamless-shift gearbox, which had been three years in development (the team had wanted to fit an earlier iteration of the idea, with a twin-clutch arrangement, to the MP4-18 and MP4-19, but dropped it on account of size and weight, both addressed by the new design). During the season, McLaren also fitted an "inerter," licensed from Cambridge University, to the front suspension to maintain an even tire contact patch over bumps.

Renault and Alonso emerged as the strongest contenders, while McLaren was stymied by unreliability once again as Mercedes' FO 110R engine proved unequal to the task of lasting the newly mandated two race weekends. Räikkonen lost another potential victory at the Nürburgring when vibrations from a flat-spotted tire broke his rear suspension. New teammate Juan Pablo Montoya missed two rounds after sustaining a shoulder fracture, allegedly while playing tennis—a story greeted with great skepticism.

Despite several more victories—including a remarkable drive at Suzuka, charging through to win after rain in qualifying left him 17th on the grid—Räikkonen couldn't make up the championship ground lost to Alonso through car failures. Montoya contributed three wins, bringing McLaren's total to ten versus Renault's eight, but this was not enough to win the constructors' title.

←
As this Giorgio Piola illustration demonstrates, McLaren was able to lift the lower front suspension wishbone away from a crucial airflow structure by mounting it to the bottom of the chassis at one end and the middle of the hub at the other. A revised front brake location lowered the center of gravity.

↑
When Juan Pablo Montoya injured his shoulder—supposedly playing tennis—test driver Alex Wurz stepped up and claimed a fine podium in San Marino.

Fly Emirates
SIEMENS
JOHNNIE WALKER
4
at&t
Emirates
Emirates

MP4-21

The seemingly endless tinkering of the Mosley era continued in 2006 as 2.4-liter (145-cubic-inch) V-8s replaced the 3-liter (182-cubic-inch) V-10s—a move to be followed by frozen specifications for a number of years (the exact figure, start date, and the degree of permitted development was the subject of intense argument during the season) and a ban on driver aids such as traction control, to be actioned by adopting a single FIA-approved ECU.

Mosley also signaled his intention to introduce a control-tire specification starting in 2007, prompting Michelin to announce their withdrawal at the end of 2006. Relations between the French tire giant and the governing body had been strained since the farcical 2005 Indianapolis Grand Prix, where the intransigence of the FIA and (Bridgestone-supplied) Ferrari forced all the Michelin runners to pull out of the race.

Change was sweeping through McLaren too. Disenchanted by the matrix management system and what he saw as the stultifyingly sterile atmosphere of the McLaren Technology Center, Adrian Newey returned from the Chinese Grand Prix and informed Ron Dennis that he was leaving to join the Red Bull team; he was immediately escorted from the premises. The final stages of MP4-21 development therefore dovetailed with the initial meetings to determine the layout of the 2007 MP4-22, as McLaren adopted a Renault-like system of alternating chief engineers.

Dennis had also signed the world champion, Fernando Alonso, for 2007. This gave him a number of options for the other seat: one of the current drivers, Kimi Räikkonen or Juan Pablo Montoya, or the McLaren-mentored prodigy Lewis Hamilton, contesting the GP2 support series in 2006.

The MP4-21 was a nuanced evolution of its predecessor, albeit differently packaged at the rear because of the smaller engine and presented in a new chrome livery with the Diageo whisky brand Johnnie Walker boldly announced on the sidepods. After ten years as title sponsor, Reemtsma took their leave of F1 as international rules on cigarette advertising tightened.

A one-inch extension to the wheelbase aimed to shift the weight forward and cure some of the twitchiness

MP4-21 SPECIFICATIONS

Engine	Mercedes 2,398cc 90-degree V-10	**Suspension**	Double wishbones with pushrod-actuated inboard torsion bars
Power	750bhp @ 19,000 rpm	**Brakes**	Carbon discs f/r
Gearbox	Seven-speed semiautomatic	**Tires**	Michelin
Chassis	Carbon fiber and aluminum honeycomb monocoque	**Weight**	605 kilograms (1,334 pounds)

←
Following the departure of the West cigarette brand as title sponsor, McLaren shifted to a new chrome-effect paint scheme by partner AkzoNobel.

experienced by Räikkönen and Montoya during 2005. But the tires this season had different properties, as in-race changes were permitted once more. Naturally gravitating more to the French-owned team that had won the 2005 constructors' championship, Michelin was beginning to develop rubber that suited Renault's desire for a rearward weight balance. Throughout the season, the MP4-21 struggled to get its rear axle up to the right operating temperature, which made qualifying problematic.

There were also a number of failures caused by indifferent quality control, such as when Räikkönen lined up last on the grid for the opening round after a suspension breakage in qualifying. This, along with the MP4-21's shortfall in qualifying pace, some key retirements, and a worsening relationship with Dennis, sent Räikkönen into the arms of Ferrari as a replacement for the retiring Michael Schumacher. Montoya, for his part, had gained weight in the off-season, appeared to lack commitment, and was being lobbied by his wife to return to live in the US. He announced in the middle of the season that he would be racing for Chip Ganassi in NASCAR from 2007 and McLaren released him immediately, to be replaced by test driver Pedro de la Rosa.

The MP4-21 was not far off the performance of the Renault R26 and Ferrari 248, but the qualifying deficit left the drivers with too much to ground to make up in races. They failed to register a victory. Ferrari also succeeded where McLaren had failed in 2005, lodging a successful protest against the mass damper Renault was using in their front suspension.

← The season got off to a tough start as suspension failure meant Räikkönen would enter the opening round from the back of the grid.

↖ Though an evolution of its successful predecessor, the MP4-21 suffered, as Michelin prioritized the Renault team's requirement for a more rearward weight balance.

↑
Räikkönen qualified on pole in Hungary but crashed out. Pedro de la Rosa finished second to future McLaren driver Jenson Button.

RBS
Salut Gilles

MP4-22

The team's most challenging season since the death of Bruce McLaren in 1970 began optimistically with one of the most extravagant Formula 1 launches ever, parading newly signed double world champion Fernando Alonso and rookie Lewis Hamilton through the streets of Valencia, Spain, in an event underwritten by new title sponsor Vodafone. "I'm sure 2007 is going to be a year we're all going to remember," said Ron Dennis.

It would, but for few reasons that were good.

Against a backdrop of political intrigue between the manufacturers and Max Mosley, the era of homologated engines came into being: the specs were theoretically frozen in late 2006, but limited development was permitted for provable reliability reasons, a loophole Mercedes exploited to smuggle through performance gains. After the MP4-22 flew in preseason testing, rumors circulated that Mercedes had liberated at least 30 brake horsepower over winter.

The MP4-22 was also well placed to weather the change in tire specifications as F1 shifted to a fixed tire spec with Bridgestone as the only active supplier. Compounds of two different grades (soft versus hard) would be available at each round, and teams had to run both during the race. The new rubber was claimed to be less peaky than the offerings during the tire-war era, with lower peak grip but performing at a wider range of operating temperatures.

Development of the MP4-22 had occurred in parallel with its predecessor, so it bore a strong resemblance to the 2006 car. McLaren chose not to lengthen the wheelbase, which proved wise since the Bridgestone tires had different properties than the Michelins McLaren had used in 2006. Now the rear tires were prone to overheating while the fronts were weak and offered little bite on turn-in. During the season, McLaren added another element to the front wing to improve front-end performance.

Ferrari's new car, the F2007, seemed to have better aerodynamic efficiency, but its front wing was more sensitive to wake turbulence from the car ahead. On track, it was a season of punch and counterpunch, as McLaren and Ferrari fought to extract maximum points at the tracks that most suited their cars or particular tire choice: broadly speaking, Ferrari on more open tracks, McLaren on tighter ones such as Monaco.

But the destination of the world championships would be decided away from the track. Alonso arrived

MP4-22 SPECIFICATIONS

Engine	Mercedes 2,398cc 90-degree V-8	**Suspension**	Double wishbones with pushrod-actuated inboard torsion bars
Power	800bhp @ 19,000 rpm	**Brakes**	Carbon discs f/r
Gearbox	Seven-speed semiautomatic	**Tires**	Bridgestone
Chassis	Carbon fiber and aluminum honeycomb monocoque	**Weight**	605 kilograms (1,334 pounds)

←
In Canada, just six races into his F1 career, Lewis Hamilton claimed his first pole position and victory in the category.

↑
McLaren adapted well to the shift to Bridgestone tires and to the new rules that forced teams to use two different compounds per race. The softer one was distinguished by a white stripe.

↗
In the aftermath of fining McLaren a record $100 million, FIA president Max Mosley staged a public handshake by way of rapprochement with his old foe, team boss Ron Dennis. As the cameras clicked, Mosley leaned in and whispered, "$5 million for the offense, $95 million for being a ******."

expecting preferential treatment, reasonable enough if the occupant of the other garage had not been supported by the team since his karting days. Hamilton was close to Alonso's pace from day one and occasionally got the better of him, inevitably leading to paranoia and disaffection, building to a point where they spoiled each other's qualifying in Hungary. Later in the year, Alonso responded to being disqualified in China by kicking a door off its hinges.

In parallel it emerged that McLaren chief designer Mike Coughlan had illicitly obtained design blueprints from a disaffected Ferrari employee, former chief mechanic Nigel Stepney. While it was never established that McLaren used or benefited from the information, questions remained about who else knew—and how much. Dennis stubbornly maintained, and doubtless believed, that Coughlan was a rogue employee acting alone but, when it was revealed awareness of the purloined IP was more widespread, the team was fined $100 million and had their constructors' points annulled.

Alonso's behavior during the year led to his ejection from the team, who then flunked the drivers' championship run-in. Hamilton was leading with two rounds to go but got beached in a gravel trap in China when McLaren pitted him too late in changing conditions; then a gearbox glitch (caused by a temporary blockage in a hydraulic line) and an ill-conceived three-stop strategy left him short of the necessary points in the finale, where Kimi Räikkönen claimed the title for Ferrari.

↑
By the mid-2000s advances in aerodynamic research led to increasingly complex surface profiles on the wings and bargeboards. Tighter rules from 2009 brought many of these excesses to heel. *James Mann*

vodafone
JOHNNIE WALKER
vodafone
JOHNNIE WALKER
vodafone
vodafone
vodafone
JOHNNIE WALKER
22

MP4-23

McLaren had contested the closing rounds of 2007 under the explicit threat of being expelled from the world championship in 2008. Lewis Hamilton had even spoken of quitting F1 entirely: such was the perception that the harshness of the team's punishment was a consequence of the longstanding enmity between Max Mosley and Ron Dennis.

While this threat receded, the MP4-23 was subjected to an unprecedented level of forensic checks to ensure it bore no trace of the Ferrari intellectual property illicitly obtained by former McLaren chief designer Mike Coughlan. Even when it passed these examinations, innuendo continued to swirl.

McLaren continued to operate a policy of alternating between Tim Goss and Pat Fry as chief engineers of each car project, although the design and engineering team itself was not split, as at Renault. Thus Goss's MP4-23 was a clear development of Fry's MP4-22, albeit with a slightly higher nose. The increasing sophistication of wind tunnel research and the influence of CFD would be felt throughout the year as McLaren expanded the number of discrete front-wing elements from three to six, then to seven. The number of slot gaps this entailed was beneficial to downforce but required great attention to detail, owing to the complexity of the flow structures these set up. For Hungary, McLaren would add "Dumbo wings" on the nose to set up vortices that benefited the airflow further down the car.

With the aim of putting less stress on the weak rear tires, McLaren moved weight forward where possible, extending the gearbox to lengthen the wheelbase by 1.1 inch (2.8 centimeters). The lateral sidepod extensions now reached further forward and a reprofiling of the airbox, with a more aggressive undercut, improved airflow to the rear.

The engine homologation era had initiated a new development war in the fuel-and-lubes arena: by optimizing the viscosity of the engine oil to minimize friction while still affording good protection, the engine itself ran cooler and required smaller radiators, which in turn meant smaller sidepod inlets, reducing aerodynamic drag. Special fuel blends also brought combustion and response improvements without exceeding the permitted octane ratings.

←
In this final season before stricter limits on aerodynamics were brought in, McLaren and other teams experimented with airflow conditioners on the nose, nicknamed "Dumbo wings."

MP4-23 SPECIFICATIONS

Engine	Mercedes 2,398cc 90-degree V-8	**Suspension**	Double wishbones with pushrod-actuated inboard torsion bars
Power	810bhp @ 19,000 rpm	**Brakes**	Carbon discs f/r
Gearbox	Seven-speed semiautomatic	**Tires**	Bridgestone
Chassis	Carbon fiber and aluminum honeycomb monocoque	**Weight**	605 kilograms (1,334 pounds)

F1 also had to adapt to a new era without traction control, owing to the imposition of a single ECU. McLaren Electronic Systems had won the supply tender, which led, inevitably, to further innuendo and paranoia among the team's competitors.

Yet again, McLaren and Ferrari were closely matched through the season. In the early races the MP4-23 had a tendency to spin up its rear tires while accelerating out of slow corners, an effect that was ameliorated by adjusting the engine mapping.

Lewis Hamilton, now partnered with Heikki Kovalainen, won three Grands Prix in the first half of the season—surviving a cracked wheel rim and an early pit stop at Monaco—but Ferrari's Felipe Massa and Kimi Räikkönen held the advantage until the midpoint, where Hamilton drew even with a remarkable victory in the wet at Silverstone. Controversy followed in Belgium where Hamilton won, only to be handed a 25-second penalty for an on-track incident with Räikkonen.

Hamilton entered the final round seven points ahead of Massa, who needed to win with Hamilton in sixth place or lower to lift the title. A thrilling race ensued after a rain-delayed start. Massa drove exquisitely to win from pole in front of his home crowd, while rain late on left Hamilton with work to do when he pitted for intermediate tires and Toyota's Timo Glock did not. At the start of the final lap, Hamilton was sixth and the championship hung in the balance. The weather then came to Hamilton's rescue as the rain intensified and he slithered past the struggling Toyota with the finish line almost in sight. In only his second year, Hamilton was the world champion—by a single point—but Ferrari finished twenty-one points ahead in the constructors' standings.

←
Tensions escalated during the championship run-in and Hamilton was penalized—and roasted in the British press—for locking up and pushing Räikkönen wide at the start of the Japanese Grand Prix.

←
Victory in the penultimate round enabled Hamilton to fractionally extend a points lead, which had been diminishing in recent races after his dubious penalty in Belgium.

↑
Hamilton leads Toyota's Timo Glock in the Brazilian Grand Prix. Changing weather conditions—and diverging strategies—meant Hamilton had to pass Glock again on the final lap to claim the championship.

llianz
vodafone
Santander
Mobil 1
BRIDGESTONE

MP4-24

One of the most wide-reaching regulatory changes in years arrived as the aftershock of the global financial crisis hit Formula 1. Though Honda had made huge investments in research and development on their 2009 F1 machine, plummeting road-car sales prompted the company to announce an immediate withdrawal in December 2008. Toyota and BMW announced they would follow at the end of the 2009 season.

While the new technical rules had been developed with some consultation, since team representatives sat on the Overtaking Working Group committee, the new package was fundamentally flawed. Several parties to the agreement had already found loopholes to exploit, and the basic philosophy brought unintended consequences. For example, cars were to have lower and wider front wings with driver-adjustable flaps, and taller and narrower rear wings. Rules such as this aimed to create opportunities for overtaking by enabling cars to follow each other more closely around corners (through making the front wings more powerful and the rear wings less disruptive), augmented by a straightline speed boost (through the adjustable front wing and additional power from a driver-activated Kinetic Energy Recovery System, KERS).

In practice the format was useless. The cars were uglier and the adjustable front flaps proved ineffectual except to trim out understeer as the tires wore. The KERS harvested energy that would otherwise dissipate as heat under braking to provide an extra 80 brake horsepower for 6.7 seconds a lap; this was admirable in terms of boosting F1's green credentials, but the extra weight more than nullified the effect of the power boost.

Worse still, having given up on their 2008 car early and focused on 2009 development, the team formerly owned by Honda had by far the most mature car at the beginning of the season after team principal Ross Brawn executed a management buyout and McLaren helpfully furnished a customer Mercedes engine supply. Though carrying inherent compromise because of running a different V-8 to the original design, the renamed Brawn BGP 001 had benefited from at least two parallel research programs in three wind tunnels. It wiped the floor with the competition.

MP4-24 SPECIFICATIONS

Engine	Mercedes 2,398cc 90-degree V-8	**Suspension**	Double wishbones with pushrod-actuated inboard torsion bars
Power	810bhp @ 18,000 rpm	**Brakes**	Carbon discs f/r
Gearbox	Seven-speed semiautomatic	**Tires**	Bridgestone
Chassis	Carbon fiber and aluminum honeycomb monocoque	**Weight**	605 kilograms (1,334 pounds)

←
New rules in 2009 called for lower, wider front wings; simplified aerodynamics in the central area; and taller, narrower rear wings.

↑
After a new floor transformed the car's performance, Lewis Hamilton started the German Grand Prix fifth and challenged for the lead at the start.

By contrast, McLaren's MP4-24 development had been stymied by the need to throw resources at the MP4-23 in the latter races of 2008 to keep Lewis Hamilton in the championship hunt. While the new rules also mandated simplified aerodynamic furniture, especially around the sidepods, McLaren and Ferrari's 2009 offering looked notably sparse. Both teams had missed a loophole exploited by Brawn, Toyota, and Williams to fit secondary planes in the rear diffuser, boosting downforce. While this wasn't in itself a magic bullet—Brawn's front wing was also highly developed in the way it steered air around the front wheels—it gained attention and proved controversial.

The new season began poorly for McLaren: Lewis Hamilton and Heikki Kovalainen failed to crack the top ten in qualifying in Melbourne. Hamilton was then disqualified for "misleading" the stewards during an investigation into a late-race incident. The imbroglio led to the firing of team manager David Ryan and Ron Dennis's decision to step aside as team principal.

← Hamilton recorded the first victory for a KERS-equipped car in Hungary.

↑ Despite being caught out by political machinations around the double diffuser, McLaren was able to modify the existing design with a new central plate by round three. Further iterations would follow quickly.

When the FIA, bafflingly, declared double diffusers legal, everyone had to scramble to design their own version. (It is widely believed that Mosley allowed the double diffusers to damage McLaren and Ferrari, since they had formed a new alliance of teams the previous summer.) McLaren had an interim version ready in China, but the MP4-24 remained frustratingly uncompetitive until a new floor package transformed it for the German Grand Prix. From qualifying 19th for the previous race, Hamilton started fifth and was challenging for the lead when he suffered a puncture in contact with Red Bull's Mark Webber. The following round, at the Hungaroring, Hamilton raced from fourth on the grid to win—the first victory for a KERS-equipped car. Many other competitors had abandoned the technology by this point.

Another victory, in Singapore, along with pole position in the season finale, confirmed McLaren's return to the sharp end of the grid.

Pepe Jeans
Pepe Jeans

CHAPTER 6

2010s

The new decade opened in a tide of optimism, largely with the news of perennial McLaren nemesis Max Mosley being pushed out of the FIA presidency and team principal Martin Whitmarsh becoming a leading voice of reason through his position in the recently established Formula One Teams Association (FOTA). McLaren faced significant headwinds all the same.

Plans to revive McLaren Automotive, based in a state-of-the-art, brand-new factory alongside the existing Technology Center, signified the beginning of a divergence from longtime partner and shareholder Daimler Benz. At the end of 2009, Mercedes announced they would buy the championship-winning Brawn F1 team and sell back their shares in McLaren to the existing shareholders: Ron Dennis, Mansour Ojjeh, and the Mumtalakat Holding Company, the Bahraini royal family's sovereign wealth fund.

The teams' united front began to crumble as Red Bull, Toro Rosso, Ferrari, and Sauber exited FOTA over the winter of 2011. The sticking point that drove their decision was the implementation of the Resource Restriction Agreement, a cost-control initiative backed strongly by McLaren and Mercedes.

Against a backdrop of diminishing performance on track in F1, questions arose over focus, leadership, and the McLaren Group's future direction. As is often the case in such matters, boardroom battles led to great collateral damage and the revolving door of management spun freely. This constant state of flux meant that, by decade's end, few of the questions had been adequately resolved.

←
Red Bull spent the early years of the decade in the ascendant, having pushed McLaren aside.

vodafone
vodafone
JOHNNIE WALKER
JOHNNIE WALKER

MP4-25

Although the flawed 2009 rules package was unpopular, its broad structure was retained for the following season amid the political push and pull. The increasingly influential FOTA had managed to oust Max Mosley as FIA president and, with that move, consign his idea of a budget cap to the trashcan of history. In return for presenting longtime ally Mosley's head on a silver platter, Bernie Ecclestone had the teams' signatures on a new iteration of the Concorde Agreement, reducing the potential for them to form a breakaway series. The F1 world could move on.

Also agreed at FOTA's behest was a ban on in-race refueling and a voluntary moratorium on the use of KERS (even though minimum car-and-driver weight had been raised to 620 kilograms, 1,367 pounds). The system was recognized as pointless and expensive, while the controversial double diffusers would remain until 2011. While seemingly small, the changes would have a profound influence on design and, like their rivals, McLaren entered 2010 with a very different car.

Clarity over the double diffuser enabled McLaren's engineers to optimize the MP4-25's floor from the outset, rather than shoehorning in a compromise afterward as they had the MP4-24. Getting key elements of the design right at the beginning would be even more crucial this year, since various structural elements such as the safety cell and crash structures would be homologated at the start of the season.

To accommodate the larger fuel tank, the wheelbase was extended by 11.5 inches (29 centimeters). While the removal of KERS afforded greater freedom in relocating engine ancillaries and various elements of the cooling architecture to benefit weight distribution, making the car longer rather than wider was considered the better aerodynamic solution.

The outer surfaces of the MP4-25 were also different, leading from a flatter nose cone to aggressively swept-in sidepods and an engine cover with sculpted exhaust outlets and an intriguing dorsal fin. At launch, chief engineer Tim Goss waved this off as a feeding device for the repositioned cooling architecture. In fact it was a clever device that stalled the rear wing while the car was traveling at speed, reducing drag.

Christened the F-duct by outsiders because one of the inlets was positioned in the Vodafone logo on the

MP4-25 SPECIFICATIONS

Engine	Mercedes 2,398cc 90-degree V-8	**Suspension**	Double wishbones with pushrod-actuated inboard torsion bars
Power	820bhp @ 18,000 rpm	**Brakes**	Carbon discs f/r
Gearbox	Seven-speed semiautomatic	**Tires**	Bridgestone
Chassis	Carbon fiber and aluminum honeycomb monocoque	**Weight**	620 kilograms (1,367 pounds)

← Jenson Button in the season-opening Bahrain Grand Prix. The air intake for the F-duct is visible to the immediate left of the mirror.

↑ Pundits christened McLaren's clever drag reduction system the "F-duct" because of the inlet's position within the Vodafone logo.

→ Although the MP4-24 had been developed into a competitive car by the end of the previous season, very little of the design concept was retained for the MP4-25.

MP4-25's nose, "Project RW80" used a network of ducts and a fluidic switch to direct air selectively via an outlet just above the gearbox or onto the underside of the rear wing's main plane. In its first iteration it was activated by the driver covering a hole in the cockpit with their knee, but McLaren later moved this back so it could be done with the driver's elbow. The newly introduced chassis homologation regime meant that it was difficult for other teams to copy.

McLaren had lured 2009 world champion Jenson Button to join Lewis Hamilton but, though the new partnership registered five wins between them in 2010, Red Bull's Adrian Newey–designed RB6 proved to be the dominant car. Despite well-founded suggestions that the wings had been cleverly designed to flex at speed, reducing drag, Red Bull had also found great gains by positioning the exhausts at floor level and using the gases to energize the diffuser. Clever engine mapping enabled hot gas to continue to flow when the driver was off-throttle, keeping the downforce consistent. McLaren adapted the MP4-25 with a similar system from Silverstone onward . . . but the extreme heat repeatedly burned the surrounding floor areas.

Hamilton entered the final round in contention for the drivers' title but requiring great misfortune to afflict his three rivals for the crown. Second place wasn't enough, but McLaren ended the season with the consolation of finishing second in the constructors' championship.

←
Following Red Bull's example from the British Grand Prix onward, McLaren ran the MP4-25 with the exhaust at floor level rather than exiting above the rear suspension wishbones.

↑
Hamilton entered the Abu Dhabi season finale in contention for the drivers' title—but second place wasn't enough.

vodafone
vodafone
vodafone
4

MP4-26

One of the key challenges of the 2011 season—and indeed for years to come—had been inspired by one of McLaren's victories in 2010. The Canadian circuit's characteristics, with lots of straights interspersed with slow corners, combined with recent resurfacing work and cooler-than-expected conditions to destroy both of the available Bridgestone tire compounds. A race of multiple pit stops and great uncertainty unfolded in which Jenson Button and Lewis Hamilton finished 1–2. When Pirelli won the tender to become F1's sole tire supplier starting in 2011, Bernie Ecclestone requested a product that could replicate these conditions at every round.

Thus McLaren, along with the other teams, had to evolve their 2011 car concept around tires designed to lose performance rapidly after a finite period. In terms of chassis packaging there would be something else to accommodate: the return of KERS and another rise in minimum car weight. To manage balance and center of gravity, McLaren placed it below the fuel tank, inside the survival cell, rather than within the sidepods. This required the wheelbase to stretch by 2 inches (5 centimeters). The MP4-26 would also feature the newly permitted Drag Reduction System, which followed the principle of the F-duct by dropping one of the rear wing planes at the touch of a button on the steering wheel.

Since double diffusers were now banned, McLaren's engineers looked to claw back the lost downforce—and more—by pursuing an aggressive development of the exhaust-blown diffuser concept introduced midseason on the MP4-25. Among the lessons drawn from this was that the team's aerodynamic tools had failed to predict the influence of what is known as the Coandă effect, the tendency of a flow of particles to follow the curvature of a solid surface. The effect was seen in exhaust gases, which, instead of moving toward the floor edge around the rear tire as planned, had been following the base of the engine cover and scorching the unprotected surfaces. Realizing the Technology

←
Over four hours after the starting lights went out, a victorious Jenson Button returns to the pitlane in Canada. Wet weather prompted a lengthy midrace stoppage and led to a change in the rules regarding event length.

MP4-26 SPECIFICATIONS

Engine	Mercedes 2,398cc 90-degree V-8	**Suspension**	Double wishbones with pushrod-actuated inboard torsion bars
Power	820bhp @ 18,000 rpm	**Brakes**	Carbon discs f/r
Gearbox	Seven-speed semiautomatic	**Tires**	Pirelli
Chassis	Carbon fiber and aluminum honeycomb monocoque	**Weight**	640 kilograms (1,410 pounds)

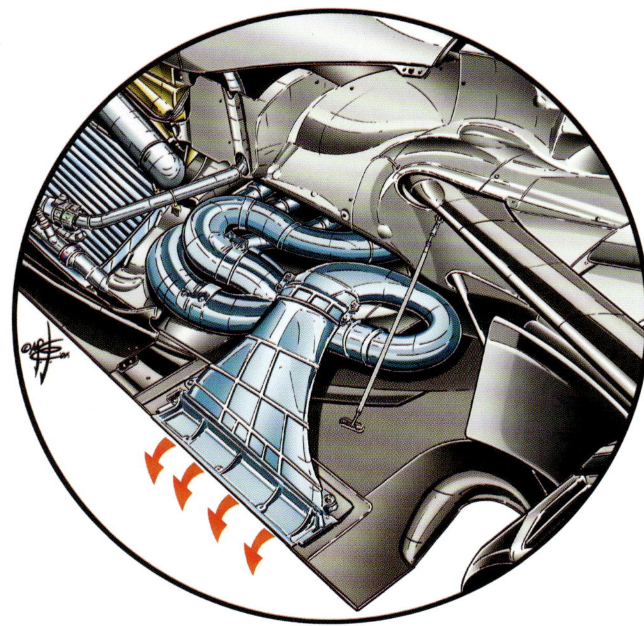

↑
The MP4-26 initially ran with an innovative fantail exhaust, illustrated here by Giorgio Piola. Intended to use the hotter air to seal the underfloor, it proved too fragile in on-track use and was dropped before the start of the season.

→
Issues in Hamilton's personal life caused unwelcome distractions on track during 2011. In Monaco he was not at fault for the incident that damaged his rear wing, but he was penalized for two other contacts and drew the stewards' ire for describing their intervention as "an absolute joke."

Center's wind tunnel was no longer suitable for the job, McLaren began to lease time in Toyota's more advanced facility in Cologne, Germany. The team hoped the larger size of this tunnel would yield a reduction in the so-called "blockage effect," which was skewing the results in the Technology Center.

The MP4-26 was the first McLaren to benefit from this new arrangement: it featured a daring sidepod treatment with L-shaped radiators, creating deep channels on either side of the cockpit to expedite airflow toward another innovative feature. Once again the aim was to generate higher downforce at the rear by using the airflow over the car to accelerate the flow passing underneath at the point of exit, increasing the suction effect. Significant gains could be found by influencing the behavior of the air at the floor edge inside the rear tires. McLaren's solution was to have slotlike fantail exhaust outlets at floor level.

Unfortunately the structure of these outlets was insufficiently strong to resist the heat surges of the exhaust gases. Repeated failures in testing reduced the number of laps the team could complete, meaning they entered the season with a less-developed understanding of the new tires' behavior. They also had to redesign the exhaust system over a period of three weeks before the season opener. Other teams were also using various means to blow the diffuser; the FIA attempted to impose a ban midseason but were forced to backtrack after lobbying from FOTA.

Compounding the MP4-26's lack of pace relative to Red Bull's RB7, Lewis Hamilton's head was not in the game, as issues in his personal life sapped his on-track focus. Hamilton claimed three wins in a season that was more generally defined by on-track incidents and run-ins with the stewards. Jenson Button won two but finished ahead of Hamilton in the standings by dint of greater consistency.

↑
Unusual L-shaped radiator inlets had an impact on the design's center of gravity, but McLaren felt the aerodynamic benefit was worth it.

Mobil 1
Mercedes-Benz
Lucozade
HILTON
HHONORS
AkzoNobel
P ZERO

MP4-27

Tweaking the technical regulations to improve safety had a major effect on car appearance in 2012—but not for McLaren. FIA race director and safety delegate Charlie Whiting wanted to lower the cars' noses to a maximum of 21.65 inches (55 centimeters) above the floor, bringing them into alignment with the mandatory side intrusion panels and thereby mitigating the effects of T-bone incidents. Several teams pushed back against the proposal since, historically, they had run high chassis to expedite airflow beneath their cars. As a concession, they were allowed to retain their previous arrangements until a point just beyond the front wishbone mountings, after which the nose had to step down to the new mandatory level.

The result was a grid comprising many visually suboptimal cars but, since McLaren had run chassis that were lower than most rivals for several years, the MP4-27 was untouched. While the front end bore a familial resemblance to the MP4-26, the aft section represented a complete rethink. The L-shaped sidepods were jettisoned, since the team felt the higher center of gravity was no longer justified by aerodynamic benefits. The FIA had moved to prevent exhaust-blown diffusers by mandating a specific (and much higher) area where the exhaust outlets could be located. Exotic engine maps were also curtailed although, as ever, suspicions would arise during the season that some competitors had found ways of circumventing the rules.

Pirelli also introduced a new range of tires to address some of the issues that had been raised in the previous season. While retaining the concept of offering good grip until a specific point, after which the tires would rapidly degrade, Pirelli aimed to provide a more stable contact patch and a longer performance peak. McLaren's wheel supplier, Enkei, produced an innovative rim design with additional holes to improve the management of brake temperatures and reduce thermal stress on the tires.

←
McLaren's new exhaust setup used the Coandă effect to induce the hot air to follow a desired path down the ramp toward the floor. This image from testing features the measuring device used to compare real-life performance with wind tunnel results.

MP4-27 SPECIFICATIONS

Engine	Mercedes 2,398cc 90-degree V-8	**Suspension**	Double wishbones with pushrod-actuated inboard torsion bars
Power	820bhp @ 18,000 rpm	**Brakes**	Carbon discs f/r
Gearbox	Seven-speed semiautomatic	**Tires**	Pirelli
Chassis	Carbon fiber and aluminum honeycomb monocoque	**Weight**	640 kilograms (1,410 pounds)

↑
Button struggled
with tire performance
throughout the season.

Returning to a conventional sidepod concept enabled McLaren to restore the undercut around the floor edges. The change in aerodynamic direction was directly influenced by the new exhaust rules, and here McLaren had an advantage over their rivals. Early awareness of the Coandă effect, following the challenges of the 2010 car, enabled the team to design the rear of the sidepod and the floor to incorporate a ramp behind the exhaust, thereby exploiting the movement of the gases and directing them along the floor as before. Other teams had to copy this innovation and, since the effect was difficult to measure in older wind tunnels, solutions varied in effect.

Hamilton and Button qualified on the front row of the grid in Australia and Button won, with Hamilton third, but the MP4-27's pace proved vexatiously track specific. This was in any case one of the most competitive seasons in years, at least in the first half of the season, where seven different drivers won the first seven races. A key problem for McLaren was tire exploitation, for the new Pirelli compounds had a narrow operating temperature range: if the car generated insufficient heat in the tires, it had no grip at all; too much heat and they degraded too rapidly. Button, Alain Prost–like in his smoothness of steering and throttle inputs, naturally suffered the most. The team suffered a number of operational issues as well, especially during pit stops.

An aerodynamic and suspension update at Silverstone seemed to be flawed—Hamilton and Button were eighth and 10th—but further upgrades to the floor and wings proved transformative and Hamilton won in Hungary, Italy, and the US. The MP4-27's late blossoming of form elevated Hamilton to championship contender status, but a number of retirements dropped him out of the title race—and shaped his decision to leave McLaren for Mercedes.

Button closed out the season with victory in Brazil, McLaren's 182nd. What no one knew at the time was that the 183rd would be a long time coming.

↖ Jenson Button (3) won the first round of the 2012 season but then struggled to recreate that form until car development unlocked more speed after the British GP. *James Mann*

↑ Mercedes' Niki Lauda had been trying to convince Hamilton to leave McLaren for months. A gearbox failure due to a manufacturing fault forced his retirement from the lead in Singapore, and this was one of several factors that led to Hamilton's final decision.

vodafone
5
SAP
Mobil 1
vodafone

MP4-28

McLaren opted for a substantial change of car concept for 2013, a decision taken in the middle of the previous season when the MP4-27 appeared to have run out of development runway. "At that point we sensed we needed to be more innovative and change more things," said Martin Whitmarsh in a contemporary interview with this author.

The most obvious visual evidence of this new approach was at the front end, where McLaren raised the chassis height and angled the wishbones more sharply, mitigating the effect of this on the car's center of gravity by mounting the torsion bars at the base of the structure and actuating them via pullrods. Adopting a similar setup at the rear entailed a substantial change in the shape of the bodywork ahead of the lower element of the rear wing.

Organizational changes followed engineering director Paddy Lowe's departure to Mercedes, replaced by McLaren veteran Tim Goss. But firefighting would be the remodeled engineering team's priority during the first half of the season, as the MP4-28 proved to be a dud. Having finished 2012 with potentially the fastest car on the grid, McLaren fell back into the midfield.

In public McLaren attributed the issue to a lack of correlation between wind tunnel research and on-track performance: the car wasn't behaving as expected. A more fundamental issue was the way it worked its tires. The suspension had been designed to address the warm-up issues experienced in 2012, but Pirelli had adopted a new construction with softer rubber. Other teams had found substantial gains in laptime, but the MP4-28 was only fractionally faster than its predecessor.

New driver Sergio Pérez also struggled to make an impact—except on teammate Jenson Button, with whom he banged wheels frequently. At the end of the season, he was dropped in favor of test driver Kevin Magnussen.

Results improved marginally when Pirelli reverted to the previous tire spec after a number of dramatic failures at the British Grand Prix. But, with an entirely new set of rules in the offing for 2014, McLaren abandoned development of the MP4-28 early and set their sights on the future—one that would include Honda, as the Japanese manufacturer committed to a return in 2015.

←
A new aerodynamic concept and pullrod suspension distinguished the MP4-28 from its predecessor. A complete change had been decided upon midway through the previous season while McLaren was struggling to develop the MP4-27.

MP4-28 SPECIFICATIONS

Engine	Mercedes 2,398cc 90-degree V-8	**Suspension**	Double wishbones with pullrod-actuated inboard torsion bars
Power	820bhp @ 18,000 rpm	**Brakes**	Carbon discs f/r
Gearbox	Seven-speed semiautomatic	**Tires**	Pirelli
Chassis	Carbon fiber and aluminum honeycomb monocoque	**Weight**	640 kilograms (1,410 pounds)

20
PIRELLI
SAP
Mobil
1
JOHNNIE WALKER
PIT LANE MARSHAL

MP4-29

After the disappointment of 2013, McLaren responded by "pragmatically framing our approach to the technical challenge" of Formula 1's new regulations, as their press release accompanying the launch of the MP4-29 put it. F1 was adopting a new format in which 1.6-liter (97-cubic-inch) turbocharged V-6s were augmented by hybrid systems. While in some regards the most wide-ranging change came in the engine department and was therefore Mercedes' bailiwick, there were still aerodynamic and packaging issues for McLaren to solve. Having ended 2013 with a car that was far from state-of-the-art, McLaren now had to accommodate a heavier engine package with different cooling requirements while adapting to updated crash-structure regulations that required a new nose cone and therefore altered the entire aerodynamic map of the car.

Change was brewing behind the scenes, too, as longtime shareholder Mansour Ojjeh required a double lung transplant over the winter. Ron Dennis, having removed himself from the racing side since 2009, took the opportunity to step in and oust team principal Martin Whitmarsh, a close friend of Ojjeh. Relations between Ojjeh and Dennis had already been deteriorating for reasons that were the subject of gossip in the F1 paddock, and this boardroom coup pushed their feud beyond the point of repair.

"There will be changes," Dennis told employees in an all-hands meeting that January. "We will win again." Only one of these statements would come to fruition: in the first of many restructurings, former Adrian Newey lieutenant Peter Prodromou was poached from Red Bull to head up the aerodynamics department, soon joined by Lotus recruit Guillaume Cattelani.

The new rules mandating a lower nose height had been poorly phrased, and all teams exploited this by building the required surface area to the exact dimensions and no more, while attempting to retain maximum airflow to the underside of the nose. The result was a proliferation of so-called "anteater noses." McLaren's solution, while aesthetically disagreeable, was actually among the least ghastly.

Other changes made in the name of safety, such as a lower chassis height and a narrower front wing (to avoid punctures and cuts incurred by contact) were less visually obvious. But engine performance was the biggest differentiator in this first year of the hybrid regulations, and the teams supplied by Mercedes had the advantage. All the same, the MP4-29 never surpassed its performance in the opening race of the year, where Kevin Magnussen and Jenson Button claimed second and third after one of the factory Mercedes was sidelined with a spark plug issue and Red Bull's Daniel Ricciardo was disqualified for a fuel-flow irregularity.

MP4-29 SPECIFICATIONS

Engine	Mercedes 1,598cc 90-degree turbocharged hybrid V-6	**Suspension**	Double wishbones with pushrod-actuated (f) and pullrod-actuated (r) inboard torsion bars
Power	840bhp @ 15,000 rpm	**Brakes**	Carbon discs f/r
Gearbox	Seven-speed semiautomatic	**Tires**	Pirelli
Chassis	Carbon fiber and aluminum honeycomb monocoque	**Weight**	691 kilograms (1,523 pounds)

← Kevin Magnussen finished on the podium in his first Grand Prix, but this was the best position the MP4-29 would achieve.

KPMG
JOHNNIE WALKER
14

MP4-30

The announcement that Fernando Alonso would return to McLaren was greeted with astonishment by those whose memories of his rancorous exit from the team in 2007 remained fresh. But Alonso's relationship with Ron Dennis would prove to be among the least challenging aspects of the 2015 campaign. Before the first MP4-30 monocoque had been struck from the mold, Dennis and his fellow shareholders were at loggerheads over the identity of the driver who would partner Alonso. Dennis favored Kevin Magnussen; Mansour Ojjeh used his casting vote to frustrate Dennis and side with the Bahrainis, who wanted Jenson Button.

Driver choice would prove irrelevant, as Honda's first hybrid engine—the RA615H—fell far short of the required power and reliability, while the MP4-30's concept was fundamentally flawed. McLaren could and should have recognized the car's shortcomings, but it was easier to blame Honda for the failure of the project—a policy that would sour the relationship between the partners and allow hubris to flourish unchecked in McLaren's engineering department.

At launch Dennis was delighted to highlight the MP4-30's "size zero" design concept, the focal point of which was the aggressively tight packaging of the engine cover and rear bodywork. Though the team would later claim there had been no attempt to dictate a form factor to Honda, prioritizing aerodynamics in this way indicated a fundamental misunderstanding of the delicate design compromises required in the hybrid era.

For their part, Honda had underestimated the technical challenges involved in building a competitive hybrid engine, particularly the Motor Generator Unit-Heat (MGU-H). This element of the hybrid system reclaimed energy from heat and could be used to spin the turbo compressor, thus reducing lag, but the torsional forces and high rotational speeds (up to around 120,000 rpm) made it difficult to engineer reliably. Adopting an axial rather than centrifugal turbo compressor so it could be located within the cylinder vee exacerbated the challenges.

Despite a series of upgrades through the year for both engine and car (including a new nose design), this was McLaren's least successful campaign since the miserable 1980 season, which had precipitated the merger with Project 4. Alonso's pointed description of Honda's product as a "GP2 engine"—fit only for the support series—during qualifying for the Japanese Grand Prix was particularly humiliating.

MP4-30 SPECIFICATIONS

Engine	Honda 1,598cc 90-degree turbocharged hybrid V-6	**Suspension**	Double wishbones with pushrod-actuated (f) and pullrod-actuated (r) inboard torsion bars
Power	760bhp @ 15,000 rpm	**Brakes**	Carbon discs f/r
Gearbox	Seven-speed semiautomatic	**Tires**	Pirelli
Chassis	Carbon fiber and aluminum honeycomb monocoque	**Weight**	702 kilograms (1,548 pounds)

←
The MP4-30's ambitiously tight "size zero" packaging was asking too much of a manufacturer entering the hybrid power unit regulations relatively late.

PIRELLI
Mobil 1
HONDA
NRF
Segafredo
Hilton
Esso
PIRELLI
P ZERO
P ZERO
CNN

MP4-31

Honda was determined to demonstrate change on all fronts and, to that end, motorsports chief Yasuhisa Arai was replaced by Yusuke Hasegawa in an announcement that coincided with the unveiling of the new RA616H power unit. Despite the company's vast engineering resources, it remained constrained by the system of development tokens introduced by racing's governing body in 2014 to limit the scope of performance improvements. Laudable though this was, Mercedes' clear advantage had moved powerful voices among their rivals to lobby for change. Come April 2016 the FIA announced a package of measures guaranteeing the principle of customer engine supply at lower cost and eliminating the token system from 2017.

Though an evolution of its predecessor in terms of the internal combustion element, the RA616H was larger overall owing to a major redesign of the turbo and hybrid elements, which were considered responsible for the poor straightline speed of the MP4-30. The turbine also required revision to comply with an amendment to the technical regulations stipulating additional wastegate exits in line with the exhaust pipe. This was an attempt to answer critics of the hybrid engines (Bernie Ecclestone among the most vocal) who felt the exhaust noise was insufficiently visceral.

Combined with a revised intake plenum, the larger turbocharger assembly came at the cost of a higher center of gravity and more overall bulk. A conventional multibranch exhaust in place of the RA615H's log slightly increased the unit's girth but was believed to improve breathing. All-up weight increased by 4.2 kilograms (9.3 pounds).

Aerodynamically the MP4-31 was an evolution of its predecessor since McLaren remained confident that Honda's engine was solely to blame for the MP4-30's underperformance. Though still tightly packaged at the rear, it was necessarily bulkier in this area since the engine was now larger than before. The front end retained a number of design philosophies introduced during the MP4-30's development, including the S-duct connecting

MP4-31 SPECIFICATIONS

Engine	Honda 1,598cc 90-degree turbocharged hybrid V-6	**Suspension**	Double wishbones with pushrod-actuated (f) and pullrod-actuated (r) inboard torsion bars
Power	800bhp @ 15,000 rpm	**Brakes**	Carbon discs f/r
Gearbox	Seven-speed semiautomatic	**Tires**	Pirelli
Chassis	Carbon fiber and aluminum honeycomb monocoque	**Weight**	702 kilograms (1,548 pounds)

←
Fifth place for Alonso in Monaco and the US was poor by McLaren standards, but it was an uplift from previous seasons.

the underside of the nose with the upper surface behind the driver's race number, and the hollow front wheel hubs that worked with the brake ducts to augment the front wing's outwashing effect. An interesting new touch was the close positioning of the rear legs of the front wishbones, an attempt to influence airflow toward the sidepod undercuts.

As the calendar grew to twenty-one races, each driver was now permitted to use up to five different power units per season rather than four. Another significant competitive change was the introduction of three possible tire compounds per weekend, though drivers still had to use only two during a race. There was also a short-lived revision to the three-session qualifying format, which had been happily in use since 2006; now, during each of the three phases, the slowest driver would be eliminated every 90 seconds rather than at the end of the session. Not one of Bernie Ecclestone's finest ideas, it was dropped after a farcical introduction at the season-opening Australian Grand Prix.

That weekend was also notable for a high-speed accident in which Fernando Alonso was injured badly enough to be forced to sit out the following round, replaced by test driver Stoffel Vandoorne. He was 10th in Bahrain, claiming the team's best finish since the 2015 US Grand Prix, while Button retired with engine failure. While McLaren and Honda continued to bring developments through the year, including new engine specs in Belgium and Malaysia, there were still too many retirements. The drivers were occasionally able to crack the top ten in qualifying and finish in the points more regularly than before—but going from ninth to sixth in the constructors' standings was not enough of an improvement to prevent further change.

In September Button announced his retirement and then, in November, Dennis's fellow shareholders forced him to step down. After thirty-six years, ten drivers' titles, and seven constructors' championships, this was a brutal and merciless termination.

←
McLaren's season got off to a dramatic start with this high-speed accident for Fernando Alonso in Melbourne.

→
Increasingly elaborate front wings were a feature of this era, but McLaren's aero package was producing too much drag.

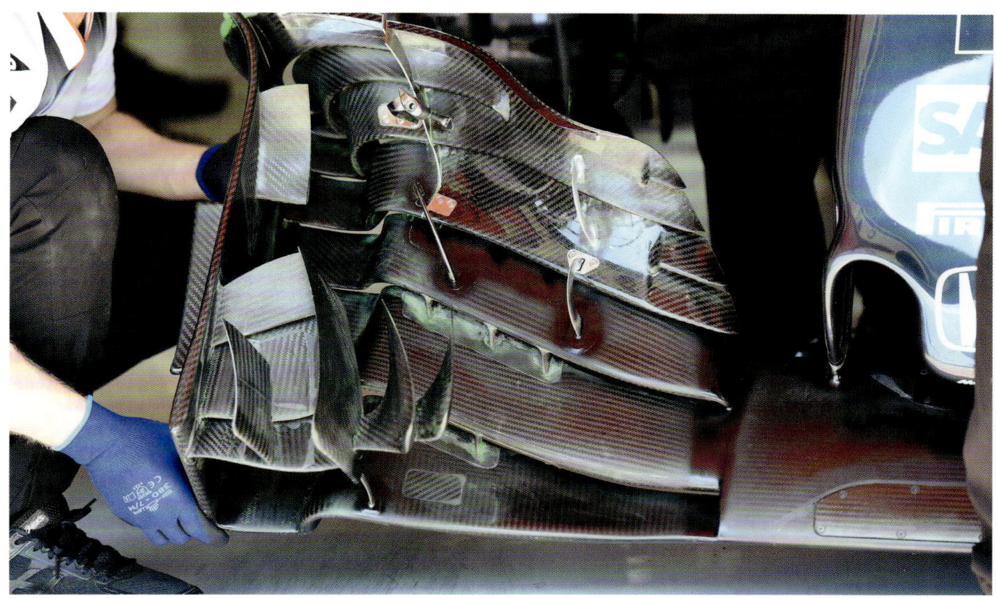

↓
It says a lot about the state of the team's competitiveness in 2016 that Stoffel Vandoorne (standing in for the injured Alonso) should find himself battling with Pascal Wehrlein's underfunded Manor car.

MCL32

A rift had been forming between McLaren and Honda, and the events of the 2017 season served to render the relationship irreparable. While the challenges experienced here set Honda on the path to world championship glory—with a different team—swapping to a new engine partner exposed grave weaknesses in McLaren's engineering approach, of which the team had chosen to remain ignorant.

To replace Ron Dennis, McLaren's shareholders recruited Zak Brown, the former head of the Just Marketing International agency that had brought so many sponsors to the team, including Diageo. Brown had long been tipped as a potential successor to Bernie Ecclestone—though of course Ecclestone believed he would remain at the commercial reins forever. In fact F1's commercial rights were in the process of being sold to the US Liberty Media Corporation for $4.6 billion by the venture capitalists who had owned them since 2006 and drawn vast profits while burdening the business with debt. But if Ecclestone thought the new owners would keep him at his post, he was disabused of the notion when they promptly clamped the gold watch on his wrist and banished him to the non job of chairman emeritus.

F1 would nevertheless have to live through the consequences of one of Ecclestone's last agitations: making the cars faster again and more dramatic looking. He had also wanted to dispose of the hybrid engines, which had by this point achieved close to 50 percent fuel efficiency but were expensive and difficult to develop. There was no consensus over this but, against a background of Mercedes dominance and audience fatigue, the stakeholders agreed to a new technical package of lower, wider cars with bigger tires. Among the unforeseen effects was that overtaking became *more* difficult because the cars occupied more on-track real estate and produced more wake turbulence.

For both McLaren and Honda, the changes created opportunities to push new concepts through. Honda took advantage of the relaxation of engine-development restrictions to produce an all-new power unit with a split turbo arrangement, like the class-leading Mercedes. Despite this the RA617H was 10 kilograms (22 pounds) lighter and ½ inch (1.27 centimeters) lower than the 2016 package. Honda also worked with spark plug supplier NGK to arrive at a precombustion chamber concept that was similar to the Mahle Jet Ignition system used by Ferrari since 2015. Program manager Yusuke Hasegawa acknowledged that wrapping all these adventurous elements into an all-new package was "very high risk."

MCL32 SPECIFICATIONS

Engine	Honda 1,598cc 90-degree turbocharged hybrid V-6	**Suspension**	Double wishbones with pushrod-actuated (f) and pullrod-actuated (r) inboard torsion bars
Power	820bhp @ 15,000 rpm	**Brakes**	Carbon discs f/r
Gearbox	Seven-speed semiautomatic	**Tires**	Pirelli
Chassis	Carbon fiber and aluminum honeycomb monocoque	**Weight**	702 kilograms (1,548 pounds)

← Performance picked up toward the end of the season. In Singapore Alonso qualified 10th while Vandoorne raced to seventh place.

↑
More orange and a new naming formula underlined the change of regime at McLaren.

Under Brown, McLaren dropped the Dennis-era MP4 nomenclature and predominantly black palette of recent cars, launching the MCL32 with a bold splash of orange. Brown also wanted to distance his team from the clinical perfectionism of the Dennis era by showing a new openness; this was perhaps premature, since the Amazon TV documentary crew he invited in captured a season defined by behind-the-scenes chaos. On launch day the MCL32 was incomplete and its engine didn't fit properly.

The first test was no better as the RA617H was punished by the higher loadings of the new generation of cars as well as by vibrations not experienced during dyno testing. Several changes of engines later, Fernando Alonso declaimed one of the issues—the structural weakness of the oil tank—as "an amateur problem."

Lack of testing mileage affected McLaren's ability to optimize the MCL32 and the RA617H had to be detuned to run reliably in the early races. Like several other teams, McLaren struggled to find a sweet spot where the car would bring the tires on both axles into the right temperature window. By midseason both sides were openly briefing against one another, citing GPS data to argue shortcomings in power and chassis performance. The inevitable divorce was made official in the aftermath of an Italian Grand Prix weekend, where Alonso had received a notional 35-place grid penalty for exceeding his quota of new power unit elements.

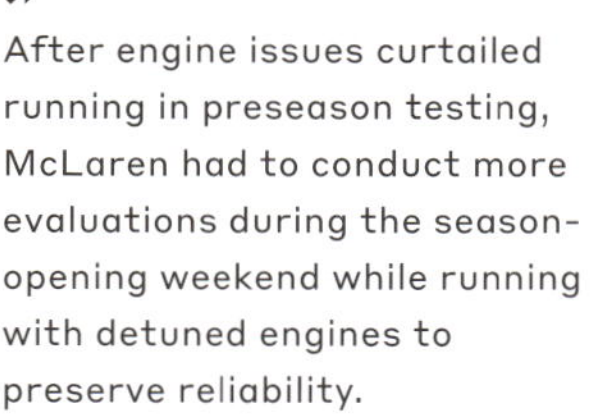

↗
After engine issues curtailed running in preseason testing, McLaren had to conduct more evaluations during the season-opening weekend while running with detuned engines to preserve reliability.

→
Replacement power unit components over the Monza weekend would trigger a notional grid penalty of thirty-five places for Fernando Alonso. McLaren's separation from Honda was made official just days later.

WALKER
NTT Communications
NRF
P ZERO
RENAULT
kimoa
RICHARD MILLE
P ZERO
PIRELLI
Hilton
Schweiz Suisse Svizzera
RICHARD MILLE
16
POWER

MCL33

Changing to a new engine supplier for 2018 meant inherent compromise for the MCL33 because, although it was conceptually an evolution of the MCL32, the car's hard points had been set before the engine call was made. McLaren had pressed Honda to adopt the class-leading Mercedes split turbo, where the compressor was at the front of the engine and the turbine at the back (Renault had resisted this and kept the two elements together at the rear). The design meant that the bulk of the engine could sit further forward, but it required a change of cooling architecture as well as a different exhaust layout, all of which affected the outer surfaces of the car around the engine cover, sidepods, and gearbox.

The MCL33 launched in another new color palette, a different shade of orange that harked back to the team's Can-Am years and the F1 cars of the late 1960s. To put a positive gloss on the change of engine supplier, the team adopted the social media hashtag "#BeBrave."

As with the MCL32, the new car followed the "high rake" philosophy pioneered by Red Bull, with a clear nose-down stance. In theory this produced more downforce at speed by providing a larger area behind the floor edge for air to expand into, accelerating its flow toward the diffuser (the effect is roughly analogous to partially covering the end of a hosepipe with your thumb). But to exploit it as well as Red Bull required finely tuned aerodynamics and suspension kinematics. In slow corners, where the rear of the car would be higher—given less downforce acting upon it—the chassis could pass a critical height threshold and cause the diffuser to stall. Addressing this effect required setting elaborate surfaces at the floor edge to generate vortices that helped maintain an aerodynamic seal for the underfloor.

Since Honda could no longer be used as an excuse for underperformance, it was now obvious that various elements of the car were not working as expected. While much of the MCL33 was new—including aggressive vanes on the front wing pylons and sidepod leading edges, and conjoined upper rear wishbone legs—the team had to spend much of the season unpicking where they had gone wrong historically. It rapidly became clear that

←
Alonso's accident at Spa demonstrated the effectiveness of the new "halo" cockpit safety feature, as Sauber's Charles Leclerc avoided injury in the impact.

MCL33 SPECIFICATIONS

Engine	Renault 1,598cc 90-degree turbocharged hybrid V-6	**Suspension**	Double wishbones with pushrod-actuated (f) and pullrod-actuated (r) inboard torsion bars
Power	900bhp @ 15,000 rpm	**Brakes**	Carbon discs f/r
Gearbox	Seven-speed semiautomatic	**Tires**	Pirelli
Chassis	Carbon fiber and aluminum honeycomb monocoque	**Weight**	733 kilograms (1,616 pounds)

↑
McLaren adopted a shade of orange closer to the team's 1960s Can-Am heyday. The new "halo" cockpit protection system divided opinion on its aesthetics—McLaren's solution was to paint it black.

→ A more elaborate nose and front wing with lateral channels and a pronounced "cape," fitted at the start of the European season, failed to deliver on expectations.

↘ McLaren, like several other teams, struggled to simulate accurately the turbulent wake of the wider post-2017 front wheels and had to turn to practical techniques to measure the effect.

on-track performance was not reflecting the results in the wind tunnel—and, as Brown would acknowledge midseason, neither could the problems with the car's behavior be reproduced in the tunnel.

McLaren was not alone in struggling to model the wake of the wider post-2017 front wheels, particularly when steering lock was applied. The MCL33's key weakness was the proximity of the front axle and suspension to the sidepods, which left less room for the bargeboards and flow conditioners necessary to set up vortices that could optimize flow down the car and divert the turbulent wake of the front wheels. But to change this would have required a new chassis and crash structure. For this reason, once it was understood, McLaren was in effect forced to shelve development of the car. But by this point several upgrade packages had been added and then removed again when they failed to deliver the anticipated results.

More humiliating still was the fact that the Toro Rosso car now powered by Honda was often faster, particularly in a straight line. As is ever the case when a project is deemed to be failing, human sacrifice was required: senior engineers Tim Goss and Matt Morris were shown the door during the season, as was racing director Eric Boullier. Fernando Alonso also announced he would be taking a sabbatical, and his ennui with the entire situation was writ large when he was running 11th in the closing laps of the final round and engineer Tom Stallard told him, "There's a point up for grabs here, mate."

Alonso's response: "I already have 1,800."

DELL Technologies
KAUST
RENAULT
RICHARD MILLE
logitech
RENAULT
PETROBRAS
RICHARD MILLE
logitech
RICHARD MILLE
KAUST

MCL34

McLaren's first big reveal of 2019 was not the new MCL34 but the recruitment of a new managing director to take full responsibility for the F1 program as the company set its sights on expansion into IndyCar and Formula E. Andreas Seidl had worked for BMW's F1 team and most recently supervised Porsche's successful World Endurance Championship campaigns.

Having shed several members of the engineering team in 2018, McLaren brought back former chief engineer Pat Fry as a consultant while incoming technical director James Key observed a period of gardening leave from his former team. The MCL34 bore much evidence of fresh thinking in addition to well-considered borrowings from other teams. At the front, as well as moving the axle line forward (and extending the wheelbase in the process) to create more space for aerodynamic furniture ahead of the sidepods, McLaren adopted Mercedes-style high-mounted wishbones, the upper of which connected to the wheel hubs via curved links. The intended function of this was to allow freer airflow from the new front wing arrangement.

F1's stakeholders had agreed on the principle of a new technical package to come into force in 2021. The finer details were yet to be worked out, but, in response to concerns about audience disenchantment with Mercedes' ongoing dominance and the lack of on-track overtaking, the FIA agreed to introduce new rules with a flavor of what was to come. Several teams contributed wind tunnel time to maximize the chances of this change being successful.

As well as enlarging the rear wings and their endplates, and establishing limits on the size of bargeboards and front brake ducts, the changes called for a different front-wing geometry. This aimed to reduce the volume of air pushed outward and limit the influence of the so-called Y250 vortex, an airflow system set up by the tips of the winglets that lie 250 millimeters (9.8 inches) from the car's centerline. Reshuffling the front suspension was one way McLaren and rivals tried to mitigate the effects of this change, since the Y250 vortex passed through that area between the nose and front wheels. The MCL34 also had narrower sidepods than before, with only the floor, a flow conditioner, and the mandatory side-impact structure extending to the minimum car width.

←
Rookie Lando Norris acquitted himself well alongside the more experienced Carlos Sainz. The MCL34 was a much more advanced design, although it was still just a midfield runner.

MCL34 SPECIFICATIONS

Engine	Renault 1,598cc 90-degree turbocharged hybrid V-6	**Suspension**	Double wishbones with pushrod-actuated (f) and pullrod-actuated (r) inboard torsion bars
Power	900bhp @ 15,000 rpm	**Brakes**	Carbon discs f/r
Gearbox	Seven-speed semiautomatic	**Tires**	Pirelli
Chassis	Carbon fiber and aluminum honeycomb monocoque	**Weight**	743 kilograms (1,638 pounds)

↑
The MCL34's front-end featured a narrow nose with the mandatory TV camera decoupled from it, plus high-mounted wishbones with a curving step down to the top of the wheel carrier.

↗
New rules, intended to restrict both the outwashing effect of the front wings and the influence of vortices shed by the winglet tips, required a great deal of experimentation with different wing profiles.

McLaren also had two new drivers, former Red Bull junior Carlos Sainz and rookie Lando Norris. Just as significant, after a number of years in which the team's share of F1's commercial income had shrunk drastically as their on-track fortunes had declined, there was a host of new sponsors on display. While Zak Brown had experience wrangling big names, he was not averse to smaller "contra" deals and B2B partnerships. Thus the arrival of the likes of Dell and CNBC in 2018, followed by FXPro, Huski Chocolate, and Deloitte, set a trend the rest of the grid would follow in the coming years.

On track the MCL34 was a vast improvement over its predecessor, showing strong pace in the opening two rounds although Sainz suffered mechanical failures in both. But in China neither driver reached the top-ten shootout in qualifying, which led Sainz to remark that the nature of the Chinese circuit—lots of corners and major stress on the front-left tire—exposed the car's "weaknesses" more. McLaren introduced small development steps in each of the opening races, focusing on the front-end aerodynamics, before bringing a larger update built around an entirely new front-wing geometry in Spain. Clearly influenced by Ferrari, it had flatter winglet profiles at the outside edges, sacrificing some downforce generation to encourage more outwashing.

McLaren spent much of the season at the leading edge of the midfield and, in Brazil, Sainz claimed the team's first podium since the beginning of 2014. A great improvement, if not yet where the team aspired to be.

↑
By the final round of 2019, the MCL34 had evolved considerably and Sainz claimed McLaren's first podium in over four years.

RICHARD MILLE
DP WORLD

CHAPTER 7

2020s

The Covid-19 pandemic touched the lives of everyone on the planet. McLaren was the first Formula 1 team to record a member of staff with the virus, precipitating their withdrawal from the 2020 season-opening race. As countries around the world called for people to stay at home, economic activity—including sports events—went on hiatus, with inevitable effects on businesses.

During this period, the McLaren Group hit financial difficulties that required cutting 1,200 jobs and financial engineering to make up for lost revenue, including the sale and leaseback of the Technology Center facility, the sale of the McLaren Applied technology business, and welcoming investment from a consortium led by MSP Sports Capital in exchange for a substantial stake in the racing company. Having headed off this existential threat, McLaren's leaders pressed on with rebuilding. In the Ron Dennis era F1 had been the sole focus of the racing organization, but under Zak Brown, the company expanded into IndyCar, Formula E, and Extreme E—structured in such a way that these activities did not detract from the F1 team's work.

Developments in F1 also worked in McLaren's favor as the Netflix series *Drive to Survive* massively expanded audience engagement in the US market. And post-Ecclestone, F1's commercial rights holders reached a more equitable deal with the teams and governing body in the form of a new Concorde Agreement that enshrined a budget cap and barriers to entry. A more level playing field and franchise values up to a billion dollars lay within reach.

←
Besides a global pandemic, the new decade would usher in a complete change in Formula 1 car design philosophy.

VELO

MCL35M

Within months of slipping his feet under the desk, Andreas Seidl was ready to make sweeping changes across the McLaren Racing organization. In January 2020 the team announced a senior management restructure: Among other changes, performance director Andrea Stella took on a new racing director role, adding responsibility for trackside engineering and operations to his remit. "We've taken the politics out of the organization," said Zak Brown.

McLaren Racing's managing director had already signaled a return to Mercedes power from 2021, as well as convincing Brown and the shareholders to make significant capital expenditure investments in the aging facilities at the Technology Center. Among these was to rebuild the wind tunnel and cease using the Toyota facility in Germany.

Though similar to the MCL34 at first glance, the MCL35 differed in several key areas (not least its matte-effect paintwork with more black in the mix, a weight-saving measure). Its nose was much narrower and no longer featured "nostrils" at the tip, with a simplified version of the Mercedes-style cape behind it. New front suspension geometry also featured more aggressively aerodynamic wishbones, almost conjoined on the top surfaces. New brake ducts and revised Enkei wheels were a further evolution in the delicate science of employing heat from the brakes to keep the front tires in the right temperature window. The sidepods were more aggressively undercut and, to the rear of the driver, the engine cover, gearbox casing, and rear suspension geometry had been reprofiled to allow a larger floor area. This was now punctuated with slots and strakes to create a sealing effect at the edge and encourage more air over the top of the diffuser ramp.

Owing to the onset of the Covid-19 pandemic, the MCL35 was parked after the cancellation of the Australian Grand Prix and did not see action until the truncated season resumed with a double-header in Austria in July. Despite the McLaren Group's financial issues, the team brought upgrades, including a new floor, to the Austrian rounds and continued to introduce new aerodynamic elements at most races. However, none of these dialed out its sensitivity to wind direction and below-par slow-speed corner performance, and Norris's podium in Austria was the only one of the season. Thanks to the inconsistency of rivals, though, McLaren were able to finish third in the constructors' championship.

←
The Red Bull Ring hosted races on two successive weekends as F1 restarted after a pandemic-induced hiatus. Norris finished third and fifth and registered a fastest lap.

MCL35, MCL35M SPECIFICATIONS

Engine	Renault, Mercedes 1,598cc 90-degree turbocharged hybrid V-6	**Suspension**	Double wishbones with pushrod-actuated (f) and pullrod-actuated (r) inboard torsion bars
Power	900bhp @ 15,000 rpm; 950bhp @ 15,000 rpm	**Brakes**	Carbon discs f/r
Gearbox	Seven-speed semiautomatic	**Tires**	Pirelli
Chassis	Carbon fiber and aluminum honeycomb monocoque	**Weight**	746 kilograms (1,645 pounds)

↑
Tire failure robbed Sainz of fourth place in the British Grand Prix. Race winner Lewis Hamilton was lucky, crossing the finishing line on three wheels after experiencing a similar delamination.

↓
While the pandemic led to F1's stakeholders agreeing on development restrictions into 2021, McLaren were able to modify the MCL35 to house a Mercedes engine. *James Mann*

→
Daniel Ricciardo celebrates McLaren's first win in nine years in his own inimitable style: drinking sparkling wine from his race boot.

The economic effects of the pandemic wrought an outbreak of unity among the stakeholders, enabling them to sign a new Concorde Agreement, which gave the existing teams a fairer share of commercial revenues, and to require new entries to pay a $200 million antidilution fee. This and a delay to the planned 2021 regulations enabled the show to go on.

Thus F1 carried on into 2021 with carryover machinery, albeit adapted to a handful of aerodynamic rule changes clearly aimed at pegging back the Mercedes team. McLaren received a concession to make further adaptations to the MCL35 in order to accommodate the Mercedes power unit.

While in-season development was permitted in 2021, McLaren were mindful of the need to direct resources to the 2022 project while trying to consolidate third place in the constructors' championship. The Mercedes power unit enabled the MCL35M to achieve a higher level of performance but, despite incremental upgrades to the front wing, floor edges, and rear wing furniture, McLaren was outdeveloped by a resurgent Ferrari.

Daniel Ricciardo, in for Ferrari-bound Carlos Sainz, led a McLaren 1–2 in Italy and Lando Norris would have won in Sochi but for disjointed decision-making when it rained in the closing stages. Ferrari's drivers scored more consistently, though—Ricciardo struggled to adapt to the MCL35M's characteristics over the first half of the season—so McLaren slipped to fourth in the constructors' standings.

OKX
Chrome
webex
by CISCO
smartsheet
Tezos
RICHARD MILLE
DEWALT
cadence
Gulf
OXXO
PIRELLI
Cinturato
KAUST
rent-a-jet

MCL36

Formula 1's new technical era should have begun in 2021, but the Covid-19 pandemic put those plans on hold, in light of the financial issues many of the teams were suffering. The new concept was defined by a return to a philosophy outlawed in 1983: ground effect. Since the middle of the 1990s, F1's rule makers had been attempting to create an on-track environment in which cars could follow each other closely through corners, thereby making overtaking opportunities more likely. But none of the solutions offered had worked.

Now that the various stakeholders were working together more harmoniously, the chances of success were greater. No other technical change in the history of F1 had been implemented with such intensive aerodynamic research to prove out the concept beforehand.

The principal theme of the new formula was to shift the balance of downforce generation so that the front and rear wings were less influential and produced less turbulence. The majority of the aerodynamic grip would now be created by two large underbody venturi: wide openings narrowed to central throats on each side before the channels widened again. Air squirting through this expansion area then created negative pressure.

Given the opportunity for divergence created by the all-new rules, many of the 2022 cars looked surprisingly similar to one another—at least in launch spec. The MCL36 was relatively unusual in that James Key's design team had opted for a high front to the chassis to maximize airflow to the underfloor venturi. They had achieved this by configuring the front suspension with pullrod actuation for the torsion bars—unseen on the front of a McLaren since the disastrous MP4-28. During testing in Bahrain, the MCL36 was one of the few cars not to suffer severe porpoising. While some observers put this down to an unusual winglike feature on the floor edge ahead of each rear wheel, it was also a factor of the McLarens not completing many high-speed laps because the brakes kept overheating.

This behavior was a limiting factor in the opening races as fitting larger brake ducts added to the drag-inducing factors on what was already proving to be a very draggy car. In common with several previous McLarens, it was also poor in slow corners and unstable on corner entry. Daniel Ricciardo, a late braker who required such stability

MCL36 SPECIFICATIONS

Engine	Mercedes 1,598cc 90-degree turbocharged hybrid V-6	**Suspension**	Double wishbones with pullrod-actuated (f) and pushrod-actuated (r) inboard torsion bars
Power	950bhp @ 15,000 rpm	**Brakes**	Carbon discs f/r
Gearbox	Seven-speed semiautomatic	**Tires**	Pirelli
Chassis	Carbon fiber and aluminum honeycomb monocoque	**Weight**	795 kilograms (1,753 pounds)

← The final update package, revising the leading edge of the sidepods and the underfloor, arrived in Singapore along with a one-off stealth livery by partner OKX.

to be confident at turn-in, found this particularly difficult. McLaren made several small tweaks to the front and rear wings and front suspension in the opening races, to little effect, before bringing a major update to the Azerbaijan Grand Prix. This included yet more wing changes along with revised sidepods and a new floor design. Lando Norris remarked that it was the car with which McLaren should have started the season.

All cars were now heavier because of the move to 18-inch (46-centimeter) wheels. This contributed to another consequence of the shift to ground effect: a tendency toward ponderous understeer in very slow corners.

McLaren briefly paused development midseason as spending came close to the newly instituted budget cap of $140 million per year, then restarted when the stakeholders agreed to raise the cap slightly to account for inflation. In Singapore the team introduced the biggest update of the season, featuring another conceptual change around the leading edge of the sidepod.

Ricciardo continued to struggle and was released at the end of the season, while Norris could not add to the podium he grabbed in poor weather conditions at Imola. Fifth place in the constructors' championship was a disappointment given the upbeat end of the previous two years.

↖
Though the MCL36 was plagued by brake issues, draggy aerodynamics, and inconsistent handling, wet weather was a great leveler. Norris finished on the podium at Imola.

←
Although Norris qualified fifth in France, the latest car upgrade was considered underwhelming, which triggered McLaren Chief Executive Zak Brown to launch an internal inquiry.

↑
McLaren's IndyCar star Pato O'Ward got an opportunity to drive in practice for the Abu Dhabi Grand Prix.

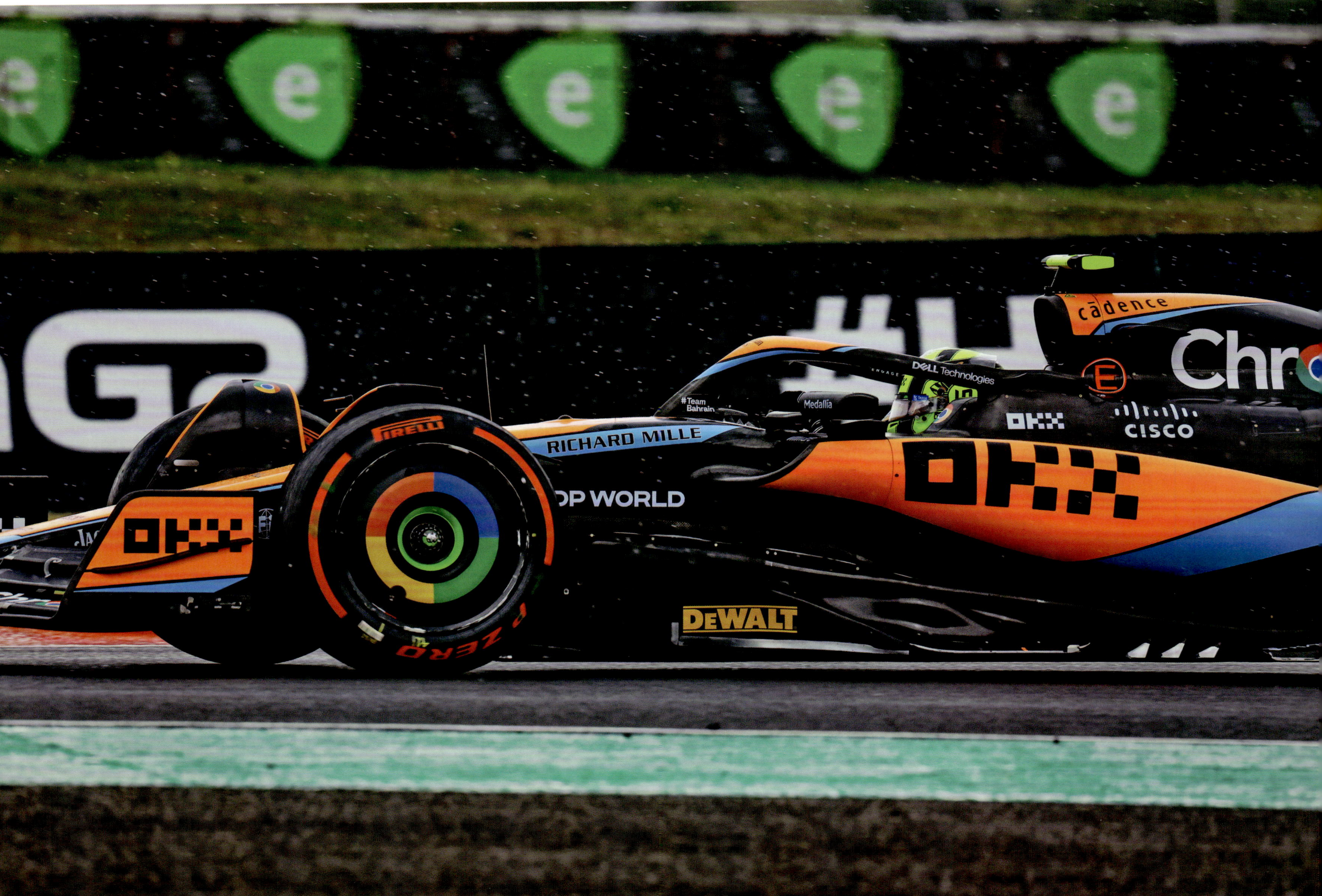

cadence
DELL Technologies
#Team Bahrain
Medallia
cisco
PIRELLI
RICHARD MILLE
DEWALT

MCL60

Over the winter of 2022 McLaren went through another leadership change as Andreas Seidl left to become CEO of the Sauber Group, soon to become the platform for Audi's Formula 1 entry. McLaren replaced him by promoting from within, as Andrea Stella stepped up from his racing director role to become team principal.

But if outsiders believed this would entail seamless continuity, they were to be surprised, for Stella had his own ideas about how the team ought to be run. Further restructuring followed the disappointing birth of the MCL60. At launch Stella conceded the team was "not entirely happy" with the first iteration of the car, since it had fallen short of the aerodynamic benchmarks set for it.

As the underfloor was the most important downforce-generating area in these ground effect cars, the outward differences between the MCL60—named for the company's sixtieth anniversary—and the MCL36 were relatively few and geared toward exploiting the underfloor. A redesigned sidepod area with a deeper undercut and a Red Bull–style undershot radiator aperture pointed toward a significant change in the cooling architecture. This was purely for aerodynamic purposes, creating more space for the vanes that fed the underfloor venturi. Expediting airflow around the floor area and over the top of the sidepod also had an influence on the sealing effect of the floor edges and the overall performance of the diffuser. The upper front suspension wishbones were also repositioned to optimize airflow toward the radiator inlets and upper sidepod surfaces.

With the notable exception of Mercedes, the rest of the grid was beginning to converge around the Red Bull approach to sidepod design—but imitation was no shortcut to faster lap times. What was not widely understood through 2022—or even in the early races of 2023—was how Red Bull had optimized their suspension kinematics, particularly at the rear, to make their car relatively benign and less prone to porpoising. This quality also enabled them to run a rear wing with a slim lower beam element. With the upper element generating more downforce and drag, this made the car even quicker when its Drag Reduction System was activated, since this involved flattening that surface. Excess drag had long been a characteristic of McLaren F1 cars, and the MCL60 was no exception. It also lacked grip and balance, particularly in slow corners.

←
Following a minor update in Baku, McLaren rolled out the first two stages of a major upgrade package to the MCL60's wings, floor, sidepod profile, and radiator inlets for both cars over the course of the Austrian, British, and Hungarian Grands Prix.

MCL60 SPECIFICATIONS

Engine	Mercedes 1,598cc 90-degree turbocharged hybrid V-6	**Suspension**	Double wishbones with pullrod-actuated (f) and pushrod-actuated (r) inboard torsion bars
Power	950bhp @ 15,000 rpm	**Brakes**	Carbon discs f/r
Gearbox	Seven-speed semiautomatic	**Tires**	Pirelli
Chassis	Carbon fiber and aluminum honeycomb monocoque	**Weight**	798 kilograms (1,759 pounds)

During 2022 McLaren had recruited Oscar Piastri, the 2021 Formula 2 champion, to replace the underperforming Daniel Ricciardo. Though Piastri was part of the rival Alpine team's young driver program, their management had failed to sign a binding onward contract and appeared to be expecting him to warm the bench as reserve driver until a race seat became available. Andreas Seidl had swooped like the eagle homing in on Prometheus's liver.

Piastri was much more closely matched to Lando Norris in pace terms, but in the early rounds of the season the MCL60 didn't look like a car capable of scoring points. The official reasoning was that rule tweaks raising the rear floor edge and diffuser had affected McLaren more than others—but the subsequent restructuring where James Key was shown the door indicated a different interpretation inside the company.

In Baku McLaren introduced a new floor-edge geometry and a lower-drag rear wing, but a much larger upgrade was in the works—so large, in fact, that it had to be rolled out over the course of three races in the middle of the season. Norris immediately claimed two podium finishes, but he cautioned that, while the car had gotten faster, it was not any easier to drive. Even so the MCL60's transformation from tail-ender to genuine contender was confirmed when Piastri won the Sprint event in Qatar.

↖
A close encounter with former McLaren driver Carlos Sainz's Ferrari ruined Oscar Piastri's Belgian Grand Prix after an excellent performance in the previous day's sprint event.

←
The team admitted at launch that they had missed a key aerodynamic design direction on the MCL60. It endured a few troubled races.

↑
Stage three of the MCL60's conceptual upgrade, a total reprofiling of the sidepods with a steeply dished internal curve, was held back until the Singapore Grand Prix.

APPENDIX: RESULTS

1966

GRAND PRIX	DRIVER	CAR	GRID	RESULT
Monaco	Bruce McLaren	M2B	10th	DNF—oil leak
Belgium	Bruce McLaren	M2B	N/A	DNS—bearings
Britain	Bruce McLaren	M2B	13th	6th
US	Bruce McLaren	M2B	11th	5th
Mexico	Bruce McLaren	M2B	15th	DNF—engine

Championship positions: McLaren 16th (3 points)

1967

GRAND PRIX	DRIVER	CAR	GRID	RESULT
Monaco	Bruce McLaren	M4B	10th	4th
Netherlands	Bruce McLaren	M5A	14th	DNF—accident
Canada	Bruce McLaren	M5A	6th	7th
Italy	Bruce McLaren	M5A	3rd	DNF—engine
US	Bruce McLaren	M5A	9th	DNF—water leak
Mexico	Bruce McLaren	M5A	8th	DNF—oil pressure

Championship positions: McLaren 14th (3 points)

1968

GRAND PRIX	DRIVER	CAR	GRID	RESULT
South Africa	Denny Hulme	M5A	9th	5th
Spain	Bruce McLaren	M7A	4th	DNF—oil leak
	Denny Hulme	M7A	3rd	2nd
Monaco	Bruce McLaren	M7A	7th	DNF—accident
	Denny Hulme	M7A	10th	5th
Belgium	Bruce McLaren	M7A	6th	1st
	Denny Hulme	M7A	5th	DNF—driveshaft
Netherlands	Bruce McLaren	M7A	8th	DNF—accident
	Denny Hulme	M7A	7th	DNF—ignition
France	Bruce McLaren	M7A	6th	8th
	Denny Hulme	M7A	4th	5th
Britain	Bruce McLaren	M7A	10th	7th
	Denny Hulme	M7A	11th	4th
Germany	Bruce McLaren	M7A	16th	13th
	Denny Hulme	M7A	11th	7th
Italy	Bruce McLaren	M7A	2nd	DNF—oil leak
	Denny Hulme	M7A	7th	1st
Canada	Bruce McLaren	M7A	8th	2nd
	Denny Hulme	M7A	6th	1st
US	Bruce McLaren	M7A	10th	6th
	Denny Hulme	M7A	5th	DNF—accident
Mexico	Bruce McLaren	M7A	9th	2nd
	Denny Hulme	M7A	4th	DNF—suspension

Championship positions: Hulme 3rd (33 points); McLaren 5th (22 points)

1969

GRAND PRIX	DRIVER	CAR	GRID	RESULT
South Africa	Bruce McLaren	M7B	8th	5th
	Denny Hulme	M7A	3rd	3rd
Spain	Bruce McLaren	M7C	13th	2nd
	Denny Hulme	M7A	9th	4th
Monaco	Bruce McLaren	M7C	11th	5th
	Denny Hulme	M7A	12th	6th
Netherlands	Bruce McLaren	M7C	6th	DNF—suspension
	Denny Hulme	M7A	7th	4th
France	Bruce McLaren	M7C	7th	4th
	Denny Hulme	M7A	2nd	8th
Britain	Bruce McLaren	M7C	7th	3rd
	Denny Hulme	M7A	3rd	DNF—ignition
	Derek Bell	M9A	15th	DNF—suspension
Germany	Bruce McLaren	M7C	8th	3rd
	Denny Hulme	M7A	5th	DNF—transmission
Italy	Bruce McLaren	M7C	5th	4th
	Denny Hulme	M7A	2nd	7th
Canada	Bruce McLaren	M7C	9th	5th
	Denny Hulme	M7A	5th	DNF—distributor
US	Bruce McLaren	M7C	6th	DNS—engine
	Denny Hulme	M7A	2nd	DNF—gearbox
Mexico	Bruce McLaren	M7C	7th	DNF—fuel system
	Denny Hulme	M7A	4th	1st

Championship positions: McLaren 3rd (26 points); Hulme 6th (20 points)

1970

GRAND PRIX	DRIVER	CAR	GRID	RESULT
South Africa	Bruce McLaren	M14A	10th	DNF—engine
	Denny Hulme	M14A	6th	2nd
Spain	Bruce McLaren	M14A	11th	2nd
	Denny Hulme	M14A	2nd	DNF—electrical
	Andrea de Adamich	M7D	DNQ	N/A
Monaco	Bruce McLaren	M14A	10th	DNF—suspension
	Denny Hulme	M14A	3rd	4th
	Andrea de Adamich	M7D	DNQ	N/A
Netherlands	Dan Gurney	M14A	19th	DNF—engine
	Peter Gethin	M14A	11th	DNF—accident
	Andrea de Adamich	M14D	DNQ	N/A
France	Dan Gurney	M14A	17th	6th
	Denny Hulme	M14D	7th	4th
	Andrea de Adamich	M7D	15th	Not classified
Britain	Dan Gurney	M14A	12th	DNF—oil pressure
	Denny Hulme	M14D	5th	3rd
	Andrea de Adamich	M7D	19th	DNS—fuel leak
Netherlands	Peter Gethin	M14A	17th	DNF—throttle
	Denny Hulme	M14A	16th	3rd
	Andrea de Adamich	M14D	DNQ	N/A
Austria	Peter Gethin	M14A	21st	10th
	Denny Hulme	M14A	11th	DNF—engine
	Andrea de Adamich	M14D	15th	12th
Italy	Peter Gethin	M14A	17th	Not classified
	Denny Hulme	M14A	9th	4th
	Andrea de Adamich	M14D	13th	8th
	Nanni Galli	M7D	DNQ	N/A
Canada	Peter Gethin	M14A	11th	6th
	Denny Hulme	M14A	15th	DNF—engine
	Andrea de Adamich	M14D	12th	DNF—oil pressure
US	Peter Gethin	M14A	21st	14th
	Denny Hulme	M14A	11th	7th
	Andrea de Adamich	M14D	DNQ	N/A
Mexico	Peter Gethin	M14A	10th	DNF—engine
	Denny Hulme	M14A	14th	3rd

Championship positions: Hulme 4th (27 points); Gethin 23rd (1 point); Gurney 24th (1 point)

1971

GRAND PRIX	DRIVER	CAR	GRID	RESULT
South Africa	Denny Hulme	M19A	7th	6th
	Peter Gethin	M14A	11th	DNF—fuel leak
Spain	Denny Hulme	M19A	5th	6th
	Peter Gethin	M14A	8th	DNF—fuel leak
Monaco	Denny Hulme	M19A	6th	14th
	Peter Gethin	M14A	14th	DNF—accident
Netherlands	Denny Hulme	M19A	14th	12th
	Peter Gethin	M19A	23rd	Not classified
France	Denny Hulme	M19A	11th	DNF—electrical
	Peter Gethin	M19A	19th	9th
Britain	Denny Hulme	M19A	8th	DNF—engine
	Peter Gethin	M19A	14th	DNF—engine
	Jackie Oliver	M14A	22nd	DNF—accident
Germany	Denny Hulme	M19A	6th	DNF—fuel leak
	Peter Gethin	M19A	19th	DNF—accident
Austria	Denny Hulme	M19A	9th	DNF—engine
	Jackie Oliver	M19A	22nd	9th
Italy	Jackie Oliver	M14A	13th	7th
Canada	Denny Hulme	M19A	10th	4th
US	Denny Hulme	M19A	3rd	DNF—accident

Championship positions: Gethin 9th (9 points); Hulme 13th (9 points)*
**All points scored with BRM*

1972

Argentina	Denny Hulme	M19A	4th	2nd
	Peter Revson	M19A	3rd	DNF—engine
South Africa	Denny Hulme	M19A	5th	1st
	Peter Revson	M19A	12th	3rd
Spain	Denny Hulme	M19A	2nd	DNF—gearbox
	Peter Revson	M19A	11th	5th
Monaco	Denny Hulme	M19C	7th	15th
	Brian Redman	M19A	10th	5th
Belgium	Denny Hulme	M19C	3rd	3rd
	Peter Revson	M19A	7th	7th
France	Denny Hulme	M19C	2nd	7th
	Brian Redman	M19A	14th	9th
Britain	Denny Hulme	M19C	11th	5th
	Peter Revson	M19A	3rd	3rd
Germany	Denny Hulme	M19C	10th	DNF—engine
	Brian Redman	M19A	19th	5th
Austria	Denny Hulme	M19C	7th	2nd
	Peter Revson	M19C	4th	3rd
Italy	Denny Hulme	M19C	5th	3rd
	Peter Revson	M19C	8th	4th
Canada	Denny Hulme	M19C	2nd	3rd
	Peter Revson	M19C	1st	2nd
US	Denny Hulme	M19C	3rd	3rd
	Peter Revson	M19C	2nd	18th—electrical
	Jody Scheckter	M19A	8th	9th

Championship positions: Hulme 3rd (39 points); Revson 5th (23 points); Redman 14th (4 points)

1973

Argentina	Denny Hulme	M19C	8th	5th
	Peter Revson	M19C	11th	8th
Brazil	Denny Hulme	M19C	5th	3rd
	Peter Revson	M19C	12th	DNF—gearbox
South Africa	Denny Hulme	M23	1st	5th
	Peter Revson	M19C	6th	2nd
	Jody Scheckter	M19C	3rd	9th—engine
Spain	Denny Hulme	M23	2nd	6th
	Peter Revson	M23	5th	4th
Belgium	Denny Hulme	M23	2nd	7th
	Peter Revson	M23	10th	DNF—accident
Monaco	Denny Hulme	M23	3rd	6th
	Peter Revson	M23	15th	5th
Sweden	Denny Hulme	M23	6th	1st
	Peter Revson	M23	7th	7th
France	Denny Hulme	M23	6th	8th
	Jody Scheckter	M23	2nd	DNF—accident
Britain	Denny Hulme	M23	2nd	3rd
	Peter Revson	M23	3rd	1st
	Jody Scheckter	M23	6th	DNF—accident
Netherlands	Denny Hulme	M23	4th	DNF—engine
	Peter Revson	M23	6th	4th
Germany	Denny Hulme	M23	12th	1st
	Peter Revson	M23	9th	7th
	Jacky Ickx	M23	4th	3rd
Austria	Denny Hulme	M23	3rd	8th
	Peter Revson	M23	4th	DNF—clutch
Italy	Denny Hulme	M23	3rd	15th
	Peter Revson	M23	2nd	3rd
Canada	Denny Hulme	M23	7th	3rd
	Peter Revson	M23	2nd	13th
	Jody Scheckter	M23	3rd	DNF—accident
US	Denny Hulme	M23	9th	4th
	Peter Revson	M23	8th	5th
	Jody Scheckter	M23	11th	DNF—suspension

*Championship positions: Revson 5th (38 points); Hulme 6th (26 points); Ickx 9th (12 points)**
**4 points scored with McLaren*

1974

Argentina	Emerson Fittipaldi	M23	3rd	10th
	Denny Hulme	M23	10th	1st
	Mike Hailwood	M23	9th	4th
Brazil	Emerson Fittipaldi	M23	1st	1st
	Denny Hulme	M23	11th	12th
	Mike Hailwood	M23	7th	5th
South Africa	Emerson Fittipaldi	M23	5th	7th
	Denny Hulme	M23	9th	9th
	Mike Hailwood	M23	12th	3rd
Spain	Emerson Fittipaldi	M23	4th	3rd
	Denny Hulme	M23	8th	6th
	Mike Hailwood	M23	18th	9th
Belgium	Emerson Fittipaldi	M23	4th	1st
	Denny Hulme	M23	12th	6th
	Mike Hailwood	M23	13th	7th
Monaco	Emerson Fittipaldi	M23	13th	5th
	Denny Hulme	M23	12th	DNF—accident
	Mike Hailwood	M23	10th	DNF—accident
Sweden	Emerson Fittipaldi	M23	9th	4th
	Denny Hulme	M23	12th	DNF—suspension
	Mike Hailwood	M23	11th	DNF—fuel leak
Netherlands	Emerson Fittipaldi	M23	3rd	3rd
	Denny Hulme	M23	9th	DNF—electrical
	Mike Hailwood	M23	4th	4th
France	Emerson Fittipaldi	M23	5th	DNF—engine
	Denny Hulme	M23	11th	6th
	Mike Hailwood	M23	6th	7th
Britain	Emerson Fittipaldi	M23	8th	2nd
	Denny Hulme	M23	19th	7th
	Mike Hailwood	M23	11th	DNF—spin
Germany	Emerson Fittipaldi	M23	3rd	DNF—accident
	Denny Hulme	M23	7th	DSQ
	Mike Hailwood	M23	12th	15th—accident
Austria	Emerson Fittipaldi	M23	3rd	DNF—engine
	Denny Hulme	M23	10th	2nd
	David Hobbs	M23	17th	7th
Italy	Emerson Fittipaldi	M23	6th	2nd
	Denny Hulme	M23	19th	6th
	David Hobbs	M23	23rd	9th
Canada	Emerson Fittipaldi	M23	1st	1st
	Denny Hulme	M23	14th	6th
	Jochen Mass	M23	12th	16th
US	Emerson Fittipaldi	M23	8th	4th
	Denny Hulme	M23	17th	DNF—engine
	Jochen Mass	M23	20th	7th

Championship positions: Fittipaldi 1st (55 points); Hulme 7th (20 points); Hailwood 10th (12 points)

1975

Argentina	Emerson Fittipaldi	M23	5th	1st
	Jochen Mass	M23	13th	14th
Brazil	Emerson Fittipaldi	M23	2nd	2nd
	Jochen Mass	M23	10th	3rd
South Africa	Emerson Fittipaldi	M23	11th	Not classified
	Jochen Mass	M23	16th	6th
Spain	Emerson Fittipaldi	M23	26th	DNS
	Jochen Mass	M23	11th	1st
Monaco	Emerson Fittipaldi	M23	9th	2nd
	Jochen Mass	M23	15th	6th
Belgium	Emerson Fittipaldi	M23	8th	7th
	Jochen Mass	M23	15th	DNF—accident
Sweden	Emerson Fittipaldi	M23	11th	8th
	Jochen Mass	M23	14th	DNF—overheating
Netherlands	Emerson Fittipaldi	M23	6th	DNF—engine
	Jochen Mass	M23	8th	DNF—accident
France	Emerson Fittipaldi	M23	10th	4th
	Jochen Mass	M23	7th	3rd
Britain	Emerson Fittipaldi	M23	7th	1st
	Jochen Mass	M23	10th	7th
Germany	Emerson Fittipaldi	M23	8th	DNF—suspension
	Jochen Mass	M23	6th	DNF—accident
Austria	Emerson Fittipaldi	M23	3rd	9th
	Jochen Mass	M23	9th	4th
Italy	Emerson Fittipaldi	M23	3rd	2nd
	Jochen Mass	M23	5th	DNF—accident
US	Emerson Fittipaldi	M23	2nd	2nd
	Jochen Mass	M23	9th	3rd

Championship positions: Fittipaldi 2nd (45 points); Mass 8th (20 points)

1976

Brazil	James Hunt	M23	1st	DNF—accident
	Jochen Mass	M23	6th	6th
South Africa	James Hunt	M23	1st	2nd
	Jochen Mass	M23	4th	3rd
US West	James Hunt	M23	3rd	DNF—accident
	Jochen Mass	M23	14th	5th
Spain	James Hunt	M23	1st	1st
	Jochen Mass	M23	4th	DNF—engine
Belgium	James Hunt	M23	3rd	DNF—gearbox
	Jochen Mass	M23	18th	6th
Monaco	James Hunt	M23	14th	DNF—engine
	Jochen Mass	M23	11th	5th
Sweden	James Hunt	M23	8th	5th
	Jochen Mass	M23	13th	11th
France	James Hunt	M23	1st	1st
	Jochen Mass	M23	14th	15th
Britain	James Hunt	M23	2nd	DSQ
	Jochen Mass	M23	12th	DNF—clutch
Germany	James Hunt	M23	1st	1st
	Jochen Mass	M23	9th	3rd
Austria	James Hunt	M23	1st	4th
	Jochen Mass	M23	12th	7th
Netherlands	James Hunt	M23	2nd	1st
	Jochen Mass	M26	15th	9th
Italy	James Hunt	M23	27th	DNF—spin
	Jochen Mass	M23	28th	DNF—electrical
Canada	James Hunt	M23	1st	1st
	Jochen Mass	M23	11th	5th
Japan	James Hunt	M23	2nd	3rd
	Jochen Mass	M23	12th	DNF—accident

Championship positions: Hunt 1st (69 points); Mass 9th (19 points)

1977

Argentina	James Hunt	M23	1st	DNF—suspension
	Jochen Mass	M23	5th	DNF—spin
Brazil	James Hunt	M23	1st	2nd
	Jochen Mass	M23	4th	DNF—accident
South Africa	James Hunt	M23	1st	4th
	Jochen Mass	M23	13th	5th
US West	James Hunt	M23	8th	7th
	Jochen Mass	M23	15th	DNF—handling
Spain	James Hunt	M26	7th	DNF—engine
	Jochen Mass	M23	9th	4th
Monaco	James Hunt	M23	7th	DNF—engine
	Jochen Mass	M23	9th	4th
Belgium	James Hunt	M26	9th	7th
	Jochen Mass	M23	6th	DNF—accident
Sweden	James Hunt	M26	3rd	12th
	Jochen Mass	M23	9th	2nd
France	James Hunt	M26	2nd	3rd
	Jochen Mass	M23	7th	9th
Britain	James Hunt	M26	1st	1st
	Jochen Mass	M26	11th	4th
	Gilles Villeneuve	M23	9th	11th
Germany	James Hunt	M26	4th	DNF—fuel pump
	Jochen Mass	M26	13th	DNF—gearbox
Austria	James Hunt	M26	2nd	DNF—engine
	Jochen Mass	M26	9th	6th
Netherlands	James Hunt	M26	3rd	DNF—accident
	Jochen Mass	M26	14th	DNF—accident
Italy	James Hunt	M26	1st	DNF—spin
	Jochen Mass	M26	9th	4th
	Bruno Giacomelli	M23	15th	DNF—engine
US	James Hunt	M26	1st	1st
	Jochen Mass	M26	15th	DNF—fuel system
Canada	James Hunt	M26	2nd	DNF—accident
	Jochen Mass	M26	5th	3rd
Japan	James Hunt	M26	2nd	1st
	Jochen Mass	M26	8th	DNF—engine

Championship positions: Hunt 5th (40 points); Mass 6th (25 points)

1978

Argentina	James Hunt	M26	6th	4th
	Patrick Tambay	M26	9th	6th
Brazil	James Hunt	M26	2nd	DNF—spin
	Patrick Tambay	M26	5th	DNF—spin
South Africa	James Hunt	M26	3rd	DNF—engine
	Patrick Tambay	M26	4th	DNF—accident
US West	James Hunt	M26	7th	DNF—accident
	Patrick Tambay	M26	11th	12th—accident
Monaco	James Hunt	M26	6th	DNF—handling
	Patrick Tambay	M26	11th	7th
Belgium	James Hunt	M26	6th	DNF—accident
	Bruno Giacomelli	M26	21st	8th
Spain	James Hunt	M26	4th	6th
	Patrick Tambay	M26	14th	DNF—spin
Sweden	James Hunt	M26	14th	8th
	Patrick Tambay	M26	15th	4th
France	James Hunt	M26	4th	3rd
	Patrick Tambay	M26	6th	8th
	Bruno Giacomelli	M26	22nd	DNF—engine
Britain	James Hunt	M26	14th	DNF—accident
	Patrick Tambay	M26	20th	6th
	Bruno Giacomelli	M26	16th	7th
Germany	James Hunt	M26	8th	DSQ
	Patrick Tambay	M26	11th	DNF—accident
Austria	James Hunt	M26	8th	DNF—accident
	Patrick Tambay	M26	14th	DNF—accident
Netherlands	James Hunt	M26	7th	10th
	Patrick Tambay	M26	14th	9th
	Bruno Giacomelli	M26	19th	DNF—spin
Italy	James Hunt	M26	10th	DNF—electrical
	Patrick Tambay	M26	19th	5th
	Bruno Giacomelli	M26	20th	14th
US	James Hunt	M26	6th	7th
	Patrick Tambay	M26	18th	6th
Canada	James Hunt	M26	19th	DNF—spin
	Patrick Tambay	M26	17th	8th

Championship positions: Hunt 13th (8 points); Tambay 13th (8 points)

1979

Argentina	John Watson	M28	6th	3rd
	Patrick Tambay	M28	9th	DNF—accident
Brazil	John Watson	M28	14th	DNF—steering
	Patrick Tambay	M26	18th	DNF—accident
South Africa	John Watson	M28	14th	DNF—electrical
	Patrick Tambay	M28	17th	10th
US West	John Watson	M28	18th	DNF—fuel system
	Patrick Tambay	M28	19th	DNF—accident
Spain	John Watson	M28	18th	DNF—engine
	Patrick Tambay	M28	20th	13th
Belgium	John Watson	M28	19th	6th
	Patrick Tambay	M26	DNQ	N/A
Monaco	John Watson	M28	14th	4th
	Patrick Tambay	M28	DNQ	N/A
France	John Watson	M28	15th	11th
	Patrick Tambay	M28	20th	10th
Britain	John Watson	M29	7th	4th
	Patrick Tambay	M28	18th	7th
Germany	John Watson	M29	12th	5th
	Patrick Tambay	M29	15th	DNF—suspension
Austria	John Watson	M29	16th	9th
	Patrick Tambay	M29	14th	10th
Netherlands	John Watson	M29	12th	DNF—engine
	Patrick Tambay	M29	14th	DNF—engine
Italy	John Watson	M29	19th	DNF—accident
	Patrick Tambay	M29	14th	DNF—engine
Canada	John Watson	M29	17th	6th
	Patrick Tambay	M29	20th	DNF—engine
US	John Watson	M29	13th	6th
	Patrick Tambay	M29	22nd	DNF—engine

Championship positions: Watson 9th (15 points)

1980

Argentina	John Watson	M29B	6th	3rd
	Alain Prost	M29B	9th	DNF—accident
Brazil	John Watson	M29B	23rd	11th
	Alain Prost	M29B	13th	5th
South Africa	John Watson	M29B	21st	11th
	Alain Prost	M29B	22nd	DNS
US West	John Watson	M29C	21st	4th
	Stephen South	M29C	DNQ	N/A
Belgium	John Watson	M29C	20th	Not classified
	Alain Prost	M29C	19th	DNF—transmission
Monaco	John Watson	M29C	DNQ	N/A
	Alain Prost	M29C	10th	DNF—accident
France	John Watson	M29C	13th	7th
	Alain Prost	M29C	7th	DNF—transmission
Britain	John Watson	M29C	12th	8th
	Alain Prost	M29C	7th	6th
Germany	John Watson	M29C	20th	DNF—engine
	Alain Prost	M29C	14th	11th
Austria	John Watson	M29C	21st	DNF—engine
	Alain Prost	M29C	12th	7th
Netherlands	John Watson	M29C	9th	DNF—engine
	Alain Prost	M30	18th	6th
Italy	John Watson	M29C	14th	DNF—wheel bearing
	Alain Prost	M30	24th	7th
Canada	John Watson	M29C	7th	4th
	Alain Prost	M30	12th	DNF—suspension
US	John Watson	M29C	9th	Not classified
	Alain Prost	M30	13th	DNS

Championship positions: Watson 11th (6 points); Prost 16th (5 points)

1981

US West	John Watson	M29F	23rd	DNF—brakes
	Andrea de Cesaris	M29F	22nd	DNF—accident
Brazil	John Watson	M29F	15th	8th
	Andrea de Cesaris	M29F	20th	DNF—engine
Argentina	John Watson	MP4/1	11th	DNF—electrical
	Andrea de Cesaris	M29F	18th	11th
San Marino	John Watson	MP4/1	7th	10th
	Andrea de Cesaris	M29F	14th	6th
Belgium	John Watson	MP4/1	5th	7th
	Andrea de Cesaris	M29F	23rd	DNF—gearbox
Monaco	John Watson	MP4/1	10th	DNF—engine
	Andrea de Cesaris	MP4/1	11th	DNF—accident
Spain	John Watson	MP4/1	4th	3rd
	Andrea de Cesaris	MP4/1	14th	DNF—accident
France	John Watson	MP4/1	2nd	2nd
	Andrea de Cesaris	MP4/1	5th	11th
Britain	John Watson	MP4/1	5th	1st
	Andrea de Cesaris	MP4/1	6th	DNF—spin
Germany	John Watson	MP4/1	9th	6th
	Andrea de Cesaris	MP4/1	10th	DNF—accident
Austria	John Watson	MP4/1	12th	6th
	Andrea de Cesaris	MP4/1	18th	8th
Netherlands	John Watson	MP4/1	8th	DNF—electrical
	Andrea de Cesaris	MP4/1	13th	DNS
Italy	John Watson	MP4/1	7th	DNF—accident
	Andrea de Cesaris	MP4/1	16th	7th
Canada	John Watson	MP4/1	9th	2nd
	Andrea de Cesaris	MP4/1	13th	DNF—spin
Caesars Palace	John Watson	MP4/1	6th	7th
	Andrea de Cesaris	MP4/1	14th	12th

Championship positions: Watson 6th (27 points); de Cesaris 18th (1 point)

1982

South Africa	Niki Lauda	MP4/1B	13th	4th
	John Watson	MP4/1B	9th	6th
Brazil	Niki Lauda	MP4/1B	5th	DNF—accident
	John Watson	MP4/1B	12th	2nd
US West	Niki Lauda	MP4/1B	2nd	1st
	John Watson	MP4/1B	11th	6th
Belgium	Niki Lauda	MP4/1B	4th	DSQ
	John Watson	MP4/1B	12th	1st
Monaco	Niki Lauda	MP4/1B	12th	DNF—engine
	John Watson	MP4/1B	10th	DNF—electrical
Detroit	Niki Lauda	MP4/1B	10th	DNF—accident
	John Watson	MP4/1B	17th	1st
Canada	Niki Lauda	MP4/1B	11th	DNF—clutch
	John Watson	MP4/1B	6th	3rd
Netherlands	Niki Lauda	MP4/1B	5th	4th
	John Watson	MP4/1B	11th	9th
Britain	Niki Lauda	MP4/1B	5th	1st
	John Watson	MP4/1B	12th	DNF—spin
France	Niki Lauda	MP4/1B	9th	8th
	John Watson	MP4/1B	12th	DNF—electrical
Germany	Niki Lauda	MP4/1B	Withdrawn	N/A
	John Watson	MP4/1B	10th	DNF—spin
Austria	Niki Lauda	MP4/1B	10th	5th
	John Watson	MP4/1B	18th	9th—engine
Switzerland	Niki Lauda	MP4/1B	4th	3rd
	John Watson	MP4/1B	11th	13th
Italy	Niki Lauda	MP4/1B	10th	DNF—brakes
	John Watson	MP4/1B	12th	4th
Caesars Palace	Niki Lauda	MP4/1B	13th	DNF—engine
	John Watson	MP4/1B	9th	2nd

Championship positions: Watson 3rd (39 points); Lauda 5th (30 points)

1983

Brazil	Niki Lauda	MP4/1C	9th	3rd
	John Watson	MP4/1C	16th	DNF—engine
US West	Niki Lauda	MP4/1C	23rd	2nd
	John Watson	MP4/1C	22nd	1st
France	Niki Lauda	MP4/1C	12th	DNF—wheel bearing
	John Watson	MP4/1C	14th	DNF—engine
San Marino	Niki Lauda	MP4/1C	18th	DNF—spin
	John Watson	MP4/1C	24th	5th
Monaco	Niki Lauda	MP4/1C	DNQ	N/A
	John Watson	MP4/1C	DNQ	N/A
Belgium	Niki Lauda	MP4/1C	15th	DNF—gearbox
	John Watson	MP4/1C	20th	DNF—accident
Detroit	Niki Lauda	MP4/1C	18th	DNF—suspension
	John Watson	MP4/1C	21st	3rd
Canada	Niki Lauda	MP4/1C	19th	DNF—spin
	John Watson	MP4/1C	20th	6th
Britain	Niki Lauda	MP4/1C	15th	6th
	John Watson	MP4/1C	24th	9th
Germany	Niki Lauda	MP4/1C	18th	DSQ
	John Watson	MP4/1C	23rd	5th
Brazil	Niki Lauda	MP4/1C	9th	3rd
	John Watson	MP4/1C	16th	DNF—engine
Austria	Niki Lauda	MP4/1C	14th	6th
	John Watson	MP4/1C	17th	9th
Netherlands	Niki Lauda	MP4/1E	19th	DNF—brakes
	John Watson	MP4/1C	15th	3rd
Italy	Niki Lauda	MP4/1E	13th	DNF—electrical
	John Watson	MP4/1E	15th	DNF—electrical
Europe	Niki Lauda	MP4/1E	13th	DNF—engine
	John Watson	MP4/1E	10th	DNF—spin
South Africa	Niki Lauda	MP4/1E	12th	11th—electrical
	John Watson	MP4/1E	15th	DSQ

Championship positions: Watson 6th (22 points); Lauda 10th (12 points)

1984

Brazil	Alain Prost	MP4/2	4th	1st
	Niki Lauda	MP4/2	6th	DNF—electrical
South Africa	Alain Prost	MP4/2	5th	2nd
	Niki Lauda	MP4/2	8th	1st
Belgium	Alain Prost	MP4/2	8th	DNF—electrical
	Niki Lauda	MP4/2	14th	DNF—water pump
San Marino	Alain Prost	MP4/2	2nd	1st
	Niki Lauda	MP4/2	5th	DNF—engine
France	Alain Prost	MP4/2	5th	7th
	Niki Lauda	MP4/2	9th	1st
Monaco	Alain Prost	MP4/2	1st	1st
	Niki Lauda	MP4/2	8th	DNF—spin

Canada	Alain Prost	MP4/2	2nd	3rd
	Niki Lauda	MP4/2	8th	2nd
Detroit	Alain Prost	MP4/2	2nd	4th
	Niki Lauda	MP4/2	10th	DNF—electrical
Dallas	Alain Prost	MP4/2	7th	DNF—puncture
	Niki Lauda	MP4/2	5th	DNF—spin
Britain	Alain Prost	MP4/2	2nd	DNF—gearbox
	Niki Lauda	MP4/2	3rd	1st
Germany	Alain Prost	MP4/2	1st	1st
	Niki Lauda	MP4/2	7th	2nd
Austria	Alain Prost	MP4/2	2nd	DNF—spin
	Niki Lauda	MP4/2	4th	1st
Netherlands	Alain Prost	MP4/2	1st	1st
	Niki Lauda	MP4/2	6th	2nd
Italy	Alain Prost	MP4/2	2nd	DNF—engine
	Niki Lauda	MP4/2	4th	1st
Europe	Alain Prost	MP4/2	2nd	1st
	Niki Lauda	MP4/2	15th	4th
Portugal	Alain Prost	MP4/2	2nd	1st
	Niki Lauda	MP4/2	11th	2nd

Championship positions: Lauda 1st (72 points); Prost 2nd (71.5 points)

1985

Brazil	Niki Lauda	MP4/2B	9th	DNF—fuel system
	Alain Prost	MP4/2B	6th	1st
Portugal	Niki Lauda	MP4/2B	7th	DNF—engine
	Alain Prost	MP4/2B	2nd	DNF—spin
San Marino	Niki Lauda	MP4/2B	8th	4th
	Alain Prost	MP4/2B	6th	DSQ
Monaco	Niki Lauda	MP4/2B	14th	DNF—spin
	Alain Prost	MP4/2B	5th	1st
Canada	Niki Lauda	MP4/2B	17th	DNF—engine
	Alain Prost	MP4/2B	5th	3rd
Detroit	Niki Lauda	MP4/2B	12th	DNF—brakes
	Alain Prost	MP4/2B	4th	DNF—accident
France	Niki Lauda	MP4/2B	6th	DNF—gearbox
	Alain Prost	MP4/2B	4th	3rd
Britain	Niki Lauda	MP4/2B	10th	DNF—electrical
	Alain Prost	MP4/2B	3rd	1st
Germany	Niki Lauda	MP4/2B	12th	5th
	Alain Prost	MP4/2B	3rd	2nd
Austria	Niki Lauda	MP4/2B	3rd	DNF—engine
	Alain Prost	MP4/2B	1st	1st
Netherlands	Niki Lauda	MP4/2B	10th	1st
	Alain Prost	MP4/2B	3rd	2nd
Italy	Niki Lauda	MP4/2B	16th	DNF—transmission
	Alain Prost	MP4/2B	5th	1st
Belgium	Niki Lauda	MP4/2B	Withdrawn	N/A
	Alain Prost	MP4/2B	1st	3rd
Europe	John Watson	MP4/2B	21st	7th
	Alain Prost	MP4/2B	6th	4th
South Africa	Niki Lauda	MP4/2B	8th	DNF—turbo
	Alain Prost	MP4/2B	9th	3rd
Australia	Niki Lauda	MP4/2B	16th	DNF—brakes
	Alain Prost	MP4/2B	4th	DNF—engine

Championship positions: Prost 1st (73 points); Lauda 10th (14 points)*
**76 before Europe result dropped under "best 11 finishes" system*

1986

Brazil	Alain Prost	MP4/2C	9th	DNF—engine
	Keke Rosberg	MP4/2C	7th	DNF—engine
Spain	Alain Prost	MP4/2C	4th	3rd
	Keke Rosberg	MP4/2C	5th	4th
San Marino	Alain Prost	MP4/2C	4th	1st
	Keke Rosberg	MP4/2C	6th	5th
Monaco	Alain Prost	MP4/2C	1st	1st
	Keke Rosberg	MP4/2C	9th	2nd
Belgium	Alain Prost	MP4/2C	3rd	6th
	Keke Rosberg	MP4/2C	8th	DNF—engine
Canada	Alain Prost	MP4/2C	4th	2nd
	Keke Rosberg	MP4/2C	6th	4th
Detroit	Alain Prost	MP4/2C	7th	3rd
	Keke Rosberg	MP4/2C	9th	DNF—transmission
France	Alain Prost	MP4/2C	5th	2nd
	Keke Rosberg	MP4/2C	7th	4th
Britain	Alain Prost	MP4/2C	6th	3rd
	Keke Rosberg	MP4/2C	5th	DNF—gearbox
Germany	Alain Prost	MP4/2C	2nd	5th
	Keke Rosberg	MP4/2C	1st	6th
Hungary	Alain Prost	MP4/2C	3rd	DNF—electrical
	Keke Rosberg	MP4/2C	5th	DNF—suspension
Austria	Alain Prost	MP4/2C	5th	1st
	Keke Rosberg	MP4/2C	3rd	9th—electrical
Italy	Alain Prost	MP4/2C	2nd	DSQ
	Keke Rosberg	MP4/2C	8th	4th
Portugal	Alain Prost	MP4/2C	3rd	2nd
	Keke Rosberg	MP4/2C	7th	DNF—electrical
Mexico	Alain Prost	MP4/2C	6th	2nd
	Keke Rosberg	MP4/2C	11th	DNF—puncture
Australia	Alain Prost	MP4/2C	4th	1st
	Keke Rosberg	MP4/2C	7th	DNF—tire

Championship positions: Prost 1st (72 points); Rosberg 6th (22 points)*
**74 points before Belgium result dropped under "best 11 finishes" system*

1987

Brazil	Alain Prost	MP4/3	5th	1st
	Stefan Johansson	MP4/3	10th	3rd
San Marino	Alain Prost	MP4/3	4th	DNF—electrical
	Stefan Johansson	MP4/3	9th	4th
Belgium	Alain Prost	MP4/3	6th	1st
	Stefan Johansson	MP4/3	10th	2nd
Monaco	Alain Prost	MP4/3	4th	9th—engine
	Stefan Johansson	MP4/3	7th	DNF—engine
Detroit	Alain Prost	MP4/3	5th	3rd
	Stefan Johansson	MP4/3	11th	7th
France	Alain Prost	MP4/3	2nd	3rd
	Stefan Johansson	MP4/3	9th	8th
Britain	Alain Prost	MP4/3	4th	DNF—engine
	Stefan Johansson	MP4/3	10th	DNF—engine
Germany	Alain Prost	MP4/3	3rd	7th
	Stefan Johansson	MP4/3	8th	2nd
Hungary	Alain Prost	MP4/3	4th	3rd
	Stefan Johansson	MP4/3	8th	DNF—gearbox
Austria	Alain Prost	MP4/3	9th	6th
	Stefan Johansson	MP4/3	14th	7th
Italy	Alain Prost	MP4/3	5th	15th
	Stefan Johansson	MP4/3	11th	6th
Portugal	Alain Prost	MP4/3	3rd	1st
	Stefan Johansson	MP4/3	8th	5th
Spain	Alain Prost	MP4/3	7th	2nd
	Stefan Johansson	MP4/3	11th	3rd
Mexico	Alain Prost	MP4/3	5th	DNF—accident
	Stefan Johansson	MP4/3	15th	DNF—accident
Japan	Alain Prost	MP4/3	2nd	7th
	Stefan Johansson	MP4/3	10th	3rd
Australia	Alain Prost	MP4/3	2nd	DNF—brakes
	Stefan Johansson	MP4/3	8th	DNF—brakes

Championship positions: Prost 4th (46 points); Johansson 6th (30 points)

1988

Brazil	Alain Prost	MP4/4	3rd	1st
	Ayrton Senna	MP4/4	1st	DSQ
San Marino	Alain Prost	MP4/4	2nd	2nd
	Ayrton Senna	MP4/4	1st	1st
Monaco	Alain Prost	MP4/4	2nd	1st
	Ayrton Senna	MP4/4	1st	DNF—spin
Mexico	Alain Prost	MP4/4	2nd	1st
	Ayrton Senna	MP4/4	1st	2nd
Canada	Alain Prost	MP4/4	2nd	2nd
	Ayrton Senna	MP4/4	1st	1st
Detroit	Alain Prost	MP4/4	4th	2nd
	Ayrton Senna	MP4/4	1st	1st
France	Alain Prost	MP4/4	1st	1st
	Ayrton Senna	MP4/4	2nd	2nd
Britain	Alain Prost	MP4/4	4th	DNF—handling
	Ayrton Senna	MP4/4	3rd	1st
Germany	Alain Prost	MP4/4	2nd	2nd
	Ayrton Senna	MP4/4	1st	1st
Hungary	Alain Prost	MP4/4	7th	2nd
	Ayrton Senna	MP4/4	1st	1st

Belgium	Alain Prost	MP4/4	2nd	2nd
	Ayrton Senna	MP4/4	1st	1st
Italy	Alain Prost	MP4/4	2nd	DNF—engine
	Ayrton Senna	MP4/4	1st	10th—accident
Belgium	Alain Prost	MP4/4	1st	1st
	Ayrton Senna	MP4/4	2nd	6th
Spain	Alain Prost	MP4/4	2nd	1st
	Ayrton Senna	MP4/4	1st	4th
Japan	Alain Prost	MP4/4	2nd	2nd
	Ayrton Senna	MP4/4	1st	1st
Australia	Alain Prost	MP4/4	2nd	1st
	Ayrton Senna	MP4/4	1st	2nd

Championship positions: Senna 1st (90 points); Prost 2nd (87 points**)*
**94 points before Portugal and Spain results dropped under "best 11 finishes" system*
***105 points before Hungary, Belgium, and Japan results dropped*

1989

Brazil	Ayrton Senna	MP4/5	1st	11th
	Alain Prost	MP4/5	5th	2nd
San Marino	Ayrton Senna	MP4/5	1st	1st
	Alain Prost	MP4/5	2nd	2nd
Monaco	Ayrton Senna	MP4/5	1st	1st
	Alain Prost	MP4/5	2nd	2nd
Mexico	Ayrton Senna	MP4/5	1st	1st
	Alain Prost	MP4/5	2nd	2nd
US	Ayrton Senna	MP4/5	1st	DNF—electrical
	Alain Prost	MP4/5	2nd	1st
Canada	Ayrton Senna	MP4/5	2nd	7th—engine
	Alain Prost	MP4/5	1st	DNF—suspension
France	Ayrton Senna	MP4/5	2nd	DNF—transmission
	Alain Prost	MP4/5	1st	1st
Britain	Ayrton Senna	MP4/5	1st	DNF—spin
	Alain Prost	MP4/5	2nd	1st
Germany	Ayrton Senna	MP4/5	1st	1st
	Alain Prost	MP4/5	2nd	2nd
Hungary	Ayrton Senna	MP4/5	2nd	2nd
	Alain Prost	MP4/5	5th	4th
Belgium	Ayrton Senna	MP4/5	1st	1st
	Alain Prost	MP4/5	2nd	2nd
Italy	Ayrton Senna	MP4/5	1st	DNF—engine
	Alain Prost	MP4/5	4th	1st
Europe	Ayrton Senna	MP4/5	1st	DNF—accident
	Alain Prost	MP4/5	4th	2nd
Spain	Ayrton Senna	MP4/5	1st	1st
	Alain Prost	MP4/5	3rd	3rd
Japan	Ayrton Senna	MP4/5	1st	DSQ
	Alain Prost	MP4/5	2nd	DNF—accident
Australia	Ayrton Senna	MP4/5	1st	DNF—accident
	Alain Prost	MP4/5	2nd	Withdrawn

Championship positions: Prost 1st (76 points); Senna 2nd (60 points)*
**81 points before Mexico and Hungary results dropped under "best 11 finishes" system*

1990

US	Ayrton Senna	MP4/5B	5th	1st
	Gerhard Berger	MP4/5B	1st	DNF—clutch
Brazil	Ayrton Senna	MP4/5B	1st	3rd
	Gerhard Berger	MP4/5B	2nd	2nd
San Marino	Ayrton Senna	MP4/5B	1st	DNF—wheel
	Gerhard Berger	MP4/5B	2nd	2nd
Monaco	Ayrton Senna	MP4/5B	1st	1st
	Gerhard Berger	MP4/5B	5th	3rd
Canada	Ayrton Senna	MP4/5B	1st	1st
	Gerhard Berger	MP4/5B	2nd	4th
Mexico	Ayrton Senna	MP4/5B	3rd	20th—tire
	Gerhard Berger	MP4/5B	1st	3rd
France	Ayrton Senna	MP4/5B	3rd	3rd
	Gerhard Berger	MP4/5B	2nd	5th
Britain	Ayrton Senna	MP4/5B	2nd	3rd
	Gerhard Berger	MP4/5B	3rd	14th—throttle
Germany	Ayrton Senna	MP4/5B	1st	1st
	Gerhard Berger	MP4/5B	2nd	3rd
Hungary	Ayrton Senna	MP4/5B	4th	2nd
	Gerhard Berger	MP4/5B	3rd	DNF—accident
Belgium	Ayrton Senna	MP4/5B	1st	1st
	Gerhard Berger	MP4/5B	2nd	3rd
Italy	Ayrton Senna	MP4/5B	1st	1st
	Gerhard Berger	MP4/5B	3rd	3rd
Portugal	Ayrton Senna	MP4/5B	3rd	2nd
	Gerhard Berger	MP4/5B	4th	4th
Spain	Ayrton Senna	MP4/5B	1st	DNF—radiator
	Gerhard Berger	MP4/5B	5th	DNF—accident
Japan	Ayrton Senna	MP4/5B	1st	DNF—accident
	Gerhard Berger	MP4/5B	4th	DNF—spin
Australia	Ayrton Senna	MP4/5B	1st	DNF—spin
	Gerhard Berger	MP4/5B	2nd	4th

Championship positions: Senna 1st (78 points); Berger 4th (43 points)

1991

US	Ayrton Senna	MP4/6	1st	1st
	Gerhard Berger	MP4/6	7th	DNF—fuel system
Brazil	Ayrton Senna	MP4/6	1st	1st
	Gerhard Berger	MP4/6	4th	3rd
San Marino	Ayrton Senna	MP4/6	1st	1st
	Gerhard Berger	MP4/6	5th	2nd
Monaco	Ayrton Senna	MP4/6	1st	1st
	Gerhard Berger	MP4/6	6th	DNF—accident
Canada	Ayrton Senna	MP4/6	3rd	DNF—electrical
	Gerhard Berger	MP4/6	6th	DNF—fuel system
Mexico	Ayrton Senna	MP4/6	3rd	3rd
	Gerhard Berger	MP4/6	5th	DNF—engine
France	Ayrton Senna	MP4/6	3rd	3rd
	Gerhard Berger	MP4/6	5th	DNF—engine
Britain	Ayrton Senna	MP4/6	2nd	4th—fuel
	Gerhard Berger	MP4/6	4th	2nd
Germany	Ayrton Senna	MP4/6	2nd	7th—fuel
	Gerhard Berger	MP4/6	3rd	4th
Hungary	Ayrton Senna	MP4/6	1st	1st
	Gerhard Berger	MP4/6	5th	4th
Belgium	Ayrton Senna	MP4/6	1st	1st
	Gerhard Berger	MP4/6	4th	2nd
Italy	Ayrton Senna	MP4/6	1st	2nd
	Gerhard Berger	MP4/6	3rd	4th
Portugal	Ayrton Senna	MP4/6	3rd	2nd
	Gerhard Berger	MP4/6	2nd	DNF—engine
Spain	Ayrton Senna	MP4/6	3rd	5th
	Gerhard Berger	MP4/6	1st	DNF—electrical
Japan	Ayrton Senna	MP4/6	2nd	2nd
	Gerhard Berger	MP4/6	1st	1st
Australia	Ayrton Senna	MP4/6	1st	1st
	Gerhard Berger	MP4/6	2nd	3rd

Championship positions: Senna 1st (96 points); Berger 4th (43 points)

1992

South Africa	Ayrton Senna	MP4/6B	2nd	3rd
	Gerhard Berger	MP4/6B	3rd	5th
Mexico	Ayrton Senna	MP4/6B	6th	DNF—transmission
	Gerhard Berger	MP4/6B	5th	4th
Brazil	Ayrton Senna	MP4/7	3rd	DNF—engine
	Gerhard Berger	MP4/7	4th	DNF—electrical
Spain	Ayrton Senna	MP4/7	3rd	9th—spin
	Gerhard Berger	MP4/7	7th	4th
San Marino	Ayrton Senna	MP4/7	3rd	3rd
	Gerhard Berger	MP4/7	4th	DNF—accident
Monaco	Ayrton Senna	MP4/7	3rd	1st
	Gerhard Berger	MP4/7	5th	DNF—gearbox
Canada	Ayrton Senna	MP4/7	1st	DNF—electrical
	Gerhard Berger	MP4/7	4th	1st
France	Ayrton Senna	MP4/7	3rd	DNF—accident
	Gerhard Berger	MP4/7	4th	DNF—engine
Britain	Ayrton Senna	MP4/7	3rd	DNF—transmission
	Gerhard Berger	MP4/7	5th	5th
Germany	Ayrton Senna	MP4/7	3rd	2nd
	Gerhard Berger	MP4/7	4th	DNF—electrical
Hungary	Ayrton Senna	MP4/7	3rd	1st
	Gerhard Berger	MP4/7	5th	3rd
Belgium	Ayrton Senna	MP4/7	2nd	5th
	Gerhard Berger	MP4/7	6th	DNF—transmission
Italy	Ayrton Senna	MP4/7	2nd	1st
	Gerhard Berger	MP4/7	5th	4th

Portugal	Ayrton Senna	MP4/7	3rd	3rd
	Gerhard Berger	MP4/7	4th	2nd
Japan	Ayrton Senna	MP4/7	3rd	DNF—engine
	Gerhard Berger	MP4/7	4th	2nd
Australia	Ayrton Senna	MP4/7	2nd	DNF—accident
	Gerhard Berger	MP4/7	4th	1st

Championship positions: Senna 4th (50 points); Berger 5th (49 points)

1993

South Africa	Ayrton Senna	MP4/8	2nd	2nd
	Michael Andretti	MP4/8	9th	DNF—accident
Brazil	Ayrton Senna	MP4/8	3rd	1st
	Michael Andretti	MP4/8	5th	DNF—accident
Europe	Ayrton Senna	MP4/8	4th	1st
	Michael Andretti	MP4/8	6th	DNF—accident
San Marino	Ayrton Senna	MP4/8	4th	DNF—hydraulics
	Michael Andretti	MP4/8	6th	DNF—spin
Spain	Ayrton Senna	MP4/8	3rd	2nd
	Michael Andretti	MP4/8	7th	5th
Monaco	Ayrton Senna	MP4/8	3rd	1st
	Michael Andretti	MP4/8	9th	8th
Canada	Ayrton Senna	MP4/8	8th	DNF—electrical
	Michael Andretti	MP4/8	12th	14th
France	Ayrton Senna	MP4/8	5th	4th
	Michael Andretti	MP4/8	16th	6th
Britain	Ayrton Senna	MP4/8	4th	5th
	Michael Andretti	MP4/8	11th	DNF—spin
Germany	Ayrton Senna	MP4/8	4th	4th
	Michael Andretti	MP4/8	12th	DNF—accident
Hungary	Ayrton Senna	MP4/8	4th	DNF—throttle
	Michael Andretti	MP4/8	11th	DNF—accident
Belgium	Ayrton Senna	MP4/8	5th	4th
	Michael Andretti	MP4/8	14th	8th
Italy	Ayrton Senna	MP4/8	4th	DNF—accident
	Michael Andretti	MP4/8	9th	3rd
Portugal	Ayrton Senna	MP4/8	4th	DNF—engine
	Mika Häkkinen	MP4/8	3rd	DNF—accident
Japan	Ayrton Senna	MP4/8	2nd	1st
	Mika Häkkinen	MP4/8	3rd	3rd
Australia	Ayrton Senna	MP4/8	1st	1st
	Mika Häkkinen	MP4/8	5th	DNF—brakes

Championship positions: Senna 2nd (73 points); Andretti 11th (7 points); Häkkinen 15th (4 points)

1994

Brazil	Mika Häkkinen	MP4/9	8th	DNF—engine
	Martin Brundle	MP4/9	18th	DNF—accident
Pacific	Mika Häkkinen	MP4/9	4th	DNF—gearbox
	Martin Brundle	MP4/9	6th	DNF—overheating
San Marino	Mika Häkkinen	MP4/9	8th	3rd
	Martin Brundle	MP4/9	13th	8th
Monaco	Mika Häkkinen	MP4/9	2nd	DNF—accident
	Martin Brundle	MP4/9	8th	2nd
Spain	Mika Häkkinen	MP4/9	3rd	DNF—engine
	Martin Brundle	MP4/9	8th	11th—clutch
Canada	Mika Häkkinen	MP4/9	7th	DNF—engine
	Martin Brundle	MP4/9	12th	DNF—electrical
France	Mika Häkkinen	MP4/9	9th	DNF—engine
	Martin Brundle	MP4/9	12th	DNF—engine
Britain	Mika Häkkinen	MP4/9	5th	3rd
	Martin Brundle	MP4/9	9th	DNF—engine
Germany	Mika Häkkinen	MP4/9	8th	DNF—accident
	Martin Brundle	MP4/9	13th	DNF—engine
Hungary	Philippe Alliot	MP4/9	14th	DNF—coolant leak
	Martin Brundle	MP4/9	6th	4th
Belgium	Mika Häkkinen	MP4/9	8th	2nd
	Martin Brundle	MP4/9	13th	DNF—spin
Italy	Mika Häkkinen	MP4/9	7th	3rd
	Martin Brundle	MP4/9	15th	5th
Portugal	Mika Häkkinen	MP4/9	4th	3rd
	Martin Brundle	MP4/9	7th	6th
Europe	Mika Häkkinen	MP4/9	9th	3rd
	Martin Brundle	MP4/9	15th	DNF—engine
Japan	Mika Häkkinen	MP4/9	8th	7th
	Martin Brundle	MP4/9	9th	DNF—spin
Australia	Mika Häkkinen	MP4/9	4th	12th—accident
	Martin Brundle	MP4/9	9th	3rd

Championship positions: Häkkinen 4th (26 points); Brundle 7th (16 points)

1995

Brazil	Mark Blundell	MP4/10	9th	6th
	Mika Häkkinen	MP4/10	7th	4th
Argentina	Mark Blundell	MP4/10	17th	DNF—engine
	Mika Häkkinen	MP4/10	5th	DNF—accident
San Marino	Nigel Mansell	MP4/10B	9th	10th
	Mika Häkkinen	MP4/10B	6th	5th
Spain	Nigel Mansell	MP4/10B	10th	DNF—handling
	Mika Häkkinen	MP4/10B	9th	DNF—fuel system
Monaco	Mark Blundell	MP4/10B	10th	5th
	Mika Häkkinen	MP4/10B	6th	DNF—engine
Canada	Mark Blundell	MP4/10B	10th	DNF—engine
	Mika Häkkinen	MP4/10B	7th	DNF—accident
France	Mark Blundell	MP4/10B	13th	11th
	Mika Häkkinen	MP4/10B	8th	7th
Britain	Mark Blundell	MP4/10B	10th	5th
	Mika Häkkinen	MP4/10B	8th	DNF—electrical
Germany	Mark Blundell	MP4/10B	8th	DNF—engine
	Mika Häkkinen	MP4/10B	7th	DNF—engine
Hungary	Mark Blundell	MP4/10B	13th	DNF—engine
	Mika Häkkinen	MP4/10B	6th	DNF—engine
Belgium	Mark Blundell	MP4/10B	6th	5th
	Mika Häkkinen	MP4/10B	3rd	DNF—spin
Italy	Mark Blundell	MP4/10B	9th	4th
	Mika Häkkinen	MP4/10B	7th	2nd
Portugal	Mark Blundell	MP4/10C	12th	9th
	Mika Häkkinen	MP4/10C	13th	DNF—engine
Europe	Mark Blundell	MP4/10C	10th	DNF—accident
	Mika Häkkinen	MP4/10C	9th	8th
Pacific	Mark Blundell	MP4/10B	10th	9th
	Jan Magnussen	MP4/10B	12th	10th
Japan	Mark Blundell	MP4/10B	24th	7th
	Mika Häkkinen	MP4/10B	3rd	2nd
Australia	Mark Blundell	MP4/10B	10th	4th
	Mika Häkkinen	MP4/10B	24th	DNS

Championship positions: Häkkinen 7th (17 points); Blundell 13th (16 points)

1996

Australia	Mika Häkkinen	MP4/11	5th	5th
	David Coulthard	MP4/11	13th	DNF—throttle
Brazil	Mika Häkkinen	MP4/11	7th	4th
	David Coulthard	MP4/11	14th	DNF—spin
Argentina	Mika Häkkinen	MP4/11	8th	DNF—throttle
	David Coulthard	MP4/11	9th	7th
Europe	Mika Häkkinen	MP4/11	9th	8th
	David Coulthard	MP4/11	6th	3rd
San Marino	Mika Häkkinen	MP4/11	11th	8th
	David Coulthard	MP4/11	4th	DNF—hydraulics
Monaco	Mika Häkkinen	MP4/11	8th	6th
	David Coulthard	MP4/11	5th	2nd
Spain	Mika Häkkinen	MP4/11	10th	5th
	David Coulthard	MP4/11	14th	DNF—accident
Canada	Mika Häkkinen	MP4/11	6th	5th
	David Coulthard	MP4/11	10th	4th
France	Mika Häkkinen	MP4/11	5th	5th
	David Coulthard	MP4/11	7th	6th
Britain	Mika Häkkinen	MP4/11B	4th	3rd
	David Coulthard	MP4/11B	9th	5th
Germany	Mika Häkkinen	MP4/11B	4th	DNF—gearbox
	David Coulthard	MP4/11B	7th	5th
Hungary	Mika Häkkinen	MP4/11B	7th	4th
	David Coulthard	MP4/11B	9th	DNF—engine
Belgium	Mika Häkkinen	MP4/11B	6th	3rd
	David Coulthard	MP4/11B	4th	DNF—spin
Italy	Mika Häkkinen	MP4/11B	4th	3rd
	David Coulthard	MP4/11B	5th	DNF—spin
Portugal	Mika Häkkinen	MP4/11B	7th	DNF—accident
	David Coulthard	MP4/11B	8th	13th
Japan	Mika Häkkinen	MP4/11B	5th	3rd
	David Coulthard	MP4/11B	8th	8th

Championship positions: Häkkinen 5th (31 points); Coulthard 7th (18 points)

1997

Australia	Mika Häkkinen	MP4/12	6th	3rd
	David Coulthard	MP4/12	4th	1st
Brazil	Mika Häkkinen	MP4/12	4th	4th
	David Coulthard	MP4/12	12th	10th
Argentina	Mika Häkkinen	MP4/12	17th	5th
	David Coulthard	MP4/12	10th	DNF—accident
San Marino	Mika Häkkinen	MP4/12	8th	6th
	David Coulthard	MP4/12	10th	DNF—engine
Monaco	Mika Häkkinen	MP4/12	8th	DNF—accident
	David Coulthard	MP4/12	5th	DNF—accident
Spain	Mika Häkkinen	MP4/12	5th	7th
	David Coulthard	MP4/12	3rd	6th
Canada	Mika Häkkinen	MP4/12	9th	DNF—accident
	David Coulthard	MP4/12	5th	7th
France	Mika Häkkinen	MP4/12	9th	DNF—engine
	David Coulthard	MP4/12	10th	7th—accident
Britain	Mika Häkkinen	MP4/12	3rd	DNF—engine
	David Coulthard	MP4/12	6th	4th
Germany	Mika Häkkinen	MP4/12	3rd	3rd
	David Coulthard	MP4/12	8th	DNF—transmission
Hungary	Mika Häkkinen	MP4/12	4th	DNF—hydraulics
	David Coulthard	MP4/12	8th	DNF—electrical
Belgium	Mika Häkkinen	MP4/12	5th	DSQ
	David Coulthard	MP4/12	10th	DNF—spin
Italy	Mika Häkkinen	MP4/12	5th	9th
	David Coulthard	MP4/12	6th	1st
Austria	Mika Häkkinen	MP4/12	2nd	DNF—engine
	David Coulthard	MP4/12	10th	2nd
Luxembourg	Mika Häkkinen	MP4/12	1st	DNF—engine
	David Coulthard	MP4/12	6th	DNF—engine
Japan	Mika Häkkinen	MP4/12	4th	4th
	David Coulthard	MP4/12	11th	10th
Europe	Mika Häkkinen	MP4/12	5th	1st
	David Coulthard	MP4/12	6th	2nd

Championship positions: Coulthard 3rd (36 points); Häkkinen 6th (27 points)

1998

Australia	Mika Häkkinen	MP4/13	1st	1st
	David Coulthard	MP4/13	2nd	2nd
Brazil	Mika Häkkinen	MP4/13	1st	1st
	David Coulthard	MP4/13	2nd	2nd
Argentina	Mika Häkkinen	MP4/13	3rd	2nd
	David Coulthard	MP4/13	1st	6th
San Marino	Mika Häkkinen	MP4/13	2nd	1st
	David Coulthard	MP4/13	1st	DNF—gearbox
Spain	Mika Häkkinen	MP4/13	1st	1st
	David Coulthard	MP4/13	2nd	2nd
Monaco	Mika Häkkinen	MP4/13	1st	1st
	David Coulthard	MP4/13	2nd	DNF—engine
Canada	Mika Häkkinen	MP4/13	2nd	DNF—gearbox
	David Coulthard	MP4/13	1st	DNF—throttle
France	Mika Häkkinen	MP4/13	1st	3rd
	David Coulthard	MP4/13	3rd	6th
Britain	Mika Häkkinen	MP4/13	1st	2nd
	David Coulthard	MP4/13	4th	DNF—spin
Austria	Mika Häkkinen	MP4/13	3rd	1st
	David Coulthard	MP4/13	14th	2nd
Germany	Mika Häkkinen	MP4/13	1st	1st
	David Coulthard	MP4/13	2nd	2nd
Hungary	Mika Häkkinen	MP4/13	1st	6th
	David Coulthard	MP4/13	2nd	2nd
Belgium	Mika Häkkinen	MP4/13	1st	DNF—accident
	David Coulthard	MP4/13	2nd	7th
Italy	Mika Häkkinen	MP4/13	3rd	4th
	David Coulthard	MP4/13	4th	DNF—engine
Luxembourg	Mika Häkkinen	MP4/13	3rd	1st
	David Coulthard	MP4/13	5th	3rd
Japan	Mika Häkkinen	MP4/13	2nd	1st
	David Coulthard	MP4/13	3rd	3rd

Championship positions: Häkkinen 1st (100 points); Coulthard 3rd (56 points)

1999

Australia	Mika Häkkinen	MP4/14	1st	DNF—throttle
	David Coulthard	MP4/14	2nd	DNF—hydraulics
Brazil	Mika Häkkinen	MP4/14	1st	1st
	David Coulthard	MP4/14	2nd	DNF—gearbox
San Marino	Mika Häkkinen	MP4/14	1st	DNF—accident
	David Coulthard	MP4/14	2nd	2nd
Monaco	Mika Häkkinen	MP4/14	1st	3rd
	David Coulthard	MP4/14	3rd	DNF—gearbox
Spain	Mika Häkkinen	MP4/14	1st	1st
	David Coulthard	MP4/14	3rd	2nd
Canada	Mika Häkkinen	MP4/14	2nd	1st
	David Coulthard	MP4/14	4th	7th
France	Mika Häkkinen	MP4/14	14th	2nd
	David Coulthard	MP4/14	4th	DNF—electrical
Britain	Mika Häkkinen	MP4/14	1st	DNF—wheel
	David Coulthard	MP4/14	3rd	1st
Austria	Mika Häkkinen	MP4/14	1st	3rd
	David Coulthard	MP4/14	2nd	2nd
Germany	Mika Häkkinen	MP4/14	1st	DNF—accident
	David Coulthard	MP4/14	3rd	5th
Hungary	Mika Häkkinen	MP4/14	1st	1st
	David Coulthard	MP4/14	3rd	2nd
Belgium	Mika Häkkinen	MP4/14	1st	2nd
	David Coulthard	MP4/14	2nd	1st
Italy	Mika Häkkinen	MP4/14	1st	DNF—spin
	David Coulthard	MP4/14	3rd	5th
Europe	Mika Häkkinen	MP4/14	3rd	5th
	David Coulthard	MP4/14	2nd	DNF—spin
Malaysia	Mika Häkkinen	MP4/14	4th	3rd
	David Coulthard	MP4/14	3rd	DNF—fuel system
Japan	Mika Häkkinen	MP4/14	2nd	1st
	David Coulthard	MP4/14	3rd	DNF—hydraulics

Championship positions: Häkkinen 1st (76 points); Coulthard 4th (48 points)

2000

Australia	Mika Häkkinen	MP4/15	1st	DNF—engine
	David Coulthard	MP4/15	2nd	DNF—engine
Brazil	Mika Häkkinen	MP4/15	1st	DNF—oil pressure
	David Coulthard	MP4/15	2nd	DSQ
San Marino	Mika Häkkinen	MP4/15	1st	2nd
	David Coulthard	MP4/15	3rd	3rd
Britain	Mika Häkkinen	MP4/15	3rd	2nd
	David Coulthard	MP4/15	4th	1st
Spain	Mika Häkkinen	MP4/15	2nd	1st
	David Coulthard	MP4/15	4th	2nd
Europe	Mika Häkkinen	MP4/15	3rd	2nd
	David Coulthard	MP4/15	1st	3rd
Monaco	Mika Häkkinen	MP4/15	5th	6th
	David Coulthard	MP4/15	3rd	1st
Canada	Mika Häkkinen	MP4/15	4th	4th
	David Coulthard	MP4/15	2nd	7th
France	Mika Häkkinen	MP4/15	4th	2nd
	David Coulthard	MP4/15	2nd	1st
Austria	Mika Häkkinen	MP4/15	1st	1st
	David Coulthard	MP4/15	2nd	2nd
Germany	Mika Häkkinen	MP4/15	4th	2nd
	David Coulthard	MP4/15	1st	3rd
Hungary	Mika Häkkinen	MP4/15	3rd	1st
	David Coulthard	MP4/15	2nd	3rd
Belgium	Mika Häkkinen	MP4/15	1st	1st
	David Coulthard	MP4/15	5th	4th
Italy	Mika Häkkinen	MP4/15	3rd	2nd
	David Coulthard	MP4/15	5th	DNF—accident
US	Mika Häkkinen	MP4/15	3rd	DNF—engine
	David Coulthard	MP4/15	2nd	5th
Japan	Mika Häkkinen	MP4/15	2nd	2nd
	David Coulthard	MP4/15	3rd	3rd
Malaysia	Mika Häkkinen	MP4/15	2nd	4th
	David Coulthard	MP4/15	3rd	2nd

Championship positions: Häkkinen 2nd (89 points); Coulthard 3rd (73 points)

2001

Australia	Mika Häkkinen	MP4-16	3rd	DNF—accident
	David Coulthard	MP4-16	6th	2nd
Malaysia	Mika Häkkinen	MP4-16	4th	6th
	David Coulthard	MP4-16	8th	3rd
Brazil	Mika Häkkinen	MP4-16	3rd	DNF—gearbox
	David Coulthard	MP4-16	5th	1st
San Marino	Mika Häkkinen	MP4-16	2nd	4th
	David Coulthard	MP4-16	1st	2nd
Spain	Mika Häkkinen	MP4-16	2nd	DNF—engine
	David Coulthard	MP4-16	3rd	5th
Austria	Mika Häkkinen	MP4-16	8th	DNF—transmission
	David Coulthard	MP4-16	7th	1st
Monaco	Mika Häkkinen	MP4-16	3rd	DNF—steering
	David Coulthard	MP4-16	1st	5th
Canada	Mika Häkkinen	MP4-16	8th	3rd
	David Coulthard	MP4-16	3rd	DNF—engine
Europe	Mika Häkkinen	MP4-16	6th	6th
	David Coulthard	MP4-16	5th	3rd
France	Mika Häkkinen	MP4-16	4th	DNF—gearbox
	David Coulthard	MP4-16	3rd	4th
Britain	Mika Häkkinen	MP4-16	2nd	1st
	David Coulthard	MP4-16	3rd	DNF—spin
Germany	Mika Häkkinen	MP4-16	3rd	DNF—engine
	David Coulthard	MP4-16	5th	DNF—engine
Hungary	Mika Häkkinen	MP4-16	6th	5th
	David Coulthard	MP4-16	2nd	3rd
Belgium	Mika Häkkinen	MP4-16	7th	4th
	David Coulthard	MP4-16	9th	2nd
Italy	Mika Häkkinen	MP4-16	7th	DNF—gearbox
	David Coulthard	MP4-16	6th	DNF—engine
US	Mika Häkkinen	MP4-16	4th	1st
	David Coulthard	MP4-16	7th	3rd
Japan	Mika Häkkinen	MP4-16	5th	4th
	David Coulthard	MP4-16	7th	3rd

Championship positions: Coulthard 2nd (65 points); Häkkinen 5th (37 points)

2002

Australia	David Coulthard	MP4-17	4th	DNF—gearbox
	Kimi Räikkönen	MP4-17	5th	3rd
Malaysia	David Coulthard	MP4-17	6th	DNF—engine
	Kimi Räikkönen	MP4-17	5th	DNF—engine
Brazil	David Coulthard	MP4-17	4th	3rd
	Kimi Räikkönen	MP4-17	5th	12th—wheel
San Marino	David Coulthard	MP4-17	6th	6th
	Kimi Räikkönen	MP4-17	5th	DNF—exhaust
Spain	David Coulthard	MP4-17	7th	3rd
	Kimi Räikkönen	MP4-17	5th	DNF—wing
Austria	David Coulthard	MP4-17	8th	6th
	Kimi Räikkönen	MP4-17	6th	DNF—engine
Monaco	David Coulthard	MP4-17	2nd	1st
	Kimi Räikkönen	MP4-17	7th	DNF—accident
Canada	David Coulthard	MP4-17	8th	2nd
	Kimi Räikkönen	MP4-17	5th	4th
Europe	David Coulthard	MP4-17	5th	DNF—accident
	Kimi Räikkönen	MP4-17	6th	3rd
Britain	David Coulthard	MP4-17	6th	10th
	Kimi Räikkönen	MP4-17	5th	DNF—engine
France	David Coulthard	MP4-17	6th	3rd
	Kimi Räikkönen	MP4-17	4th	2nd
Germany	David Coulthard	MP4-17	9th	5th
	Kimi Räikkönen	MP4-17	5th	DNF—spin
Hungary	David Coulthard	MP4-17	10th	5th
	Kimi Räikkönen	MP4-17	11th	4th
Belgium	David Coulthard	MP4-17	6th	4th
	Kimi Räikkönen	MP4-17	2nd	DNF—engine
Italy	David Coulthard	MP4-17	7th	7th
	Kimi Räikkönen	MP4-17	6th	DNF—engine
US	David Coulthard	MP4-17	3rd	3rd
	Kimi Räikkönen	MP4-17	6th	DNF—engine
Japan	David Coulthard	MP4-17	3rd	DNF—throttle
	Kimi Räikkönen	MP4-17	4th	3rd

Championship positions: Coulthard 5th (41 points); Räikkönen 6th (24 points)

2003

Australia	David Coulthard	MP4-17D	11th	1st
	Kimi Räikkönen	MP4-17D	15th	3rd
Malaysia	David Coulthard	MP4-17D	4th	DNF—electrical
	Kimi Räikkönen	MP4-17D	7th	1st
Brazil	David Coulthard	MP4-17D	2nd	4th
	Kimi Räikkönen	MP4-17D	4th	2nd
San Marino	David Coulthard	MP4-17D	12th	5th
	Kimi Räikkönen	MP4-17D	6th	2nd
Spain	David Coulthard	MP4-17D	8th	DNF—accident
	Kimi Räikkönen	MP4-17D	20th	DNF—accident
Austria	David Coulthard	MP4-17D	14th	5th
	Kimi Räikkönen	MP4-17D	2nd	2nd
Monaco	David Coulthard	MP4-17D	6th	7th
	Kimi Räikkönen	MP4-17D	2nd	2nd
Canada	David Coulthard	MP4-17D	11th	DNF—gearbox
	Kimi Räikkönen	MP4-17D	20th	6th
Europe	David Coulthard	MP4-17D	9th	15th—spin
	Kimi Räikkönen	MP4-17D	1st	DNF—engine
France	David Coulthard	MP4-17D	5th	5th
	Kimi Räikkönen	MP4-17D	4th	4th
Britain	David Coulthard	MP4-17D	12th	5th
	Kimi Räikkönen	MP4-17D	3rd	3rd
Germany	David Coulthard	MP4-17D	10th	2nd
	Kimi Räikkönen	MP4-17D	5th	DNF—accident
Hungary	David Coulthard	MP4-17D	9th	5th
	Kimi Räikkönen	MP4-17D	7th	2nd
Italy	David Coulthard	MP4-17D	8th	DNF—fuel system
	Kimi Räikkönen	MP4-17D	4th	4th
US	David Coulthard	MP4-17D	8th	DNF—gearbox
	Kimi Räikkönen	MP4-17D	1st	2nd
Japan	David Coulthard	MP4-17D	7th	3rd
	Kimi Räikkönen	MP4-17D	8th	2nd

Championship positions: Räikkönen 2nd (91 points); Coulthard 7th (51 points)

2004

Australia	David Coulthard	MP4-19	12th	8th
	Kimi Räikkönen	MP4-19	10th	DNF—spin
Malaysia	David Coulthard	MP4-19	9th	6th
	Kimi Räikkönen	MP4-19	5th	DNF—engine
Bahrain	David Coulthard	MP4-19	10th	DNF—hydraulics
	Kimi Räikkönen	MP4-19	20th	DNF—engine
San Marino	David Coulthard	MP4-19	11th	12th
	Kimi Räikkönen	MP4-19	20th	8th
Spain	David Coulthard	MP4-19	10th	10th
	Kimi Räikkönen	MP4-19	13th	11th
Monaco	David Coulthard	MP4-19	9th	DNF—accident
	Kimi Räikkönen	MP4-19	6th	DNF—hydraulics
Europe	David Coulthard	MP4-19	18th	DNF—engine
	Kimi Räikkönen	MP4-19	4th	DNF—engine
Canada	David Coulthard	MP4-19	9th	6th
	Kimi Räikkönen	MP4-19	8th	5th
US	David Coulthard	MP4-19	12th	7th
	Kimi Räikkönen	MP4-19	7th	6th
France	David Coulthard	MP4-19B	3rd	6th
	Kimi Räikkönen	MP4-19B	9th	7th
Britain	David Coulthard	MP4-19B	7th	7th
	Kimi Räikkönen	MP4-19B	1st	2nd
Germany	David Coulthard	MP4-19B	5th	4th
	Kimi Räikkönen	MP4-19B	4th	DNF—wing
Hungary	David Coulthard	MP4-19B	12th	9th
	Kimi Räikkönen	MP4-19B	10th	DNF—electrical
Belgium	David Coulthard	MP4-19B	4th	7th
	Kimi Räikkönen	MP4-19B	10th	1st
Italy	David Coulthard	MP4-19B	10th	6th
	Kimi Räikkönen	MP4-19B	7th	DNF—overheating
China	David Coulthard	MP4-19B	10th	9th
	Kimi Räikkönen	MP4-19B	2nd	3rd
Japan	David Coulthard	MP4-19B	8th	DNF—accident
	Kimi Räikkönen	MP4-19B	12th	6th
Brazil	David Coulthard	MP4-19B	13th	11th
	Kimi Räikkönen	MP4-19B	3rd	2nd

Championship positions: Räikkönen 7th (45 points); Coulthard 10th (24 points)

2005

Australia	Kimi Räikkönen	MP4-20	10th	8th
	Juan Pablo Montoya	MP4-20	9th	6th
Malaysia	Kimi Räikkönen	MP4-20	6th	9th
	Juan Pablo Montoya	MP4-20	11th	4th
Bahrain	Kimi Räikkönen	MP4-20	9th	3rd
	Pedro de la Rosa	MP4-20	8th	5th
San Marino	Kimi Räikkönen	MP4-20	1st	DNF—transmission
	Alex Wurz	MP4-20	7th	3rd
Spain	Kimi Räikkönen	MP4-20	1st	1st
	Juan Pablo Montoya	MP4-20	7th	7th
Monaco	Kimi Räikkönen	MP4-20	1st	1st
	Juan Pablo Montoya	MP4-20	18th	5th
Europe	Kimi Räikkönen	MP4-20	2nd	11th—suspension
	Juan Pablo Montoya	MP4-20	5th	7th
Canada	Kimi Räikkönen	MP4-20	7th	1st
	Juan Pablo Montoya	MP4-20	5th	DSQ
US	Kimi Räikkönen	MP4-20	2nd	DNS
	Juan Pablo Montoya	MP4-20	11th	DNS
France	Kimi Räikkönen	MP4-20	13th	2nd
	Juan Pablo Montoya	MP4-20	8th	DNF—engine
Britain	Kimi Räikkönen	MP4-20	12th	3rd
	Juan Pablo Montoya	MP4-20	3rd	1st
Germany	Kimi Räikkönen	MP4-20	1st	DNF—hydraulics
	Juan Pablo Montoya	MP4-20	20th	2nd
Hungary	Kimi Räikkönen	MP4-20	4th	1st
	Juan Pablo Montoya	MP4-20	2nd	DNF—transmission
Turkey	Kimi Räikkönen	MP4-20	1st	1st
	Juan Pablo Montoya	MP4-20	4th	3rd
Italy	Kimi Räikkönen	MP4-20	11th	4th
	Juan Pablo Montoya	MP4-20	1st	1st
Belgium	Kimi Räikkönen	MP4-20	2nd	1st
	Juan Pablo Montoya	MP4-20	1st	14th—accident
Brazil	Kimi Räikkönen	MP4-20	5th	2nd
	Juan Pablo Montoya	MP4-20	2nd	1st
Japan	Kimi Räikkönen	MP4-20	17th	1st
	Juan Pablo Montoya	MP4-20	18th	DNF—accident
China	Kimi Räikkönen	MP4-20	3rd	2nd
	Juan Pablo Montoya	MP4-20	5th	DNF—engine

Championship positions: Räikkönen 2nd (112 points); Montoya 4th (60 points)

2006

Bahrain	Kimi Räikkönen	MP4-21	22nd	3rd
	Juan Pablo Montoya	MP4-21	5th	5th
Malaysia	Kimi Räikkönen	MP4-21	6th	DNF—accident
	Juan Pablo Montoya	MP4-21	5th	4th
Australia	Kimi Räikkönen	MP4-21	4th	2nd
	Juan Pablo Montoya	MP4-21	5th	DNF—electrical
San Marino	Kimi Räikkönen	MP4-21	8th	5th
	Juan Pablo Montoya	MP4-21	7th	3rd
Europe	Kimi Räikkönen	MP4-21	5th	4th
	Juan Pablo Montoya	MP4-21	8th	DNF—engine
Spain	Kimi Räikkönen	MP4-21	9th	5th
	Juan Pablo Montoya	MP4-21	12th	DNF—spin
Monaco	Kimi Räikkönen	MP4-21	3rd	DNF—fire
	Juan Pablo Montoya	MP4-21	4th	2nd
Britain	Kimi Räikkönen	MP4-21	2nd	3rd
	Juan Pablo Montoya	MP4-21	8th	6th
Canada	Kimi Räikkönen	MP4-21	3rd	3rd
	Juan Pablo Montoya	MP4-21	7th	DNF—accident
US	Kimi Räikkönen	MP4-21	9th	DNF—accident
	Juan Pablo Montoya	MP4-21	11th	DNF—accident
France	Kimi Räikkönen	MP4-21	6th	5th
	Pedro de la Rosa	MP4-21	8th	7th
Germany	Kimi Räikkönen	MP4-21	1st	3rd
	Pedro de la Rosa	MP4-21	9th	DNF—fuel system
Hungary	Kimi Räikkönen	MP4-21	1st	DNF—accident
	Pedro de la Rosa	MP4-21	4th	2nd
Turkey	Kimi Räikkönen	MP4-21	7th	DNF—accident
	Pedro de la Rosa	MP4-21	11th	5th
Italy	Kimi Räikkönen	MP4-21	1st	2nd
	Pedro de la Rosa	MP4-21	7th	DNF—engine
China	Kimi Räikkönen	MP4-21	5th	DNF—throttle
	Pedro de la Rosa	MP4-21	7th	5th
Japan	Kimi Räikkonen	MP4-21	11th	5th
	Pedro de la Rosa	MP4-21	13th	11th
Brazil	Kimi Räikkönen	MP4-21	2nd	5th
	Pedro de la Rosa	MP4-21	12th	8th

Championship positions: Räikkönen 5th (65 points); Montoya 8th (26 points); de la Rosa 11th (19 points)

2007

Australia	Fernando Alonso	MP4-22	2nd	2nd
	Lewis Hamilton	MP4-22	4th	3rd
Malaysia	Fernando Alonso	MP4-22	2nd	1st
	Lewis Hamilton	MP4-22	4th	2nd
Bahrain	Fernando Alonso	MP4-22	4th	5th
	Lewis Hamilton	MP4-22	2nd	2nd
Spain	Fernando Alonso	MP4-22	2nd	3rd
	Lewis Hamilton	MP4-22	4th	2nd
Monaco	Fernando Alonso	MP4-22	1st	1st
	Lewis Hamilton	MP4-22	2nd	2nd
Canada	Fernando Alonso	MP4-22	2nd	7th
	Lewis Hamilton	MP4-22	1st	1st
US	Fernando Alonso	MP4-22	2nd	2nd
	Lewis Hamilton	MP4-22	1st	1st
France	Fernando Alonso	MP4-22	10th	7th
	Lewis Hamilton	MP4-22	2nd	3rd
Britain	Fernando Alonso	MP4-22	3rd	2nd
	Lewis Hamilton	MP4-22	1st	3rd
Europe	Fernando Alonso	MP4-22	2nd	1st
	Lewis Hamilton	MP4-22	10th	9th
Hungary	Fernando Alonso	MP4-22	6th	4th
	Lewis Hamilton	MP4-22	1st	1st
Turkey	Fernando Alonso	MP4-22	4th	3rd
	Lewis Hamilton	MP4-22	2nd	5th
Italy	Fernando Alonso	MP4-22	1st	1st
	Lewis Hamilton	MP4-22	2nd	2nd
Belgium	Fernando Alonso	MP4-22	3rd	3rd
	Lewis Hamilton	MP4-22	4th	4th
Japan	Fernando Alonso	MP4-22	2nd	DNF—accident
	Lewis Hamilton	MP4-22	1st	1st
China	Fernando Alonso	MP4-22	1st	DNF—spin
	Lewis Hamilton	MP4-22	4th	2nd
Brazil	Fernando Alonso	MP4-22	4th	3rd
	Lewis Hamilton	MP4-22	2nd	7th

Championship positions: Hamilton 2nd (109 points); Alonso 3rd (109 points)

2008

Australia	Lewis Hamilton	MP4-23	1st	1st
	Heikki Kovalainen	MP4-23	3rd	5th
Malaysia	Lewis Hamilton	MP4-23	9th	5th
	Heikki Kovalainen	MP4-23	8th	3rd
Bahrain	Lewis Hamilton	MP4-23	3rd	13th
	Heikki Kovalainen	MP4-23	5th	5th
Spain	Lewis Hamilton	MP4-23	5th	3rd
	Heikki Kovalainen	MP4-23	6th	DNF—accident
Turkey	Lewis Hamilton	MP4-23	3rd	2nd
	Heikki Kovalainen	MP4-23	2nd	12th
Monaco	Lewis Hamilton	MP4-23	3rd	1st
	Heikki Kovalainen	MP4-23	4th	8th

Canada	Lewis Hamilton	MP4-23	1st	DNF—accident
	Heikki Kovalainen	MP4-23	7th	9th
France	Lewis Hamilton	MP4-23	13th	10th
	Heikki Kovalainen	MP4-23	10th	4th
Britain	Lewis Hamilton	MP4-23	4th	1st
	Heikki Kovalainen	MP4-23	1st	4th
Germany	Lewis Hamilton	MP4-23	1st	1st
	Heikki Kovalainen	MP4-23	3rd	5th
Hungary	Lewis Hamilton	MP4-23	1st	5th
	Heikki Kovalainen	MP4-23	2nd	1st
Europe	Lewis Hamilton	MP4-23	2nd	2nd
	Heikki Kovalainen	MP4-23	5th	4th
Belgium	Lewis Hamilton	MP4-23	1st	3rd
	Heikki Kovalainen	MP4-23	3rd	10th—gearbox
Italy	Lewis Hamilton	MP4-23	15th	7th
	Heikki Kovalainen	MP4-23	2nd	2nd
Singapore	Lewis Hamilton	MP4-23	2nd	3rd
	Heikki Kovalainen	MP4-23	5th	10th
Japan	Lewis Hamilton	MP4-23	1st	12th
	Heikki Kovalainen	MP4-23	3rd	DNF—engine
China	Lewis Hamilton	MP4-23	1st	1st
	Heikki Kovalainen	MP4-23	5th	DNF—engine
Brazil	Lewis Hamilton	MP4-23	4th	5th
	Heikki Kovalainen	MP4-23	5th	7th

Championship positions: Hamilton 1st (98 points); Kovalainen 7th (53 points)

2009

Australia	Lewis Hamilton	MP4-24	18th	DSQ
	Heikki Kovalainen	MP4-24	12th	DNF—accident
Malaysia	Lewis Hamilton	MP4-24	12th	7th
	Heikki Kovalainen	MP4-24	14th	DNF—spin
China	Lewis Hamilton	MP4-24	9th	6th
	Heikki Kovalainen	MP4-24	12th	5th
Bahrain	Lewis Hamilton	MP4-24	5th	4th
	Heikki Kovalainen	MP4-24	11th	12th
Spain	Lewis Hamilton	MP4-24	14th	9th
	Heikki Kovalainen	MP4-24	18th	DNF—gearbox
Monaco	Lewis Hamilton	MP4-24	19th	12th
	Heikki Kovalainen	MP4-24	7th	DNF—accident
Turkey	Lewis Hamilton	MP4-24	16th	13th
	Heikki Kovalainen	MP4-24	14th	14th
Britain	Lewis Hamilton	MP4-24	18th	16th
	Heikki Kovalainen	MP4-24	13th	DNF—accident
Germany	Lewis Hamilton	MP4-24	5th	18th
	Heikki Kovalainen	MP4-24	6th	8th
Hungary	Lewis Hamilton	MP4-24	4th	1st
	Heikki Kovalainen	MP4-24	6th	5th
Europe	Lewis Hamilton	MP4-24	1st	2nd
	Heikki Kovalainen	MP4-24	2nd	4th
Belgium	Lewis Hamilton	MP4-24	12th	DNF—accident
	Heikki Kovalainen	MP4-24	15th	6th
Italy	Lewis Hamilton	MP4-24	1st	DNF—accident
	Heikki Kovalainen	MP4-24	4th	6th
Singapore	Lewis Hamilton	MP4-24	1st	1st
	Heikki Kovalainen	MP4-24	8th	7th
Japan	Lewis Hamilton	MP4-24	3rd	3rd
	Heikki Kovalainen	MP4-24	11th	11th
Brazil	Lewis Hamilton	MP4-24	17th	3rd
	Heikki Kovalainen	MP4-24	16th	12th
Abu Dhabi	Lewis Hamilton	MP4-24	1st	DNF—brakes
	Heikki Kovalainen	MP4-24	13th	11th

Championship positions: Hamilton 5th (49 points); Kovalainen 12th (22 points)

2010

Bahrain	Jenson Button	MP4-25	8th	7th
	Lewis Hamilton	MP4-25	4th	3rd
Australia	Jenson Button	MP4-25	4th	1st
	Lewis Hamilton	MP4-25	11th	6th
Malaysia	Jenson Button	MP4-25	17th	8th
	Lewis Hamilton	MP4-25	20th	6th
China	Jenson Button	MP4-25	5th	1st
	Lewis Hamilton	MP4-25	6th	2nd
Spain	Jenson Button	MP4-25	5th	5th
	Lewis Hamilton	MP4-25	3rd	14th—accident
Monaco	Jenson Button	MP4-25	8th	DNF—overheating
	Lewis Hamilton	MP4-25	5th	5th
Turkey	Jenson Button	MP4-25	4th	2nd
	Lewis Hamilton	MP4-25	2nd	1st
Europe	Jenson Button	MP4-25	7th	3rd
	Lewis Hamilton	MP4-25	3rd	2nd
Britain	Jenson Button	MP4-25	14th	4th
	Lewis Hamilton	MP4-25	4th	2nd
Germany	Jenson Button	MP4-25	5th	5th
	Lewis Hamilton	MP4-25	6th	4th
Hungary	Jenson Button	MP4-25	11th	8th
	Lewis Hamilton	MP4-25	5th	DNF—gearbox
Belgium	Jenson Button	MP4-25	5th	DNF—accident
	Lewis Hamilton	MP4-25	2nd	1st
Italy	Jenson Button	MP4-25	2nd	2nd
	Lewis Hamilton	MP4-25	5th	DNF—accident
Singapore	Jenson Button	MP4-25	4th	4th
	Lewis Hamilton	MP4-25	3rd	DNF—accident
Japan	Jenson Button	MP4-25	6th	4th
	Lewis Hamilton	MP4-25	3rd	5th
Korea	Jenson Button	MP4-25	7th	12th
	Lewis Hamilton	MP4-25	4th	2nd
Brazil	Jenson Button	MP4-25	11th	5th
	Lewis Hamilton	MP4-25	4th	4th
Abu Dhabi	Jenson Button	MP4-25	4th	3rd
	Lewis Hamilton	MP4-25	2nd	2nd

Championship positions: Hamilton 4th (240 points); Button 5th (214 points)

2011

Australia	Lewis Hamilton	MP4-26	2nd	2nd
	Jenson Button	MP4-26	4th	6th
Malaysia	Lewis Hamilton	MP4-26	2nd	8th
	Jenson Button	MP4-26	4th	2nd
China	Lewis Hamilton	MP4-26	3rd	1st
	Jenson Button	MP4-26	2nd	4th
Turkey	Lewis Hamilton	MP4-26	4th	4th
	Jenson Button	MP4-26	6th	6th
Spain	Lewis Hamilton	MP4-26	3rd	2nd
	Jenson Button	MP4-26	5th	3rd
Monaco	Lewis Hamilton	MP4-26	9th	6th
	Jenson Button	MP4-26	2nd	3rd
Canada	Lewis Hamilton	MP4-26	5th	DNF—accident
	Jenson Button	MP4-26	7th	1st
Europe	Lewis Hamilton	MP4-26	3rd	4th
	Jenson Button	MP4-26	6th	6th
Britain	Lewis Hamilton	MP4-26	10th	4th
	Jenson Button	MP4-26	5th	DNF—wheel
Germany	Lewis Hamilton	MP4-26	2nd	1st
	Jenson Button	MP4-26	7th	DNF—hydraulics
Hungary	Lewis Hamilton	MP4-26	2nd	4th
	Jenson Button	MP4-26	3rd	1st
Belgium	Lewis Hamilton	MP4-26	2nd	DNF—accident
	Jenson Button	MP4-26	13th	3rd
Italy	Lewis Hamilton	MP4-26	2nd	4th
	Jenson Button	MP4-26	3rd	2nd
Singapore	Lewis Hamilton	MP4-26	4th	5th
	Jenson Button	MP4-26	3rd	2nd
Japan	Lewis Hamilton	MP4-26	3rd	5th
	Jenson Button	MP4-26	2nd	1st
Korea	Lewis Hamilton	MP4-26	1st	2nd
	Jenson Button	MP4-26	3rd	4th
India	Lewis Hamilton	MP4-26	2nd	7th
	Jenson Button	MP4-26	5th	2nd
Abu Dhabi	Lewis Hamilton	MP4-26	2nd	1st
	Jenson Button	MP4-26	3rd	3rd
Brazil	Lewis Hamilton	MP4-26	4th	DNF—gearbox
	Jenson Button	MP4-26	3rd	3rd

Championship positions: Button 2nd (270 points); Hamilton 5th (227 points)

2012

Australia	Jenson Button	MP4-27	2nd	1st
	Lewis Hamilton	MP4-27	1st	3rd
Malaysia	Jenson Button	MP4-27	2nd	14th
	Lewis Hamilton	MP4-27	1st	3rd
China	Jenson Button	MP4-27	5th	2nd
	Lewis Hamilton	MP4-27	7th	3rd
Bahrain	Jenson Button	MP4-27	4th	DNF—exhaust
	Lewis Hamilton	MP4-27	2nd	8th

Spain	Jenson Button	MP4-27	10th	9th
	Lewis Hamilton	MP4-27	24th	8th
Monaco	Jenson Button	MP4-27	13th	16th—accident
	Lewis Hamilton	MP4-27	4th	5th
Canada	Jenson Button	MP4-27	10th	16th
	Lewis Hamilton	MP4-27	2nd	1st
Europe	Jenson Button	MP4-27	9th	8th
	Lewis Hamilton	MP4-27	2nd	DNF—accident
Britain	Jenson Button	MP4-27	16th	10th
	Lewis Hamilton	MP4-27	8th	8th
Germany	Jenson Button	MP4-27	7th	2nd
	Lewis Hamilton	MP4-27	8th	DNF—puncture
Hungary	Jenson Button	MP4-27	4th	6th
	Lewis Hamilton	MP4-27	1st	1st
Belgium	Jenson Button	MP4-27	1st	1st
	Lewis Hamilton	MP4-27	7th	DNF—accident
Italy	Jenson Button	MP4-27	2nd	DNF—fuel system
	Lewis Hamilton	MP4-27	1st	3rd
Singapore	Jenson Button	MP4-27	4th	2nd
	Lewis Hamilton	MP4-27	1st	DNF—gearbox
Japan	Jenson Button	MP4-27	8th	4th
	Lewis Hamilton	MP4-27	9th	5th
Korea	Jenson Button	MP4-27	11th	DNF—accident
	Lewis Hamilton	MP4-27	3rd	10th
India	Jenson Button	MP4-27	4th	5th
	Lewis Hamilton	MP4-27	3rd	4th
Abu Dhabi	Jenson Button	MP4-27	5th	4th
	Lewis Hamilton	MP4-27	1st	DNF—fuel system
US	Jenson Button	MP4-27	12th	5th
	Lewis Hamilton	MP4-27	2nd	1st
Brazil	Jenson Button	MP4-27	2nd	1st
	Lewis Hamilton	MP4-27	1st	DNF—accident

Championship positions: Hamilton 4th (190 points); Button 5th (188 points)

2013

Australia	Jenson Button	MP4-28	10th	9th
	Sergio Pérez	MP4-28	15th	11th
Malaysia	Jenson Button	MP4-28	7th	DNF—wheel
	Sergio Pérez	MP4-28	9th	9th
China	Jenson Button	MP4-28	8th	5th
	Sergio Pérez	MP4-28	12th	11th
Bahrain	Jenson Button	MP4-28	10th	10th
	Sergio Pérez	MP4-28	12th	6th
Spain	Jenson Button	MP4-28	14th	8th
	Sergio Pérez	MP4-28	8th	9th
Monaco	Jenson Button	MP4-28	9th	6th
	Sergio Pérez	MP4-28	7th	16th—accident
Canada	Jenson Button	MP4-28	14th	12th
	Sergio Pérez	MP4-28	12th	11th
Britain	Jenson Button	MP4-28	10th	13th
	Sergio Pérez	MP4-28	13th	20th—puncture
Germany	Jenson Button	MP4-28	9th	6th
	Sergio Pérez	MP4-28	13th	8th
Hungary	Jenson Button	MP4-28	13th	7th
	Sergio Pérez	MP4-28	9th	9th
Belgium	Jenson Button	MP4-28	6th	6th
	Sergio Pérez	MP4-28	13th	11th
Italy	Jenson Button	MP4-28	9th	10th
	Sergio Pérez	MP4-28	8th	12th
Singapore	Jenson Button	MP4-28	8th	7th
	Sergio Pérez	MP4-28	14th	8th
Korea	Jenson Button	MP4-28	11th	8th
	Sergio Pérez	MP4-28	10th	10th
Japan	Jenson Button	MP4-28	10th	9th
	Sergio Pérez	MP4-28	11th	15th
India	Jenson Button	MP4-28	10th	14th
	Sergio Pérez	MP4-28	9th	5th
Abu Dhabi	Jenson Button	MP4-28	12th	12th
	Sergio Pérez	MP4-28	8th	9th
US	Jenson Button	MP4-28	15th	10th
	Sergio Pérez	MP4-28	7th	7th
Brazil	Jenson Button	MP4-28	14th	4th
	Sergio Pérez	MP4-28	19th	6th

Championship positions: Button 9th (73 points); Pérez 11th (49 points)

2014

Australia	Kevin Magnussen	MP4-29	4th	2nd
	Jenson Button	MP4-29	10th	3rd
Malaysia	Kevin Magnussen	MP4-29	8th	9th
	Jenson Button	MP4-29	10th	6th
Bahrain	Kevin Magnussen	MP4-29	8th	DNF—clutch
	Jenson Button	MP4-29	6th	17th—clutch
China	Kevin Magnussen	MP4-29	15th	13th
	Jenson Button	MP4-29	12th	11th
Spain	Kevin Magnussen	MP4-29	14th	12th
	Jenson Button	MP4-29	8th	11th
Monaco	Kevin Magnussen	MP4-29	8th	10th
	Jenson Button	MP4-29	12th	6th
Canada	Kevin Magnussen	MP4-29	12th	9th
	Jenson Button	MP4-29	9th	4th
Austria	Kevin Magnussen	MP4-29	6th	7th
	Jenson Button	MP4-29	11th	11th
Britain	Kevin Magnussen	MP4-29	5th	7th
	Jenson Button	MP4-29	3rd	4th
Germany	Kevin Magnussen	MP4-29	4th	9th
	Jenson Button	MP4-29	11th	8th
Hungary	Kevin Magnussen	MP4-29	Pitlane	12th
	Jenson Button	MP4-29	7th	10th
Belgium	Kevin Magnussen	MP4-29	7th	12th*
	Jenson Button	MP4-29	10th	6th
Italy	Kevin Magnussen	MP4-29	5th	10th*
	Jenson Button	MP4-29	6th	8th
Singapore	Kevin Magnussen	MP4-29	9th	10th
	Jenson Button	MP4-29	11th	DNF—electrical
Japan	Kevin Magnussen	MP4-29	7th	14th
	Jenson Button	MP4-29	8th	5th
Russia	Kevin Magnussen	MP4-29	11th	5th
	Jenson Button	MP4-29	4th	4th
US	Kevin Magnussen	MP4-29	7th	8th
	Jenson Button	MP4-29	12th	12th
Brazil	Kevin Magnussen	MP4-29	7th	9th
	Jenson Button	MP4-29	5th	4th
Abu Dhabi	Kevin Magnussen	MP4-29	9th	11th
	Jenson Button	MP4-29	6th	5th

Championship positions: Button 8th (126 points); Magnussen 11th (55 points)
**Penalized for pushing another driver off-track*

2015

Australia	Kevin Magnussen	MP4-30	17th	DNF—engine
	Jenson Button	MP4-30	16th	11th
Malaysia	Fernando Alonso	MP4-30	18th	DNF—engine
	Jenson Button	MP4-30	17th	DNF—turbo
China	Fernando Alonso	MP4-30	18th	12th
	Jenson Button	MP4-30	17th	14th*
Bahrain	Fernando Alonso	MP4-30	14th	11th
	Jenson Button	MP4-30	Pitlane	DNS
Spain	Fernando Alonso	MP4-30	13th	DNF—brakes
	Jenson Button	MP4-30	14th	16th
Monaco	Fernando Alonso	MP4-30	13th	DNF—gearbox
	Jenson Button	MP4-30	10th	8th
Canada	Fernando Alonso	MP4-30	13th	DNF—exhaust
	Jenson Button	MP4-30	20th	DNF—exhaust
Austria	Fernando Alonso	MP4-30	19th	DNF—accident
	Jenson Button	MP4-30	20th	DNF—electrical
Britain	Fernando Alonso	MP4-30	17th	10th
	Jenson Button	MP4-30	18th	DNF—accident
Hungary	Fernando Alonso	MP4-30	15th	5th
	Jenson Button	MP4-30	16th	9th
Belgium	Fernando Alonso	MP4-30	20th	13th
	Jenson Button	MP4-30	19th	14th
Italy	Fernando Alonso	MP4-30	16th	18th—electrical
	Jenson Button	MP4-30	15th	14th
Singapore	Fernando Alonso	MP4-30	12th	DNF—gearbox
	Jenson Button	MP4-30	15th	DNF—gearbox
Japan	Fernando Alonso	MP4-30	12th	11th
	Jenson Button	MP4-30	14th	16th
Russia	Fernando Alonso	MP4-30	19th	11th**
	Jenson Button	MP4-30	13th	9th
US	Fernando Alonso	MP4-30	9th	11th
	Jenson Button	MP4-30	11th	6th
Mexico	Fernando Alonso	MP4-30	18th	DNF—engine
	Jenson Button	MP4-30	20th	14th

Brazil	Fernando Alonso	MP4-30	20th	15th
	Jenson Button	MP4-30	16th	14th
Abu Dhabi	Fernando Alonso	MP4-30	16th	17th
	Jenson Button	MP4-30	12th	12th

Championship positions: Button 16th (16 points); Alonso 17th (11 points)
**Penalized for causing a collision*
***Penalized for exceeding track limits*

2016

Australia	Fernando Alonso	MP4-31	11th	DNF—accident
	Jenson Button	MP4-31	12th	14th
Bahrain	Jenson Button	MP4-31	14th	DNF—engine
	Stoffel Vandoorne	MP4-31	12th	10th
China	Fernando Alonso	MP4-31	11th	12th
	Jenson Button	MP4-31	12th	13th
Russia	Fernando Alonso	MP4-31	14th	6th
	Jenson Button	MP4-31	12th	10th
Spain	Fernando Alonso	MP4-31	10th	DNF—engine
	Jenson Button	MP4-31	12th	9th
Monaco	Fernando Alonso	MP4-31	9th	5th
	Jenson Button	MP4-31	13th	9th
Canada	Fernando Alonso	MP4-31	10th	11th
	Jenson Button	MP4-31	12th	DNF—engine
Europe	Fernando Alonso	MP4-31	13th	DNF—gearbox
	Jenson Button	MP4-31	19th	11th
Austria	Fernando Alonso	MP4-31	14th	DNF—electrical
	Jenson Button	MP4-31	3rd	6th
Britain	Fernando Alonso	MP4-31	9th	13th
	Jenson Button	MP4-31	17th	12th
Hungary	Fernando Alonso	MP4-31	7th	7th
	Jenson Button	MP4-31	8th	DNF—oil leak
Germany	Fernando Alonso	MP4-31	13th	12th
	Jenson Button	MP4-31	12th	8th
Belgium	Fernando Alonso	MP4-31	22nd	7th
	Jenson Button	MP4-31	9th	DNF—accident
Italy	Fernando Alonso	MP4-31	12th	15th
	Jenson Button	MP4-31	14th	12th
Singapore	Fernando Alonso	MP4-31	9th	7th
	Jenson Button	MP4-31	12th	DNF—brakes
Malaysia	Fernando Alonso	MP4-31	22nd	7th
	Jenson Button	MP4-31	9th	9th
Japan	Fernando Alonso	MP4-31	15th	16th
	Jenson Button	MP4-31	22nd	18th
US	Fernando Alonso	MP4-31	12th	5th
	Jenson Button	MP4-31	19th	9th
Mexico	Fernando Alonso	MP4-31	11th	13th
	Jenson Button	MP4-31	13th	12th
Brazil	Fernando Alonso	MP4-31	10th	10th
	Jenson Button	MP4-31	17th	16th
Abu Dhabi	Fernando Alonso	MP4-31	9th	10th
	Jenson Button	MP4-31	12th	DNF—suspension

Championship positions: Alonso 10th (54 points); Button 15th (21 points); Vandoorne 20th (1 point)

2017

Australia	Stoffel Vandoorne	MCL32	18th	13th
	Fernando Alonso	MCL32	12th	DNF—floor
China	Stoffel Vandoorne	MCL32	15th	DNF—fuel system
	Fernando Alonso	MCL32	13th	DNF—driveshaft
Bahrain	Stoffel Vandoorne	MCL32	17th	DNS
	Fernando Alonso	MCL32	15th	DNF—engine
Russia	Stoffel Vandoorne	MCL32	20th	14th
	Fernando Alonso	MCL32	15th	DNS
Spain	Stoffel Vandoorne	MCL32	20th	DNF—accident
	Fernando Alonso	MCL32	7th	12th
Monaco	Stoffel Vandoorne	MCL32	12th	DNF—accident
	Jenson Button	MCL32	Pitlane	DNF—accident
Canada	Stoffel Vandoorne	MCL32	16th	14th
	Fernando Alonso	MCL32	12th	16th—engine
Azerbaijan	Stoffel Vandoorne	MCL32	18th	12th
	Fernando Alonso	MCL32	19th	9th
Austria	Stoffel Vandoorne	MCL32	13th	12th
	Fernando Alonso	MCL32	12th	DNF—accident
Britain	Stoffel Vandoorne	MCL32	8th	11th
	Fernando Alonso	MCL32	20th	DNF—fuel system
Hungary	Stoffel Vandoorne	MCL32	8th	10th
	Fernando Alonso	MCL32	7th	6th
Belgium	Stoffel Vandoorne	MCL32	20th	14th
	Fernando Alonso	MCL32	10th	DNF—engine
Italy	Stoffel Vandoorne	MCL32	18th	DNF—electrical
	Fernando Alonso	MCL32	19th	17th—clutch
Singapore	Stoffel Vandoorne	MCL32	9th	7th
	Fernando Alonso	MCL32	8th	DNF—accident
Malaysia	Stoffel Vandoorne	MCL32	7th	7th
	Fernando Alonso	MCL32	10th	11th
Japan	Stoffel Vandoorne	MCL32	9th	14th
	Fernando Alonso	MCL32	20th	11th
US	Stoffel Vandoorne	MCL32	20th	12th
	Fernando Alonso	MCL32	8th	DNF—engine
Mexico	Stoffel Vandoorne	MCL32	19th	12th
	Fernando Alonso	MCL32	18th	10th
Brazil	Stoffel Vandoorne	MCL32	12th	DNF—accident
	Fernando Alonso	MCL32	6th	8th
Abu Dhabi	Stoffel Vandoorne	MCL32	13th	12th
	Fernando Alonso	MCL32	11th	9th

Championship positions: Alonso 15th (17 points); Vandoorne 16th (13 points)

2018

Australia	Stoffel Vandoorne	MCL33	11th	9th
	Fernando Alonso	MCL33	10th	5th
Bahrain	Stoffel Vandoorne	MCL33	14th	8th
	Fernando Alonso	MCL33	13th	7th
China	Stoffel Vandoorne	MCL33	14th	13th
	Fernando Alonso	MCL33	13th	7th
Azerbaijan	Stoffel Vandoorne	MCL33	16th	9th
	Fernando Alonso	MCL33	12th	7th
Spain	Stoffel Vandoorne	MCL33	11th	DNF—gearbox
	Fernando Alonso	MCL33	8th	7th
Monaco	Stoffel Vandoorne	MCL33	12th	14th
	Fernando Alonso	MCL33	7th	DNF—gearbox
Canada	Stoffel Vandoorne	MCL33	15th	16th
	Fernando Alonso	MCL33	14th	DNF—exhaust
France	Stoffel Vandoorne	MCL33	18th	12th
	Fernando Alonso	MCL33	16th	DNF—suspension
Austria	Stoffel Vandoorne	MCL33	14th	15th—accident
	Fernando Alonso	MCL33	Pitlane	8th
Britain	Stoffel Vandoorne	MCL33	17th	11th
	Fernando Alonso	MCL33	13th	8th
Germany	Stoffel Vandoorne	MCL33	18th	13th
	Fernando Alonso	MCL33	11th	DNF—gearbox
Hungary	Stoffel Vandoorne	MCL33	15th	DNF—gearbox
	Fernando Alonso	MCL33	11th	8th
Belgium	Stoffel Vandoorne	MCL33	20th	15th
	Fernando Alonso	MCL33	14th	DNF—accident
Italy	Stoffel Vandoorne	MCL33	17th	12th
	Fernando Alonso	MCL33	13th	DNF—electrical
Singapore	Stoffel Vandoorne	MCL33	18th	12th
	Fernando Alonso	MCL33	11th	7th
Russia	Stoffel Vandoorne	MCL33	15th	16th
	Fernando Alonso	MCL33	16th	14th
Japan	Stoffel Vandoorne	MCL33	19th	15th
	Fernando Alonso	MCL33	18th	14th
US	Stoffel Vandoorne	MCL33	17th	11th
	Fernando Alonso	MCL33	13th	DNF—accident
Mexico	Stoffel Vandoorne	MCL33	15th	8th
	Fernando Alonso	MCL33	12th	DNF—cooling
Brazil	Stoffel Vandoorne	MCL33	20th	15th
	Fernando Alonso	MCL33	17th	17th
Abu Dhabi	Stoffel Vandoorne	MCL33	18th	14th
	Fernando Alonso	MCL33	15th	11th

Championship positions: Alonso 11th (50 points); Vandoorne 16th (12 points)

2019

Australia	Lando Norris	MCL34	8th	12th
	Carlos Sainz	MCL34	18th	DNF—engine
Bahrain	Lando Norris	MCL34	10th	6th
	Carlos Sainz	MCL34	7th	DNF—gearbox
China	Lando Norris	MCL34	15th	18th—accident
	Carlos Sainz	MCL34	14th	14th
Azerbaijan	Lando Norris	MCL34	7th	8th
	Carlos Sainz	MCL34	9th	7th
Spain	Lando Norris	MCL34	10th	DNF—accident
	Carlos Sainz	MCL34	12th	8th
Monaco	Lando Norris	MCL34	12th	11th
	Carlos Sainz	MCL34	9th	6th
Canada	Lando Norris	MCL34	8th	DNF—suspension
	Carlos Sainz	MCL34	11th	11th
France	Lando Norris	MCL34	5th	9th
	Carlos Sainz	MCL34	6th	6th
Austria	Lando Norris	MCL34	5th	6th
	Carlos Sainz	MCL34	19th	8th
Britain	Lando Norris	MCL34	8th	11th
	Carlos Sainz	MCL34	13th	6th
Germany	Lando Norris	MCL34	19th	DNF—engine
	Carlos Sainz	MCL34	7th	5th
Hungary	Lando Norris	MCL34	7th	9th
	Carlos Sainz	MCL34	8th	5th
Belgium	Lando Norris	MCL34	11th	11th—engine
	Carlos Sainz	MCL34	15th	DNF—engine
Italy	Lando Norris	MCL34	16th	10th
	Carlos Sainz	MCL34	7th	DNF—wheel
Singapore	Lando Norris	MCL34	9th	7th
	Carlos Sainz	MCL34	7th	12th
Russia	Lando Norris	MCL34	7th	8th
	Carlos Sainz	MCL34	5th	6th
Japan	Lando Norris	MCL34	8th	11th
	Carlos Sainz	MCL34	7th	5th
Mexico	Lando Norris	MCL34	8th	DNF—lug nut
	Carlos Sainz	MCL34	7th	13th
US	Lando Norris	MCL34	8th	7th
	Carlos Sainz	MCL34	7th	8th
Brazil	Lando Norris	MCL34	10th	8th
	Carlos Sainz	MCL34	20th	3rd
Abu Dhabi	Lando Norris	MCL34	6th	8th
	Carlos Sainz	MCL34	8th	10th

Championship positions: Sainz 6th (96 points); Norris 11th (49 points)

2020

Austria	Lando Norris	MCL35	3rd	3rd
	Carlos Sainz	MCL35	8th	5th
Styria	Lando Norris	MCL35	9th	5th
	Carlos Sainz	MCL35	3rd	9th
Hungary	Lando Norris	MCL35	8th	13th
	Carlos Sainz	MCL35	9th	9th
Britain	Lando Norris	MCL35	5th	5th
	Carlos Sainz	MCL35	7th	13th
70th Anniversary	Lando Norris	MCL35	10th	9th
	Carlos Sainz	MCL35	12th	13th
Spain	Lando Norris	MCL35	8th	10th
	Carlos Sainz	MCL35	7th	6th
Belgium	Lando Norris	MCL35	10th	7th
	Carlos Sainz	MCL35	7th	DNS—engine
Italy	Lando Norris	MCL35	6th	4th
	Carlos Sainz	MCL35	3rd	2nd
Tuscany	Lando Norris	MCL35	11th	6th
	Carlos Sainz	MCL35	9th	DNF—accident
Russia	Lando Norris	MCL35	8th	15th
	Carlos Sainz	MCL35	6th	DNF—accident
Eifel	Lando Norris	MCL35	8th	DNF—engine
	Carlos Sainz	MCL35	10th	5th
Portugal	Lando Norris	MCL35	8th	13th
	Carlos Sainz	MCL35	7th	6th
Emilia Romagna	Lando Norris	MCL35	9th	8th
	Carlos Sainz	MCL35	10th	7th
Turkey	Lando Norris	MCL35	14th	8th
	Carlos Sainz	MCL35	15th	5th
Austria	Lando Norris	MCL35	3rd	3rd
	Carlos Sainz	MCL35	8th	5th
Bahrain	Lando Norris	MCL35	9th	4th
	Carlos Sainz	MCL35	15th	5th
Sakhir	Lando Norris	MCL35	19th	10th
	Carlos Sainz	MCL35	8th	4th
Abu Dhabi	Lando Norris	MCL35	4th	5th
	Carlos Sainz	MCL35	6th	6th

Championship positions: Sainz 6th (105 points); Norris 9th (97 points)

2021

Bahrain	Daniel Ricciardo	MCL35M	6th	7th
	Lando Norris	MCL35M	7th	4th
Emilia Romagna	Daniel Ricciardo	MCL35M	6th	6th
	Lando Norris	MCL35M	7th	3rd
Portugal	Daniel Ricciardo	MCL35M	16th	9th
	Lando Norris	MCL35M	7th	5th
Spain	Daniel Ricciardo	MCL35M	7th	6th
	Lando Norris	MCL35M	9th	8th
Monaco	Daniel Ricciardo	MCL35M	12th	12th
	Lando Norris	MCL35M	5th	3rd
Azerbaijan	Daniel Ricciardo	MCL35M	13th	9th
	Lando Norris	MCL35M	9th	5th
France	Daniel Ricciardo	MCL35M	10th	6th
	Lando Norris	MCL35M	8th	5th
Styria	Daniel Ricciardo	MCL35M	13th	13th
	Lando Norris	MCL35M	3rd	5th
Austria	Daniel Ricciardo	MCL35M	13th	7th
	Lando Norris	MCL35M	2nd	3rd
Britain	Daniel Ricciardo	MCL35M	7th	5th
	Lando Norris	MCL35M	6th	4th
Hungary	Daniel Ricciardo	MCL35M	11th	11th
	Lando Norris	MCL35M	6th	DNF—accident
Belgium	Daniel Ricciardo	MCL35M	4th	4th
	Lando Norris	MCL35M	15th	14th
Netherlands	Daniel Ricciardo	MCL35M	10th	11th
	Lando Norris	MCL35M	13th	10th
Italy	Daniel Ricciardo	MCL35M	5th	1st
	Lando Norris	MCL35M	4th	2nd
Russia	Daniel Ricciardo	MCL35M	5th	4th
	Lando Norris	MCL35M	1st	7th
Turkey	Daniel Ricciardo	MCL35M	20th	13th
	Lando Norris	MCL35M	7th	7th
US	Daniel Ricciardo	MCL35M	6th	5th
	Lando Norris	MCL35M	7th	8th
Mexico	Daniel Ricciardo	MCL35M	7th	12th
	Lando Norris	MCL35M	18th	10th
São Paulo	Daniel Ricciardo	MCL35M	8th	DNF—engine
	Lando Norris	MCL35M	7th	10th
Qatar	Daniel Ricciardo	MCL35M	14th	12th
	Lando Norris	MCL35M	4th	9th
Saudi Arabia	Daniel Ricciardo	MCL35M	11th	5th
	Lando Norris	MCL35M	7th	10th
Abu Dhabi	Daniel Ricciardo	MCL35M	10th	12th
	Lando Norris	MCL35M	3rd	7th

Championship positions: Norris 6th (160 points); Ricciardo 8th (115 points)

2022				
Bahrain	Daniel Ricciardo	MCL36	18th	14th
	Lando Norris	MCL36	13th	15th
Saudi Arabia	Daniel Ricciardo	MCL36	14th	DNF—gearbox
	Lando Norris	MCL36	11th	7th
Australia	Daniel Ricciardo	MCL36	7th	6th
	Lando Norris	MCL36	4th	5th
Emilia Romagna	Daniel Ricciardo	MCL36	6th	6th
	Lando Norris	MCL36	3rd	5th
Miami	Daniel Ricciardo	MCL36	14th	13th
	Lando Norris	MCL36	8th	DNF—accident
Spain	Daniel Ricciardo	MCL36	9th	12th
	Lando Norris	MCL36	11th	8th
Monaco	Daniel Ricciardo	MCL36	14th	13th
	Lando Norris	MCL36	5th	6th
Azerbaijan	Daniel Ricciardo	MCL36	12th	8th
	Lando Norris	MCL36	11th	9th
Canada	Daniel Ricciardo	MCL36	9th	11th
	Lando Norris	MCL36	14th	15th
Britain	Daniel Ricciardo	MCL36	14th	13th
	Lando Norris	MCL36	6th	6th
Austria	Daniel Ricciardo	MCL36	16th	12th
	Lando Norris	MCL36	15th	11th
France	Daniel Ricciardo	MCL36	9th	9th
	Lando Norris	MCL36	5th	7th
Hungary	Daniel Ricciardo	MCL36	9th	15th
	Lando Norris	MCL36	4th	7th
Belgium	Daniel Ricciardo	MCL36	7th	15th
	Lando Norris	MCL36	17th	12th
Netherlands	Daniel Ricciardo	MCL36	17th	17th
	Lando Norris	MCL36	7th	7th
Italy	Daniel Ricciardo	MCL36	4th	DNF—oil leak
	Lando Norris	MCL36	3rd	7th
Singapore	Daniel Ricciardo	MCL36	16th	5th
	Lando Norris	MCL36	6th	4th
Japan	Daniel Ricciardo	MCL36	11th	11th
	Lando Norris	MCL36	10th	10th
US	Daniel Ricciardo	MCL36	15th	16th
	Lando Norris	MCL36	6th	6th
Mexico	Daniel Ricciardo	MCL36	11th	7th
	Lando Norris	MCL36	8th	9th
São Paulo	Daniel Ricciardo	MCL36	14th	DNF—accident
	Lando Norris	MCL36	4th	DNF—gearbox
Abu Dhabi	Daniel Ricciardo	MCL36	13th	9th
	Lando Norris	MCL36	7th	6th

Championship positions: Norris 7th (122 points); Ricciardo 11th (37 points)

2023				
Bahrain	Lando Norris	MCL60	11th	17th
	Oscar Piastri	MCL60	18th	DNF—electrical
Saudi Arabia	Lando Norris	MCL60	19th	17th
	Oscar Piastri	MCL60	8th	15th
Australia	Lando Norris	MCL60	13th	6th
	Oscar Piastri	MCL60	16th	8th
Azerbaijan	Lando Norris	MCL60	7th	9th
	Oscar Piastri	MCL60	10th	11th
Miami	Lando Norris	MCL60	16th	17th
	Oscar Piastri	MCL60	19th	19th
Monaco	Lando Norris	MCL60	10th	9th
	Oscar Piastri	MCL60	11th	10th
Spain	Lando Norris	MCL60	3rd	17th
	Oscar Piastri	MCL60	9th	13th
Canada	Lando Norris	MCL60	7th	13th
	Oscar Piastri	MCL60	8th	11th
Austria	Lando Norris	MCL60	4th	3rd
	Oscar Piastri	MCL60	13th	17th
Britain	Lando Norris	MCL60	2nd	2nd
	Oscar Piastri	MCL60	3rd	4th
Hungary	Lando Norris	MCL60	3rd	2nd
	Oscar Piastri	MCL60	4th	5th
Belgium	Lando Norris	MCL60	7th	7th
	Oscar Piastri	MCL60	5th	DNF—accident
Netherlands	Lando Norris	MCL60	2nd	7th
	Oscar Piastri	MCL60	8th	9th
Italy	Lando Norris	MCL60	9th	8th
	Oscar Piastri	MCL60	7th	12th
Singapore	Lando Norris	MCL60	4th	2nd
	Oscar Piastri	MCL60	17th	7th
Japan	Lando Norris	MCL60	3rd	2nd
	Oscar Piastri	MCL60	2nd	3rd
Qatar	Lando Norris	MCL60	10th	3rd
	Oscar Piastri	MCL60	6th	2nd
US	Lando Norris	MCL60	2nd	2nd
	Oscar Piastri	MCL60	10th	DNF—overheating
Mexico	Lando Norris	MCL60	19th	5th
	Oscar Piastri	MCL60	7th	8th
São Paulo	Lando Norris	MCL60	7th	2nd
	Oscar Piastri	MCL60	10th	14th
Las Vegas	Lando Norris	MCL60	16th	DNF—accident
	Oscar Piastri	MCL60	19th	10th
Abu Dhabi	Lando Norris	MCL60	5th	5th
	Oscar Piastri	MCL60	3rd	6th

Championship positions: Norris 6th (205 points); Piastri 9th (97 points)

INDEX

N

O

P

R

S

T

W

Y

vodafone
2
Mobil
1
DIAGEO
vodafone